RAND

Ensuring the Quality and Productivity of Education and Professional Development Activities:

A Review of Approaches and Lessons for DoD

Susan M. Gates, Catherine H. Augustine, Roger Benjamin, Tora K. Bikson, Eric Derghazarian, Tessa Kaganoff, Dina G. Levy, Joy S. Moini, Ron W. Zimmer

National Defense Research Institute

Prepared for the
Office of the Secretary of Defense

Approved for public release; distribution unlimited

This research was conducted for the DoD Office of the Chancellor for Education and Professional Development within the Forces and Resources Policy Center of RAND's National Defense Research Institute, a federally funded research and development center sponsored by the Office of the Secretary of Defense, the Joint Staff, the Unified Commands, and the defense agencies, Contract DASW01-95-C-0059.

ISBN: 0-8330-2987-8

RAND is a nonprofit institution that helps improve policy and decisionmaking through research and analysis. RAND® is a registered trademark. RAND's publications do not necessarily reflect the opinions or policies of its research sponsors.

© Copyright 2001 RAND

All rights reserved. No part of this book may be reproduced in any form by any electronic or mechanical means (including photocopying, recording, or information storage and retrieval) without permission in writing from RAND.

Published 2001 by RAND
1700 Main Street, P.O. Box 2138, Santa Monica, CA 90407-2138
1200 South Hayes Street, Arlington, VA 22202-5050
201 North Craig Street, Suite 102, Pittsburgh, PA 15213
RAND URL: http://www.rand.org/
To order RAND documents or to obtain additional information, contact Distribution Services: Telephone: (310) 451-7002; Fax: (310) 451-6915; Email: order@rand.org

Preface

A high-quality civilian workforce is an important element of a high-quality defense infrastructure. In an era of streamlining, demographic change, low unemployment, and rapid technological advances, education and professional development play a key role in maintaining and improving the quality of the workforce. In this environment, it is important for the Department of Defense to ensure that the civilian workforce receives appropriate, high-quality training and education in an efficient manner. At the request of the DoD Office of the Chancellor for Education and Professional Development, RAND undertook a study to examine the approaches used to evaluate academic quality and productivity in a variety of postsecondary education and training contexts and consider which approaches might be most relevant to the Chancellor's office. This report may also be of interest to higher education administrators and managers of corporate universities.

It provides a conceptual structure for understanding the processes used to assess quality and productivity in various higher education, corporate, and government organizations that provide education and professional development. In addition, this report includes detailed, structured appendices summarizing the assessment approach and providing examples of measures used by several different organizations involved in quality and productivity assessment. A companion report (Levy et al., forthcoming) discusses strategic planning approaches used by similar organizations and identifies potentially useful approaches for the Chancellor's office.

This research was conducted for the DoD Office of the Chancellor for Education and Professional Development within the Forces and Resources Policy Center of RAND's National Defense Research Institute, a federally funded research and development center sponsored by the Office of the Secretary of Defense, the Joint Staff, the Unified Commands, and the defense agencies.

Contents

Preface ... iii

Figures ... ix

Tables ... xi

Summary ... xiii

Acknowledgments ... xix

Acronyms ... xxi

1. INTRODUCTION ... 1
   - Background ... 1
   - Motivation ... 2
   - Objectives and Approach ... 3
   - Organization of the Report ... 5

2. FRAMEWORK ... 7
   - The System of DoD Civilian Education and Professional Development ... 8
   - Framework for Analyzing the Assessment of System Performance ... 11

3. PHASE ONE: SYSTEM-LEVEL ASSESSMENT ... 13
   - Goals of System-Level Assessment ... 13
     - Identifying Misalignment ... 13
     - Optimizing Resource Allocation at the System Level ... 14
   - How Systems Establish a Structure for Such Assessment ... 15
   - How Systems Identify Misalignments ... 16
   - How Systems Allocate Resources ... 18
   - Need for Standardized Data and Course Offerings ... 19
   - Beyond Assessment: Promoting Workforce Improvement ... 20
   - Multiple Benefits ... 21
   - Lessons for the Chancellor's Office ... 21

4. PHASE TWO: ASSESSING HOW WELL PROVIDERS MEET CUSTOMER NEEDS ... 23
   - Model 1: Intermediary Assesses or Guides Provider's Process of Assessment ... 24
     - ISO 9000 ... 25
     - The Academic Audit ... 26
   - Model 2: Intermediary Conducts the Assessment ... 28
     - State Higher Education Governing and Coordinating Boards ... 29
     - *U.S. News and World Report* ... 30
     - Accrediting Agencies ... 31
     - Malcolm Baldrige National Quality Award ... 32
     - The Problem of Compliance ... 32
   - Model 3: Provider Conducts the Assessment ... 34
     - The University of Phoenix ... 35

The Urban Universities Portfolio Project 36
Model 4: Student Competencies Are Assessed 37
Microsoft's Technical Certification Programs 38
The Department of Labor's SCANS Initiative 39
Western Governors University 39
Strengths and Weaknesses of the Four Approaches 40

5. CHOOSING THE RIGHT MODEL FOR PHASE TWO 44
Purposes of Assessment 44
Level of Authority 47
Level of Resources 48
Centralization of Operations 49
System Heterogeneity 50
System Complexity 52
Summary 53
Implications for the Chancellor's Office 53

6. THREE STEPS FOR ASSESSING PROVIDERS 55
Step One: Identifying Goals 56
Goal Setting Guides the Assessment Process 56
How to Set Goals 56
Level of Stakeholder Involvement 57
Step Two: Selecting Measures 59
Input Measures 59
Process Measures 60
Outcome Measures 61
Choosing Measures 61
Step Three: Evaluate Performance Using Measures 64
Comparison with External Peers 64
Comparison with Preset Standards 65
Comparison with Internal Peers 66
Comparison with Past Performance 66
Measurement Validity and Reliability 67
Validity 67
Reliability 69
Implications 70
Bringing It All Together: Integrating All Three Steps 71
Relevance of the Three Assessment Steps for the Chancellor's Office 73

7. CONCLUSIONS AND RECOMMENDATIONS 75
Phase One: DoD Should Devote Attention to the First Phase of Assessment 75
Phase Two: Recommendations 76
Consider the Purpose of Assessment 77
Consider Constraints Within the DoD Education and Professional Development System 77
Integrate the Three Assessment Steps 78

Appendix

A. OVERVIEW OF APPENDICES 79

B. STATE HIGHER EDUCATION BOARDS 82

B.1. TEXAS HIGHER EDUCATION COORDINATING BOARD 88

B.2. KENTUCKY COUNCIL ON POSTSECONDARY EDUCATION 95

C. PROCESS AUDITORS—ACADEMIC AUDIT 100

C.1. INTERNATIONAL ORGANIZATION FOR STANDARDIZATION 106

D. ACCREDITING AGENCIES 111

D.1. WESTERN ASSOCIATION OF SCHOOLS AND COLLEGES 123

E. PROFESSIONAL SOCIETIES 130

F.1. U.S. DEPARTMENT OF TRANSPORTATION 133

F.2. U.S. AIR FORCE TRAINING AND EDUCATION 139

F.3. U.S. NAVY INDIVIDUAL AND MISSION TRAINING 145

G. CORPORATE PROFESSIONAL DEVELOPMENT AND TRAINING 151

G.1. LUCENT TECHNOLOGIES LEARNING AND PERFORMANCE CENTER 162

H.1. *U.S. NEWS AND WORLD REPORT* 168

I.1. BALDRIGE AWARD 175

J. CERTIFIERS OF STUDENT COMPETENCIES 183

K.1. UNIVERSITY OF PHOENIX 190

K.2. U.S. AIR FORCE ACADEMY, DEPARTMENT OF MANAGEMENT 196

K.3. BALANCED SCORECARD 202

K.4. THE URBAN UNIVERSITIES PORTFOLIO PROJECT: ASSURING QUALITY FOR MULTIPLE PUBLICS 210

Bibliography 215

Figures

2.1. Different Levels of Customers of DoD Civilian Education and Professional Development 9
2.2. Different Levels of Providers of DoD Civilian Education and Professional Development 10
2.3. The DoD System Includes Customers, Their Providers, and Intermediaries 11
4.1. Four Models for Assessing Providers 24
F.1.1. DOT Learning and Professional Development System 134
K.4.1. UUPP Campus Team Structure 213

Tables

4.1. Strengths and Weaknesses of the Four Assessment Models 41
5.1. Suitability of Assessment Models to Different Circumstances 53
6.1. University of Southern California's Goals, Measures, and Benchmarks 72
A.1. Overview of Appendices 80
A.2. Map of Appendices 81
B.1. Report Card Indicators Used in Tennessee 86
B.2. Performance Measures Used in South Carolina 87
B.1.1. Examples of Measures for Texas Two-Year Colleges 94
D.1. Examples of Goals and Measures Used by the Middle States Association of Colleges and Schools 117
D.2. Examples of Goals and Measures Used by the New England Association of Schools and Colleges 117
D.3. Examples of Goals and Measures Used by the North Central Association of Colleges and Schools 118
D.4. Examples of Goals and Measures Used by the Northwest Association of Schools and Colleges 119
D.5. Examples of Goals and Measures Used by the Southern Association of Colleges and Schools 120
D.6. Examples of Goals and Measures Used by the Western Association of Schools and Colleges 121
D.7. Examples of Goals and Measures Used by the Accrediting Commission of Career Schools and Colleges of Technology 122
D.1.1. Proposed Timeline 129
F.1.1. Performance Measures Proposed by L&D Program 137
G.1. Kirkpatrick Model 159
H.1.1. Measures Used in Best Colleges Ranking 172
H.1.2. Measures Used in Professional and Academic Graduate Program Rankings 172
H.1.3. Weight Given to Different Categories of Measures by Type of School 173
I.1.1. Examples of Measures Used in the Baldrige Award 180
I.1.2. Baldrige Scoring System: Points Awarded by Area 181
K.3.1. USC School of Education Goals, by Perspective 205
K.3.2. Stakeholder Perspective: How Do Stakeholders See Us? (USC) ... 207
K.3.3. Examples of Business Operations Scorecard (UCSD) 208

Summary

Background and Approach

The Office of the Chancellor for Education and Professional Development in the Department of Defense (DoD) was established in 1998 to help raise the quality of civilian training and professional development to world-class standards. The Chancellor's office is specifically charged with ensuring the quality and productivity of education and professional development activities targeted at DoD civilians. In support of this aim, the Chancellor asked RAND to review existing approaches for assessing academic quality and productivity and to suggest approaches that might be useful for the assessment of the current DoD system of education and professional development.

The RAND study team conducted a broad review of the general literature on the assessment of quality and productivity in education and professional development. The team also reviewed the documentation of organizations engaged in such assessment, interviewed experts, attended conferences, and conducted site visits to exemplary organizations. This report synthesizes that information and provides suggestions for approaches that might be useful for DoD.

Need for System-Level Assessment

The Office of the Secretary of Defense (OSD) supports a vast and complicated system of education and professional development for civilians. In 1997, it sponsored 20 institutions as well as 36 programs within DoD and 68 programs external to DoD.[1] Beyond this, the system includes many additional institutions and programs sponsored by the Departments of the Army, Navy, and Air Force. Although the main task of assessment must focus on the quality and productivity of the services offered by specific providers of education and professional development, the study found that a higher-level assessment of the system as a whole is also crucial.

Such high-level assessment has two main purposes: (1) to determine whether the stakeholder and system-level needs are being addressed and (2) to identify

[1]DoD Management Reform Memorandum 3.

opportunities to improve efficiency in existing programs. In the first case, system-level assessment compares the needs of the population served to the programs offered by the system. In a corporate setting, for example, such an assessment might find that there are corporate-level goals that are not being addressed by education and training programs that are run by individual business units. In higher education, on the other hand, a system-level assessment might find that certain geographical regions are not being well served by existing institutions.

To achieve the second aim, the assessment examines whether the system's resources are being allocated efficiently. The report offers a number of illustrations of organizations that are improving their productivity through this process.

- The Texas Higher Education Coordinating Board, for example, conducts regular program reviews to assess whether a proposed program is based on established needs, whether it will duplicate other programs in the same area, and whether it falls within an institution's mission.
- In the private sector, training is being elevated to the corporate level in the interest of both quality and efficiency. At Lucent Technologies, for example, such corporate oversight has streamlined education and professional development by assessing whether limited education and training resources are being used in a way that promotes overall corporate goals. Its focus on business needs, rather than student demand, allowed the company to reduce the number of courses taught throughout the corporation from 70,000 to about 2,000.
- In the U.S. Air Force, the Air Force Occupational Measurement Squadron (AFOMS) surveys every person in a particular occupational specialty to identify the skills used and not used in particular jobs. Based on this information, Air Force managers assess the content of specific training programs to eliminate irrelevant instruction from courses and ensure that graduates acquire the skills and knowledge they need to do their jobs.

A clear trend in all the systems considered in this study is the development of a learning organization of some sort that is responsible for more than just the assessment of existing providers. These organizations promote communications among stakeholders and develop a clear link between education and professional development on the one hand and the basic mission of the system on the other. Corporate learning organizations describe this as "becoming a strategic partner" in the corporation. Such an organization facilitates dialog among key stakeholders, assembles information on workforce needs and existing programs, and serves as an interface between customers and providers.

The study recommends that the Chancellor's office advocate the development of a central learning organization, modeled after a corporate learning organization or a state higher education coordinating board. Creation of such an entity would require high-level DoD support and substantial collaboration among a range of stakeholders, including other organizations within DoD responsible for workforce planning and personnel policy.

Approaches to Provider Assessment or Certification of Students

In reviewing a wide variety of assessment approaches, this study identified key similarities and differences among the approaches and classified them into four basic models. The first model involves the use of an intermediary organization that is responsible for reviewing the process used by individual providers to assess their own quality and productivity. In the second model, an intermediary organization conducts the actual assessment of providers. In the third model, providers conduct their own assessment with no involvement of an intermediary. The fourth model differs from the other three in that it focuses on the learner rather than the provider and involves the certification of student competencies. Each approach has strengths and weaknesses that make it more appropriate for some circumstances than for others. For that reason, no one approach can be considered a "best practice" model. The best approach depends on the context of the assessment.

The Most Promising Approach for the Chancellor

The Chancellor's office is neither a provider of education and professional development nor a direct consumer of the services of such providers. We thus describe the role of the Chancellor's office as that of an intermediary. Models 1, 2, and 4, which allow a role for an intermediary, are therefore the most relevant to the Chancellor's office in considering an appropriate role for itself. However, the Chancellor's office might also wish to learn about the best practices under Model 3 in order to serve as a clearinghouse of information useful to provider institutions.

In considering possible assessment approaches for an intermediary, the study identified six factors as the most important to consider in choosing an approach to assessing the quality and productivity of provider services. These are (1) purpose of the assessment (accountability versus improvement of outcomes), (2) level of authority, (3) level of resources, (4) centralization of operations, (5) system heterogeneity, and (6) system complexity. Given the characteristics of the DoD system of education and professional development—a highly complex, decentralized system with heterogeneous service providers—and the establishment of a Chancellor's office with little formal authority over service providers and uncertain resources, Model 1 would probably be the most promising approach.

This model is based on quality improvement concepts that have been used in the business world for the last 25 years and were adopted by the International Organization for Standardization (ISO) in the 1980s to promote high-quality standards among manufacturing companies. To qualify for ISO 9000 certification, an organization must define and document its quality standards for producing its goods or services in a policy document or "quality manual" that is reviewed by a third party.

The academic audit, a new approach to education assessment that has been influenced by the ISO, is another example of Model 1. The audit is conducted by an intermediary organization and focuses on assuring that providers of education have effective processes in place for measuring their own quality and thus can engage in ongoing self-improvement. Because this approach is more sensitive to the different missions and characteristics of institutions than are other approaches, it is particularly useful for systems with a diverse set of providers.

The U.S. Department of Transportation (DOT) follows a modified version of Model 1. Although the central learning organization does not have the authority to assess the processes used by individual lines of business (operating agencies) that are both the providers and stakeholders of education and professional development, it does recommend certain assessment practices in a policy guide called the *Learning and Development Framework*. This variation on the model is effective in situations where the intermediary organization—in this case, the Learning and Development (L&D) Program within the DOT—has limited authority over provider or stakeholder groups. While the L&D unit can do its best to influence outcomes by offering different types of assistance, its role is to promote quality rather than ensure it.

The key advantage of Model 1 is that it delegates to provider organizations the task of defining goals, measuring outcomes, and evaluating outcomes. As a result, this approach can accommodate the many diverse providers within the DoD education and professional development system. Because they have such control over their own assessment, providers are less likely to resist the process and are more likely to use it to promote improvements.

The primary disadvantage of Model 1 relative to Model 2 is that it emphasizes improvement over accountability. The trade-off between the two purposes of assessment remains an important issue for the Chancellor's office. However, even if the Chancellor decides that its main goal is accountability, it may be too costly to develop an appropriate process for measuring quality and productivity for all providers in the system based on Model 2. An attractive alternative would be to modify Model 1 to include specific reporting requirements or standards of performance.

Three-Step Process of Assessment

Regardless of the model selected, the study found that there are three key steps that must be included in any provider or student assessment:[2]

- Identifying goals of the education activities under consideration
- Measuring the outcomes related to those goals
- Evaluating whether the outcomes meet those goals.

The literature review revealed several broad lessons concerning these steps. First, each of these steps should be linked to one another and the process as a whole should be driven by the goals. It is especially important to avoid selecting measures before or without defining goals. Practitioners in higher education, corporate, and government settings stress the tendency of people to value what is measured and focus exclusively on that information rather than linking what is measured to the purpose of the activity.

Second, developing measures that relate to goals is a crucial if difficult step. It is often difficult to find an adequate measure of achievement for a particular goal. However, it is usually better to use an imperfect measure of a specific goal than it is to use a perfect measure of something different. Engaging a broad range of stakeholders in this process helps to keep it focused on the goals of the undertaking. Such stakeholder involvement and continuous feedback is an explicit element of both the Baldrige Award process and the balanced scorecard.

[2]The terms *assessment* and *evaluation* are often used interchangeably in the literature. For purposes of internal consistency, we use the term *assessment* to refer to the start-to-finish process of examining the quality or productivity of an education or professional development activity. We use the term *evaluation* to refer to the step in the assessment process in which performance measures are examined and a judgment about performance is made on the basis of that examination.

Third, there is a broad trend in assessment to focus less on input measures and more on process and outcome measures. Measuring outcomes alone may not result in improvement, but considering the intervening processes that use resources to produce outcomes provides information more useful to program improvement. This process and outcome emphasis is reflected in the Baldrige Award process.

Finally, except for certificate or licensing programs, providers of professional development courses are not likely to be able to rely on preexisting evaluation tools with known validity and reliability characteristics. Rather, they will most likely have to develop measures of learning outcomes on their own. The literature provides some guidelines for developing such measures and for avoiding major sources of invalidity and unreliability. The Chancellor's office should be able to provide such information to service providers and help them apply it to their own assessment process.

Acknowledgments

We thank Susan Hosek and Susan Everingham for the guidance they provided as directors of the program under which this report was produced. RAND colleagues Jim Dewar, Cathy Stasz, Tom Szayna, and Al Robbert provided helpful guidance at several stages of this research. The authors benefited from conversations with Joe Beel, Estela Bensimon, David Dill, Peter Ewell, Maryann Gray, Bill Harrod, Terry Halvorsen, Jim Mingle, Laura Palmer Noone, Harry O'Neil, Karen Paulson, Matthew Peters, Steve Green, William Jennings, Joseph Tartell, and Ralph Wolff.

Maryann Gray and Larry Hanser provided helpful reviews of an earlier draft. We also benefited from comments of seminar participants at RAND. Lisa Hochman and Donna White provided helpful secretarial support. Christina Pitcher carefully edited the final copy.

Jerome Smith, James Raney, John Dill, Beverly Popelka, Leslye Fuller, and Donna Brown of the DoD Office of the Chancellor for Civilian Education and Professional Development provided useful feedback on the research leading up to this report.

Acronyms

AAU	Academic Audit Unit (UK)
ABA	American Bar Association
ABET	Accreditation Board of Engineering and Technology
ACT	American College Testing
ACCSCT	Accrediting Commission of Career Schools and Colleges of Technology
AETC	Air Education and Training Command
AFOMS	Air Force Occupational Measurement Squadron
AFSC	Air Force Specialty Code
ALOA	Adult Learning Outcomes Assessment
AMA	American Medical Association
AQIP	Academic Quality Improvement Project
AQMS	Academic Quality Management System
ASQC	American Society for Quality Control Standards
ASTD	American Society for Training and Development
BAM	Baseline Assessment Memorandum
CEO	Chief Executive Officer
CHEA	Council for Higher Education Accreditation
CLAST	College Level Academic Skills Test
CLO	chief learning officer
CMU	Carnegie Mellon University
CNA	Center for Naval Analyses
CNET	Chief of Naval Education and Training
CNO	Chief of Naval Operations
COCA	Cognitive Outcomes Comprehensive Assessment
CPE	Council on Postsecondary Education
CQI	continuous quality improvement
CRE	Association of European Universities
DFM	Department of Management, U.S. Air Force Academy
DoD	Department of Defense

DOT	U.S. Department of Transportation
DRI	Defense Reform Initiative
EBI	Educational Benchmarking Institute
ESL	English as a Second Language
ETS	Educational Testing Service
FHWA	Federal Highway Administration
FTE	full-time equivalent
GAO	U.S. General Accounting Office
GED	General Educational Development
GMAT	Graduate Management Admission Test
GPA	grade point average
GPRA	Government Performance and Results Act
GRE	Graduate Record Examination
HMI	Her Majesty's Inspector (UK)
HR	Human Resources
IAME/AACSB	International Association of Management Education/American Assembly of Collegiate Schools of Business
IR	Institutional Research
IRB	Institutional Review Board
ISD	Instructional System Development
ISO	International Organization for Standardization
ITS	Intelligent Transportation Systems
L&D	learning and development
LPC	Learning and Performance Center (Lucent Technologies)
LSAT	Legal Scholastic Aptitude Test
MCAT	Medical Colleges Admissions Test
MSA	Middle States Association of Colleges and Schools
N8	Deputy Chief of Naval Operations (Resources, Warfare, Requirements and Assessments)
N81	N8's Training and Education Assessment Division
N82	N8's Fiscal Management Division
NAB	National Advisory Board
NACUBO	National Association of Colleges and Universities Business Officers

NASC	Northwest Association of Schools and Colleges
NAVSEA	Naval Sea Systems Command
NCA	North Central Association of Colleges and Schools Commission on Institutions of Higher Education
NCHEMS	National Center for Higher Education Management Systems
NEASC (CIHE and CTCI)	New England Association of Schools and Colleges (Commission on Institutions of Higher Education and Commission on Technical and Career Institutions)
NIST	National Institute of Standards and Technology
NITRAS	Navy Integrated Training Resource Assessment System
NWA	Northwest Association of Schools and Colleges
OA	operating administration
OMB	U.S. Office of Management and Budget
OSD	Office of the Secretary of Defense
RAB	Registrar Accreditation Board
ROI	return on investment
SACS	Southern Association of Colleges and Schools
SAT	Scholastic Aptitude Test
SCANS	Secretary's Commission on Achieving Necessary Skills
SCH	Semester Credit Hours
SCOPE	Strategic Committee on Postsecondary Education
SMEs	subject matter experts
SOR	Services Operating Report
SSTAS	Standard Schoolhouse Training and Analysis System
TEAC	Teacher Education Accreditation Council
TQM	total quality management
UCLA	University of California at Los Angeles
UCSD	University of California at San Diego
UGC	University Grants Committee (Hong Kong)
UK	United Kingdom
USAFA	U.S. Air Force Academy
USC	University of Southern California
USUHS	Uniformed Services University of the Health Sciences
UUPP	The Urban Universities Portfolio Project

WASC (Jr. and Sr.)	Western Association of Schools and Colleges (Accrediting Commission for Community and Junior Colleges and Accrediting Commission for Senior Colleges and Universities)
WECM	workforce education course manual
WGU	Western Governors University

1. Introduction

Background

The Department of Defense (DoD) Office of the Chancellor for Education and Professional Development was established in October 1998 and formally chartered in September 1999 to serve as the "principal advocate for the academic quality and cost-effectiveness of all DoD civilian education and professional development activities."[1] The Chancellor is responsible for working with DoD entities that sponsor such education and professional development to ensure that appropriate standards of quality and productivity are achieved. An important role for the principal advocate of academic quality and cost-effectiveness is to identify and promote viable methods for the assessment of academic quality and productivity.

The Department of Defense is the single largest employer of civil service workers in the U.S. government. As is the case in many large organizations, DoD has developed a complex structure to provide education and professional development to a workforce of about 700,000 employees. In fiscal year 1997, the staff offices of the Office of the Secretary of Defense (OSD) sponsored 20 institutions and an additional 36 programs promoting the education and professional development of DoD civilian employees.[2] In addition, OSD sponsored 68 programs provided by organizations external to DoD. Although substantial, those numbers do not include other institutions and programs for civilian education and professional development run specifically by or for other components of DoD such as the Army, Navy, and Air Force.

---

[1]DoD Directive 5124.7, September 27, 1999, Office of the Chancellor for Education and Professional Development.

[2]These institutions, programs and courses are described in detail in DoD Management Reform Memorandum 3. Examples of OSD-sponsored institutions include the Defense Language Institute, the Uniformed Services University of the Health Sciences, and the Defense Contract Audit Institute. Programs include DoD-run programs, such as the Defense Acquisition Career Development Program, and various agency-sponsored scholarship and fellowship programs. Examples of externally provided programs include a senior executive seminar at Carnegie Mellon University and the Congressional Fellowship Program run by the American Political Science Association.

Motivation

The establishment of the Chancellor's office is an outgrowth of a larger effort, called the Defense Reform Initiative (DRI). The purpose of the DRI is to improve business affairs within DoD. The Defense Reform Initiative Report, issued in November 1997, highlighted options for reducing DoD infrastructure and improving efficiency. The report focused particular attention on the education, training, and professional development of DoD civilian employees. According to the report:

> [DoD] is a world-class organization despite rendering second-rate education, training, and professional development to its civilian employees. Among the lessons of corporate America is that every successful organization finds its people to be its most important asset, and reflects their importance in a strong, corporate-sponsored program of continuous training and professional development. DoD has many educational programs and institutions, but their quality is mixed (Cohen, 1997, p. 20).

In the report, Secretary of Defense William Cohen specifically recommends the establishment of a Chancellor for Education and Professional Development. The role of the Chancellor would be "to raise the quality of civilian training and professional development to world-class standards" (ibid.).[3]

Implicit in the DRI recommendation are several notions: that civilian education and professional development is important to DoD, that the quality of existing education and professional development is lacking and must be improved, and that oversight or intervention is necessary to improve the quality and productivity of these activities. These themes were reiterated by Secretary Cohen at Chancellor Smith's oath of office ceremony.[4]

The establishment of the Chancellor's office can also be understood as part of a more general trend toward increased demands for accountability in the federal government. In the 1990s, Congress passed several pieces of legislation, including the Government Performance and Results Act (GPRA) of 1993, that address waste and inefficiency, increase program effectiveness, and improve the internal management of the federal government. The GPRA directs the 24 largest federal agencies (including DoD) to submit five-year strategic plans as well as annual performance plans with their budget requests to Congress. The

[3]For a more detailed discussion of the current and potential challenges facing DoD with respect to the civilian workforce, see Levy et al. (forthcoming).

[4]"Secretary of Defense Hosts Oath of Office Ceremony for First Chancellor for Education and Professional Development," Office of Assistant Secretary of Defense (Public Affairs) News Release No. 516-98, October 2, 1998.

legislation promotes a results-oriented focus by requiring several specific elements in the plans, including:

- a description of general goals and objectives
- a description of the relationship between performance goals in the annual performance plan and the general goals and objectives in the strategic plan
- a description of program evaluations used, including a schedule for future evaluations.[5]

The annual performance plan requirement of GPRA offers an opportunity for the federal agency to make the link between long-term strategic plans for the agency and daily activities of managers and staff. Each annual plan must include performance targets for all activities included in agency budget requests, a description of resources that will be used to meet the targets, and a plan for how results will be measured.[6] This objective-oriented approach to assessment is being implemented within government agencies, including DoD.

Objectives and Approach

The DoD Office of the Chancellor for Education and Professional Development asked RAND to (1) conduct a broad review of the approaches currently used by other organizations to assess academic quality and productivity and (2) identify potentially promising approaches for the Chancellor's office to consider in assessing academic quality and productivity in DoD institutions, programs, and courses of instruction that provide education and professional development for DoD civilian personnel.

Our research is thus based on a review of the literature on quality and productivity in education and professional development activities and of the methods used by various organizations that assess quality and productivity. The analysis was supplemented by interviews with experts on quality and productivity assessment, attendance at conferences on quality and productivity assessment, and site visits to organizations responsible for assessing quality and productivity.

The literature on this topic falls into two categories. The first includes theoretical literature on quality and productivity and offers general frameworks for assessment, including accreditation, program review, academic audit, and such

[5]OMB, 1998.

[6]U.S. GAO, 1996.

business-based methods as the balanced scorecard, the Baldrige criteria, ISO 9000, and benchmarking. We reviewed a broad range of sources, including journal articles, published reports or manuals, and web sites.

Because the theoretical literature is so voluminous, we chose to focus on the objectives-oriented approach for evaluating quality and productivity, which is the dominant trend in higher education, business, and government. The GPRA, for example, mandates that government programs be evaluated and justified on the basis of their contribution to the performance objectives of the government agencies responsible for them. An objectives-oriented approach often includes other considerations (e.g., it might include a consumer-oriented approach to the extent that consumer demand is taken as an indicator of the quality of the program delivered).

The other body of literature on quality and productivity assessment describes the actual practices of organizations that are assessing the quality and/or productivity of education and training services. Our review of this literature focused on new developments and "best practices" used for quality and productivity assessment that appeared to have relevance for the Chancellor's office. In some areas, the existing literature included comprehensive reviews, comparisons, and evaluations of the assessment practices. Such literature existed mainly for institutions of higher education and corporate universities. In reviewing the quality and productivity assessment activities of other types of organizations, we had to rely mainly on primary source documents (e.g., reports, web sites).

In addition to the literature review, we conducted phone and in-person interviews with representatives of organizations responsible for assessing academic quality and productivity as well as with experts in the field of academic quality and productivity assessment. Such interviews helped us to identify organizations whose assessment efforts were well regarded in the assessment community at large, to identify new assessment trends, and to supplement written information. Such interviews were used to supplement the literature-based case studies for the Western Association of Schools and Colleges (WASC), the University of Phoenix, and the academic audit. More-detailed case studies were conducted to gather information on the Kentucky Council on Postsecondary Education; the Texas Higher Education Coordinating Board; the U.S. Department of Transportation; the U.S. Air Force Training and Education; the U.S. Air Force Academy, Department of Management; and Lucent Technologies Learning and Performance Center. Our case studies were selected to provide a broad review of approaches to evaluating academic quality and productivity. To the extent possible we focused on organizations that were well regarded by peers or experts in the field, were doing something novel, or faced particular challenges relevant to the Chancellor's office.

The main document synthesizes the literature review and draws lessons from the appendices. In spite of the wide variety of organizations reviewed, we were able to identify key similarities across approaches. These similarities provided a foundation for a categorization scheme that we developed and which provides a structure for this report.

Each case study and area of literature reviewed is summarized in a separate appendix. Each appendix that relied on material from interviews and case studies was reviewed by the interviewee for accuracy.

Organization of the Report

In conducting this broad literature review, we found that a number of very different activities are described by the general terms "assessment of education and professional development." As a result, a large part of the effort that went into this report involved defining terms and creating a structure for talking about the different elements of assessment used in different sectors. We are aware of no other report that brings together lessons on assessment from such a wide variety of organizations and believe that this document will prove useful not only to the DoD Chancellor, but also to those interested in assessment in universities, state higher education systems, corporations, and other government agencies.

In this document, we draw together the results of our broad review of literature and practice and highlight important themes, lessons, and best practices of potential interest to the Chancellor's office. In the next section, we present a conceptual framework for understanding the process of academic quality and productivity assessment, including definitions of key terms. Section 2 establishes the importance of conducting both a system-level assessment, which we call Phase One of the assessment process, as well as individual provider-level assessments. It also offers an introduction to the main approaches (or models) used in assessing quality and productivity of individual providers. Section 3 provides a more detailed description of the system-level assessment in Phase One, and Section 4 compares the four main models to assessing quality and productivity in Phase Two, including their relative strengths and limitations. Section 5 discusses the factors that are most important to consider in deciding on an appropriate model for assessment, with particular attention to the Chancellor's office and the DoD system within which it has responsibilities. Section 6 describes the three steps involved in any assessment process: (1)

defining goals of the system, (2) choosing appropriate measures, and (3) using those measures to evaluate progress toward those goals. Section 7 offers some final observations designed to help the Chancellor's office establish itself in this arena.

The appendices contain detailed descriptions of the methods used by various organizations in their assessment of academic quality and productivity.

2. Framework

In this section, we describe the framework we developed for analyzing the assessment of quality and productivity of education systems. First we define an educational system in general and the system of DoD civilian education and professional development in particular. These systems are highly complex, and it is important to understand their key components and the relationships between them. Then we describe three sets of distinctions that we use to analyze how assessment is conducted.

Before describing our framework, we should clarify what we mean by certain terms that are not always used consistently in the literature or in the assessment community. For example, we use the term *assessment* to refer to the multistep process of examining the quality and productivity of education and professional development activities. We use the term *evaluation* to describe the step in the assessment process in which measures of quality and productivity are examined against some standard of performance. We use the term *productivity* to mean the level and quality of service obtained from a given amount of resources (Epstein, 1992). In this sense, it is synonymous with efficiency. If the provider of education can produce a greater quantity and/or higher quality of service with the same amount of resources, it has improved its productivity or efficiency. Quality is used interchangeably with effectiveness. There is no single definition of quality: It means different things to different people. In an assessment process, the meaning of quality typically emerges through the process of identifying goals for the assessment. The quality or effectiveness of an education system is defined in terms of performance as required by multiple stakeholders including students, employers, parents, accreditors, and the government (McGuinness, 1997). In this sense, quality is in the eye of the beholder.

As can be seen by these definitions, the concept of productivity includes a consideration of quality so that productivity improvement is not synonymous with cost cutting. Both quality and productivity are thus multifaceted concepts, inextricably linked with the goals and missions of the system or institution under consideration and of its stakeholders.

The System of DoD Civilian Education and Professional Development

An education system consists of customers of education, providers of education, and intermediary organizations that mediate, oversee, or assess educational services. All these are stakeholders within the system who have an interest in the educational services provided. There are also stakeholders outside the system itself, such as taxpayers, legislatures, and the business community. Even though they are not part of DoD, they are stakeholders of the civilian education and professional development system because they provide funding for the education system or because they stand to benefit from its services, or both.

The main customers within an education system are the learners themselves. All DoD civilian employees are potential customers of the civilian education and professional development system, although at any given time only a small percentage of employees are enrolled in formal courses. Systems can contain other customers as well. Figure 2.1 illustrates different levels of customers of the civilian education and professional development system within DoD. DoD itself can be considered the highest-level customer. Within DoD, all departments and agencies are also customers because they purchase educational services for their employees. Examples are military departments, such as the Army, or agencies such as the Defense Finance and Accounting Service. Individual managers within these organizations are also customers of educational services, with a direct interest in the career development of their personnel. Although most learners work in such hierarchical organizations with managers who have the authority to direct their education and professional development, some learners may also be independent consumers of education.

All large systems of education have such layered schemes of customers. In corporations that provide education and training to their employees, the highest level of customer within their system would be the corporation. Within the corporation, different business units and managers are also customers of educational services for their employees. In state higher education systems, the state is the highest level of customer. Companies and employers are often customers as well, since they pay for educational services for their employees. Within companies, managers are also customers when they are involved in decisions that lead their employees to enroll in courses at institutions of higher education in the state. Those companies that do not directly pay for the education and professional training of their employees are not customers, but they should be considered stakeholders in the system because they stand to benefit from the creation of a well-trained workforce.

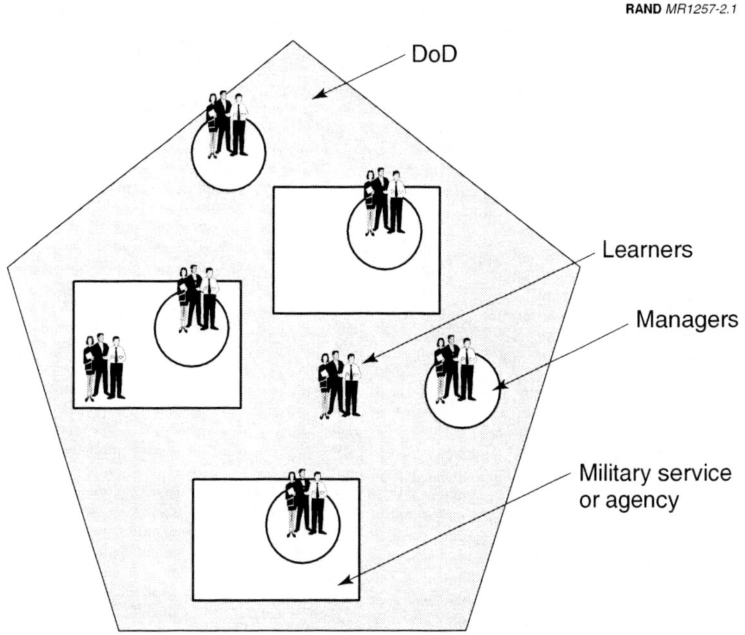

Figure 2.1—Different Levels of Customers of DoD Civilian Education and Professional Development

Providers of education services also exist at different levels of aggregation. Some providers are formal institutions offering degree programs and courses in a wide variety of areas; others offer only a single course on a specific topic. Figure 2.2 illustrates the different levels of providers within the DoD system of civilian education and professional training. It also shows that institutional providers can exist both inside and outside DoD. An example of an internal institutional provider would be the National Defense University. It serves DoD civilians and is therefore part of the system of DoD civilian education and professional development, but it also educates military personnel and is thus also part of the system of professional military education. An example of an institutional provider outside DoD would be another government agency, such as the U.S. Department of Agriculture Graduate School, or traditional colleges and universities, where DoD civilians can enroll in courses that are paid for by their employer.

These provider relationships also hold true for large state higher education systems. For example, citizens of Kentucky can attend college at a public institution in Kentucky, a private institution in Kentucky, or an institution in another state. Corporations also usually offer a mix of internally and externally provided education and training activities.

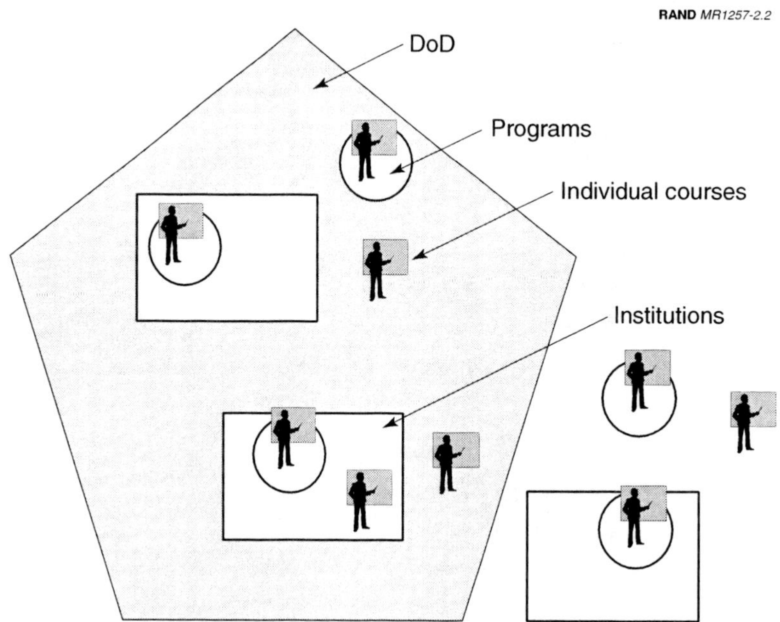

Figure 2.2—Different Levels of Providers of DoD Civilian Education and Professional Development

The system of DoD civilian education as a whole is summarized by Figure 2.3. It consists of all customers, all providers, and intermediaries as well. Intermediaries are organizations that mediate between customers and providers and provide a locus for the consideration of system-level issues. Potential roles for an intermediary include

- assessing quality and productivity
- providing useful information and guidance to customers and/or providers
- helping to aggregate the demands of many customers
- helping to resolve disagreements among different levels of customers or between customer and provider
- leading systemwide planning efforts
- providing incentives for change at the provider level.

The Chancellor's office is an example of an intermediary in the system of DoD civilian education and professional training. It is not yet clear just which role or roles that office will assume.[1] In other education systems, examples of

[1]The specific roles assumed by the Chancellor's office should be determined through a strategic planning process. See Levy et al. (forthcoming) for information on approaches to strategic planning.

intermediaries are state higher education planning boards, professional societies, and corporate learning organizations.

RAND *MR1257-2.3*

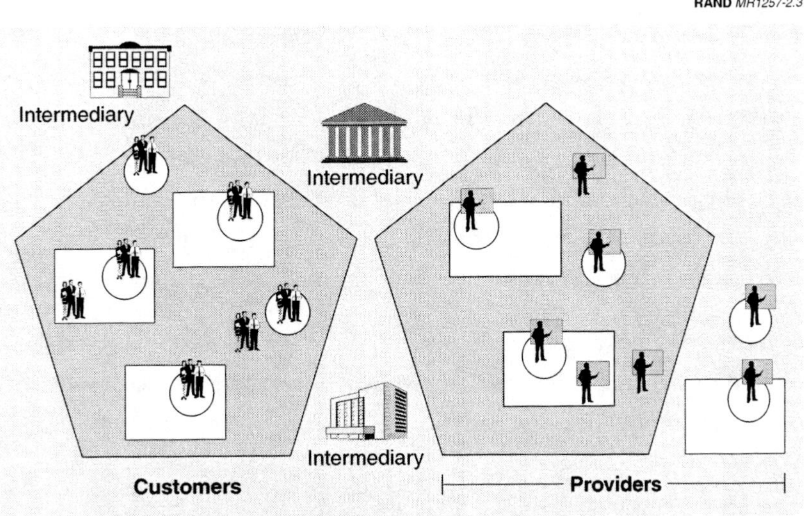

Figure 2.3—The DoD System Includes Customers, Their Providers, and Intermediaries

Framework for Analyzing the Assessment of System Performance

Assessment of the quality and productivity of such vast systems of education is a complex and multidimensional process. Our analysis of the process, as well as the organization of this report, rests on several important distinctions concerning the level of assessment, the approach to assessment, and the steps of the assessment process.

First, our analysis suggests that any assessment of system performance must proceed at two levels: the system level and the provider level. Much of the literature on assessment in higher education and corporations emphasizes provider-level assessment. However, our review of specific organizations highlights the importance of assessment that takes place at the system level. That type of assessment, which we call Phase One, poses two questions that cannot be answered by assessing individual providers: (1) Are all potential customers being served by the system? and (2) Are system-level objectives being addressed by providers? Provider-level assessment, which we call Phase Two, evaluates how well individual providers of education are meeting the needs of their customers. We found that many assessment activities simply overlook Phase

One and therefore fail to discern systemic problems. Since system-level assessment can only be carried out by an intermediary organization that stands outside provider institutions, it is particularly important for the Chancellor's office to consider.[2]

Second, for Phase Two assessment of provider institutions, we identified four main approaches to assessment that differ along several dimensions. Three of the approaches, which we call Models 1, 2, and 3, focus on assessing the performance of the provider. Model 4 focuses on assessing the competencies of the student. The models are further distinguished by such factors as who designs and carries out the assessment process and what its primary purpose is.

Third, regardless of what approach is taken to the assessment of providers, our research found that there are basically three steps in the process, each with its own important requirements:

- *Identify* the goals of education or professional development.
- *Measure* performance: Identify and implement measures of performance.
- *Evaluate* the extent to which the performance measures meet the education and professional development goals.

The first step, identifying goals, is often overlooked in system assessments. When assessors go right to the task of defining measures of performance without first identifying goals, they run the danger of committing themselves to measuring outcomes that do not clearly relate to the objectives of the education system. They may either develop extraneous measures or neglect measures that reflect core system objectives. In the first instance, time will be wasted collecting and analyzing irrelevant information. In the second instance, they will not know whether the system is meeting these objectives.

The next section describes the first of our distinctions: how system-level assessment differs from the assessment of individual providers—why it is important, how specific organizations have implemented it, and what benefits it brings.

---

[2]Because of the relative emphasis placed on Phase Two assessment in the literature (this is what most people think of when they discuss assessment), our report goes into more detail on Phase Two. However, we stress the importance of Phase One and draw lessons on Phase One from case studies.

3. Phase One: System-Level Assessment

The assessment of any education system involves more than assessing individual providers of that education. Our research revealed the importance of a higher-level assessment that addresses issues that go beyond individual institutions, such as whether the network of providers is reaching all potential customers, whether it is meeting the needs of the system as a whole, and whether the system itself, rather than any individual provider or customer, is allocating its resources efficiently. System-level assessment of this kind has not received much treatment in the literature. As a result, our research drew on the case studies of state higher education systems such as the Texas Higher Education Coordinating Board, corporations such as Lucent Technologies, and military services and government agencies, such as the U.S. Department of Transportation's system of education and professional development.

Goals of System-Level Assessment

There are two main goals of system-level assessment. One is to detect any misalignments between customer needs, system-level needs, and provider offerings. The other is to determine whether the system's resources are being allocated in a way that will optimize their effects. Each of these objectives poses its own challenges.

Identifying Misalignment

Misalignments can come in various forms. For example, system-level assessment should address whether all potential customers are being reached by the services provided. In a state higher education system, for example, certain geographical regions of a state may be underserved by the existing set of institutions. In a corporation or government agency, the needs of certain lines of business might be ignored by existing programs.

In other cases, the customer that is not being well served may be at a higher level of the hierarchy of customers. For example, the lines of business in a corporation might have narrower training objectives than the corporate officers who might be interested in building a corporate culture or other more general training. For example, in corporations where training and education are the responsibility of individual business units, no single business unit may want to take responsibility for corporate leadership training.

Another type of misalignment in the system is that the network of providers may not be fully supporting the overall mission of the system. In other words, educational services may be offered that have nothing to do with carrying out the organization's goals.[1] At Lucent Technologies, for example, educational activities are provided with one purpose in mind: to help the company achieve growth in key markets. If a program or course cannot be linked to this objective, Lucent will not offer it.

This focus on mission-driven education and professional development can also be found in public sector organizations, such as the U.S. Department of Transportation (DOT). The goal of the DOT Learning and Development Program is to "enhance the operation of the Department in accomplishing its mission by investing in the development and utilization of its human resources" (DOT, 1997). This goal is linked to DOT's overall management strategy, "ONE DOT," which is designed to develop an integrated and unified department to provide the highest-quality transportation system for the country. The Learning and Development Program sees a clear need for partnership with managers of the operating administrations who control key business areas in designing and assessing training.

Optimizing Resource Allocation at the System Level

All of the education systems we studied were dealing with limited resources. Many of the education systems are embedded within larger systems (e.g., corporations, government agencies, or states) that had primary missions other than education, training, and professional development. As a result, the leaders of the larger system had to determine how to allocate education and training resources in an efficient, effective manner. This is the crux of the system-level productivity issue: Are the system's resources being allocated in such a way as to maximize their impact? Our case studies illustrate the ways in which different systems address this issue.

---

[1]It is important to point out that many systems do not view this type of misalignment as a problem. For example, some companies might support training and education that benefits the employees as individuals (e.g., enrichment courses) even if it does not relate to their jobs. Similarly, state institutions of higher education often offer courses or sponsor research that is not of direct interest to the state.

How Systems Establish a Structure for Such Assessment

To carry out such high-level assessment, most large systems set up an entity responsible for looking at the "big picture" education and professional development issues that can be assessed only at the system level. This entity is neither a direct customer nor a provider, but an intermediary. In states, that entity is a state higher education board; in corporations, military services, and government agencies, it is a central learning organization of some type.

As our case studies showed, these intermediaries must be closely tied to the customers and providers. Although the education systems we reviewed differ in profound ways, those that were engaged in system-level assessment were surprisingly consistent on this point: They were able to operate at a strategic level because they had high-level involvement from system leaders—such as the state governor, the CEO, or the secretary of the military service—and they were fully integrated into the operating units of the organization in which they were embedded or the institutions over which they had oversight. This integration provides access to regular information on the priorities and needs of the overall system of which they are a part.

Several case studies provide examples of such integration:

- In Kentucky, the governor has made higher education a defining issue of his administration and played a key role in reshaping the Kentucky Council on Postsecondary Education (CPE). There is also a Strategic Committee on Postsecondary Education (SCOPE), which includes the governor, the state general assembly leadership, and the leadership of CPE. The purpose of SCOPE is to ensure that the elected leaders play a role in developing the strategic agenda for postsecondary education.
- In the corporate environment, central learning organizations, headed by a "chief learning officer," are replacing a model in which training was controlled by individual lines of business and each had its own training activities to meet their specific needs. This shift to more centralized planning is similar to the transition that information technology went through in the 1980s, when the term "chief information officer" was relatively new. Corporate learning organizations have recognized the importance of getting buy-in from both the company's chief executive officer and the heads of lines of business in support of their efforts.
- In the Air Force education and training establishment, many stakeholders are involved at different stages of the process: Commanders at different levels identify training requirements and priorities; Air Education and Training Command is the primary agency responsible for training development and

assessment; Major commands identify mission demands and training/personnel needs; Air Force Deputy Chiefs of Staff oversee the management and policies for training. They, along with the training managers, supervisors, and students, provide input into the quality assessment process.

- The U.S. Department of Transportation (DOT) education and professional development process is coordinated through the Learning and Development Program in the Office of Human Resource Management, as described earlier. There is continuous collaboration between this program and the operating administrations of DOT. Members of the human resources department of every operating administration sit on the Learning and Development Council and provide input and feedback on education and development policies for the department as a whole.
- Lucent Technologies established a structure for systemwide assessment by creating business performance councils that support curricula in 15 different areas, such as software, wireless, diversity, and program management. Each business performance council is composed of powerful people in the company. For example, the software committee is headed by the Vice President for Software. There are over 160 people on these councils. There is a dean for each curriculum, and about 20 subject matter experts help with curriculum design. The success of the business performance councils and of the learning and development activities in general is driven by several factors including strong, executive-level leadership and support and broad involvement with the business units. The councils are responsible for much more than education and training, highlighting the link between education and professional development and corporate goals. They consider all strategic issues related to the particular subject area.

Such integrated learning organizations are well suited to the tasks of Phase One assessment.

How Systems Identify Misalignments

One of the goals of Phase One assessment is to identify the gaps between what is needed and what is provided, determine which gaps can and should be addressed by learning solutions, and develop learning solutions to help close those gaps. As a practical matter, however, the first step in that process—often referred to as needs analysis—is difficult to accomplish.

The most structured approach to needs analysis we observed was in the Air Force. The Air Force uses the Instructional System Development model to determine what instruction is and is not needed. This step is conducted by the Air Force Occupational Measurement Squadron (AFOMS), which surveys every person in a particular occupational specialty[2] to determine the skills that are used (and not used) in different jobs. The activities of AFOMS provide the information necessary for Air Force managers to determine whether the appropriate training needs are being addressed. They do not address individual job performance or the quality of the training provided. That is done by staff at the training centers. AFOMS focuses exclusively on collecting data about the work done in every specialty in every career field and comparing that with information on the training being provided by the Air Force. AFOMS reports become the departure point for decisionmaking on key issues, including skills that are being trained but not used in the Air Force and skills that are used but not trained.

Lucent Technologies has also recognized the importance of this type of needs analysis, and the different business performance councils are at different stages in the development of tools for identifying competency gaps. At this point, only two of the councils (software and program management) have a strong needs analysis methodology in place. The software council makes use of an industrywide tool called the Kiviat. The Kiviat is a measurement tool that helps assess proficiencies and identify gaps in eight software project areas: customer focus, project management, project team variables, tools, quality focus, methodologies, physical environment, and metrics. The tool includes a detailed instrument, with 20 metrics in each area, for measuring a company's performance relative to others in the industry on a five-point scale. The performance measures are evaluated on the basis of ten years of industrywide data. The software council uses the results of the Kiviat to point out areas where Lucent's performance is not leading edge and then considers whether learning solutions might be able to help improve performance in these areas.

The two state higher education coordinating boards that we reviewed had a much less structured approach to needs analysis at the system level. Often, gaps between needs and offerings are identified when some constituency group is motivated to complain about the current offerings. For example, in the 1990s, 48 counties filed a lawsuit against the State of Texas because they felt that the region was not being provided with enough educational opportunities. This lawsuit led

[2]Every military and civilian job in the Air Force is associated with a functional Air Force Specialty Code (AFSC), which is in turn part of a career field. Each career field has a high-level manager—a person who is in charge of the enlisted, officer, and civilian workforce in that functional area. Among other things, that individual is responsible for the training and education of individuals in that career field. The career field manager is in the Pentagon (functional headquarters) or in a specific command (when the specialty is confined to one major command).

to growth in higher education spending in that region of the state. However, the State of Texas recently commissioned a study by the Council for Aid to Education to help identify state higher education needs through demographic and labor market analyses (Benjamin et al., 2000).

How Systems Allocate Resources

Of all our case studies, Lucent Technologies has the most impressive record of improving the productivity of its education and professional development system. Since 1995, the Lucent Learning Performance Center has increased the total number of learner days by over 60 percent and decreased the cost per learner day by about 50 percent. It achieved these results by taking several steps:

- Reducing redundancies in the course development and design process. For example, there were about 700 courses on fire extinguisher operation being offered. This process allowed Lucent to consolidate about 70,000 courses offered to about 2,000 courses.
- Decreasing the number of vendors from which courses were purchased.
- Improving the focus of the courses Lucent developed internally,[3] thereby reducing the number of those courses from 800 to 390.
- Eliminating high-cost programs, such as the Wharton School of Business Executive MBA Program, whose value did not justify their cost.
- Increasing the use of web-based instruction to reduce travel costs.

Compared to the Lucent Learning Performance Center or the DOT Learning and Development Program, the Texas Higher Education Coordinating Board has much less control over what education offerings are provided by the public institutions in the state. However, this board does exert some influence through its authority to approve programs as eligible for state funding. In exercising that authority, it also considers whether existing offerings are meeting state needs and whether they do so efficiently.

The Texas Higher Education Coordinating Board's strategic plan (1999–2003) emphasizes that one of the board's key functions is "to eliminate costly duplication in academic programs and technical programs." This is accomplished through a review process that is based on five criteria: need (does the state need this program at this particular institution?), quality, cost, duplication (would a proposed program duplicate existing programs within the

[3] Lucent Learning Performance Center helps coordinate courses provided by external vendors in addition to those developed internally.

geographic area?), and mission (does the program fall within the institution's mission?). In spite of these reviews, the staff of the board know that they will not be able to identify all the programs that should be eliminated (about 10 percent will be bad investments). The key is to establish a process of ongoing review so that the number of ineffective programs can be continually reduced.

The Air Force Air Education and Training Command (AETC) uses the Instructional System Development (ISD) process in developing its training programs.

> The goal of ISD is to increase effectiveness and cost efficiency of education by developing instruction on job performance requirements, eliminating irrelevant skills and knowledge instruction from courses, and ensuring that graduates acquire the necessary skills and knowledge to do the job.[4]

As a result, "ISD is a total quality process"[5] that provides a system approach to training. Similarly, in the Navy, the primary goals of education and training assessment are to provide more training to more sailors at lower cost and to provide sailors the skills that they need to do the job.

Need for Standardized Data and Course Offerings

In many systems we examined, education and professional development activities emerged over time in a decentralized manner on an "as-needed basis." There was no centralized entity coordinating and monitoring that growth and development. By the time many of these systems realized the potential value of Phase One assessment, the information required to conduct such an assessment was highly decentralized and difficult to assemble. Thus, an important task for many entities responsible for Phase One assessment has been data gathering and standardization of provider offerings.

For example, the Texas Higher Education Coordinating Board developed a workforce education course manual (WECM), a "statewide inventory of technical and workforce continuing education courses that colleges may offer in rapid response to the needs of business and industry." The creation of the manual was motivated in part by complaints from state residents about the difficulty of transferring credits among different institutions in the state, along with a recognition that there was excessive program duplication. To develop the manual, the Texas board gathered experts and faculty together and got them to

---

[4]AETC Instruction 36-2201 (1998), *Training Evaluation,* Department of the Air Force.

[5]Air Force Handbook 36-2235 (1993), *Information for Designers of Instructional Systems,* Department of the Air Force.

agree on a set of courses, appropriate content descriptions, and an appropriate range of contact hours for courses in particular course sequences. For example, in welding, they reduced the number of courses from 900 to 96. Overall, they went from over 30,000 courses to about 6,000. Now, introductory welding has the same course name at every college offering it, and the course involves the same number of total contact hours regardless of where it is delivered. A person could take the course in Del Rio, and then be ready to take the next course in the sequence in San Antonio. The WECM effort took about four years and cost approximately $150,000 per year.

An added benefit of the WECM effort is that it facilitates data gathering and tracking efforts on students. As part of the ongoing review of two-year colleges, the coordinating board has developed the Academic Performance Indicator System. The information system contains longitudinal data on courses and students (demographic information, Social Security number, what courses they are taking, and graduation and Texas employment status). Students can be tracked across colleges and into the workforce by linking Social Security numbers to Texas workforce commission data. This tracking capability and the ability to track student, course, and college performance in one system is greatly facilitated by the WECM effort. This data effort costs about $530,000 annually.

Beyond Assessment: Promoting Workforce Improvement

Phase One efforts create a structure for identifying system needs on an ongoing basis. Some of these efforts go well beyond assessment. Centralized learning organizations, for example, provide a range of services that are ultimately designed to promote workforce improvement. They help employees develop individual learning plans to meet their training needs and keep track of their training accomplishments. The consolidation of courses at Lucent Technologies has made it easier to integrate training records with personnel records. Formerly, Lucent kept training records on employees, but they were not centralized, thus making it difficult to construct a training history on an individual. Now, if a learner successfully completes a course, course completion is noted in the person's record. In addition, the system allows students to search for and enroll in courses online.

Some learning organizations, such as the one at Sun Microsystems, have introduced information "portals" that organize information functionally, allowing employees to easily find what they need about learning opportunities throughout the company. United Airlines is also developing an interactive web site that includes online tests that help an employee determine the skills (math, verbal, and leadership) he or she is lacking. The web site is a huge information clearinghouse, organized on the basis of the tests and other information for the benefit of the user. For example, the learner can pull up a list of learning opportunities, both internal and external, that are available through United. Using well-developed web tools, learning organizations can connect and coordinate learning experiences for employees.

Multiple Benefits

The process of determining whether the system is addressing the needs of the system as a whole can have many important benefits:

- It identifies where additional education and professional development is needed, as well as where redundancies have developed.
- It ties education and professional development to the primary mission of the system.
- It encourages prioritizing among competing needs.

Phase One efforts can have other useful results as well. For example, as part of a Phase One assessment, a system might conduct a needs analysis (comparing the skills, aptitudes, and abilities that are needed in specific positions with those that employees have) that can be used for other purposes. The system might also develop the capability to track a learner's skill acquisition and performance over time and integrate that information with personnel records. Finally, a Phase One effort might lead a system to standardize course content within the system, a step that also helps identify redundancies and track individual skill development.

Lessons for the Chancellor's Office

The issues that are typically addressed in Phase One assessment clearly go beyond the mission of the Chancellor's office; they address the link between workforce planning and education and professional development. Phase One assessment involves the key decisionmakers of the larger system—in this case DoD. Drawing on the lessons from state higher education coordinating boards and corporate universities, high-level support, probably from the Secretary of Defense, would be required to support a real Phase One assessment effort. It would also require input from many segments of the DoD hierarchy.

As an intermediary in the system of DoD civilian education and professional development, the Chancellor's office would be a key player since it is in a unique position to promote the type of Phase One activities described in this section. The Chancellor's office could begin an effort to build support for such assessment among key constituents, such as functional sponsors of education and professional development, managers of the civilian workforce, etc. The Chancellor's office could also partner with parallel offices responsible for workforce planning to create an organization similar to a corporate learning organization.

4. Phase Two: Assessing How Well Providers Meet Customer Needs

Phase Two of the assessment of education systems focuses on the performance of specific providers of educational services. While such assessment is sometimes driven by system-level goals, the unit of analysis for assessment is either a provider organization or the student. This section describes the main approaches used to conduct such assessments. As with the rest of this report, this section summarizes and draws key lessons from assessment approaches used in a wide variety of contexts. Although all of the literature we reviewed and all of our case studies concerned assessment, we found that each of the different assessment organizations (e.g., accrediting agencies, corporate learning organizations) uses a different language to describe what they do. We did not identify any existing literature that summarized and drew lessons about assessment from such a diverse set of assessment approaches. In this section we present such a summary, describing models of assessment that capture the key differences among approaches.

We identified four models for determining how well providers are meeting the needs of their customers. These are illustrated in Figure 4.1. In the first model and its variation, the provider conducts the assessment of education activities, and an intermediary institution reviews the process used by the provider to conduct its self-assessment. In Model 2, on the other hand, the intermediary actually conducts the assessment: It defines assessment goals, designs the assessment process, and evaluates institutional performance based on data from the provider. Model 3 differs from both these models in that there is no role for an intermediary: The provider acts independently in conducting its self-assessment. In the fourth model, either the provider or an intermediary also conducts the assessment, but in this case the focus is student competencies. The assumption behind this approach is that measuring what students have learned is the best way to assess performance of the education system as a whole.[1]

---

[1]Models 1–3 reflect traditional approaches to educational assessment that focus on the provider and implicitly assume that if the institution is good, that students who pass through the institution have learned what they needed to learn. Indeed, many provider-based assessments consider evidence of student performance, improvement, or achievement (e.g., pass rates on licensure exams) as a measure of an institution's success or failure. In that respect, information on student performance can be an element of all four assessment models. What makes Model 4 different from the others is that the assessment essentially ignores the provider. In fact, an individual need not attend a course to achieve certification. Instead, they may learn skills or concepts on the job, through

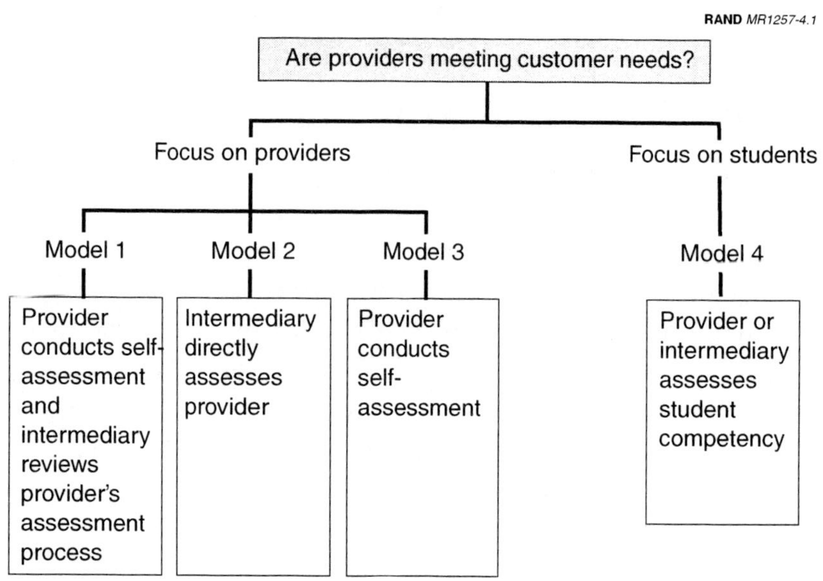

Figure 4.1—Four Models for Assessing Providers

Model 1: Intermediary Assesses or Guides Provider's Process of Assessment

What is unique about Model 1 is that an intermediary organization is responsible for overseeing the assessment process used by provider institutions. This approach, which has its origins in the business world, is receiving growing interest in the education community because it allows education institutions to develop their own assessment processes that best reflect their education and training goals. In reviewing these processes, the intermediary organization focuses on whether the goals are reasonable, and whether the measures are valid and reliable indicators of the achievement of the goals. Because this approach does not typically impose goals from the outside, each provider may be assessed against different goals.

---

a CD-ROM, or be self-taught. What further complicates the distinction between Model 4 and provider-based assessment is the fact that many professional societies require that individuals both graduate from an institution that is accredited by the society *and* pass a licensing examination to be certified as a professional in that field. In other words, these professional societies require that both the individual competencies be assessed through Model 4 and that the providers be assessed, normally through a Model 2–style assessment process.

One of the best examples of this approach is outside the education community: the International Organization for Standardization process quality standards, called ISO 9000. The clearest example of Model 1 in the academic world is the academic audit, an approach developed outside the United States that is only now attracting wide attention in this country.

ISO 9000

ISO 9000 certification is a widely recognized and highly regarded stamp of approval for manufacturing companies. Developed in the late 1980s, it was designed to provide quality standards of production worldwide and thereby facilitate business deals between producers and consumers. To achieve ISO 9000 certification, leaders within an organization must explicitly define and document their policy for quality, which ultimately becomes a "quality manual." The adopted policy should be not only a standard of quality within the organization, but also a standard of quality that can be verified and certified by a third party. The ISO 9000 process also requires that measures be developed for assessing a process and that the leaders of the organization explicitly define the quality standards for producing products or services. The organizational standards should be stated principally in terms of performance. Because evaluation is an essential part of the ISO 9000 philosophy, it is crucial that workers keep up-to-date documentation that can be used by external auditors to certify[2] the organization as an ISO organization. ISO registration does not guarantee that an organization's products are of high quality, but serves as evidence that the organization is strictly adhering to its own internal quality production standards. To become certified, a third-party organization must serve as an objective evaluator of the organization's adherence to its quality manual.[3] In theory, once an organization is certified, it is recognized around the world as having a quality system that is fully and consistently utilized. The certification lasts for three years.

Recently, the ISO has developed a new set of standards and guidelines that could be applied to service industries, including education. Some researchers argue that the ISO 9000, along with total quality management (TQM) strategies, can be used in an education context to enhance customer satisfaction, reduce student attrition, and improve graduation rates while reducing costs (Vandenberge, 1995; Spanbauer, 1992). But there has been substantial resistance to this approach from

---

[2]Also referred to as being registered.

[3]The Registrar Accreditation Board (RAB), an affiliate of the American Society for Quality Control, regulates the external audits for certification.

the academic community, due in part to their reluctance to adopt strategies from the business world.

The Academic Audit

The purpose of an academic audit is to ensure that institutions have processes in place for measuring their own quality and thus can engage in ongoing self-improvement. It is a relatively new approach to quality assessment that has been implemented abroad—in Hong Kong, Scandinavia, Great Britain, Australia, New Zealand, and the Association of European Universities (CRE)—and is beginning to receive attention in the United States, particularly from certain regional accrediting organizations. It has been influenced by the process-oriented quality assessment tradition in the private sector, such as total quality management and the Baldrige Award, but it is less adversarial and more collaborative and is therefore viewed by academics as less alien than many techniques used in the business world.

Academic audits are normally conducted by an external organization or intermediary, but that organization often brings together representatives of provider institutions and other stakeholders as well. In Hong Kong, for example, the audits are carried out by the University Grants Committee (UGC), a large advisory body including distinguished overseas academics, prominent local professionals and business people, and senior academics from local institutions.

According to David Dill, Professor of Public Policy Analysis and Education at the University of North Carolina,

> Auditors review and verify the effectiveness of an institution's basic processes of academic quality assurance and improvement, including: (1) how an institution designs, monitors, and evaluates academic programs and degrees; (2) how an institution assesses, evaluates, and improves teaching and student learning; and (3) how an institution takes account of the views of external stakeholders in improving teaching and student learning (Dill, 2000b).[4]

The process is structured somewhat like an accreditation process. It begins with the inspection of documents that describe the way the institution assesses its own performance. As a next step, a team of auditors visits the institution. Finally, the team writes a report that is made widely available. Because audit reports are

---

[4]David Dill, Professor of Public Policy Analysis and Education at the University of North Carolina, Chapel Hill, has written extensively on the academic audit. See his web site for additional information, including reviews of other countries that have implemented the process, manuals, and review instruments: www.unc.edu/courses/acaudit. Appendix C contains a more detailed description of the academic audit.

made public, they are viewed as an important tool to ensure accountability. Public release also motivates institutions to take the process seriously.

Because the academic audit allows the institutions to define their own quality-assurance processes, it is more sensitive to the different roles, missions, and characteristics of institutions than are certain other approaches. As a result, it is particularly useful for systems with a diverse set of providers. Although it has been criticized for lack of attention to inputs and outcomes, it does not so much ignore outcomes as delegate responsibility for assessing outcomes to the provider.

The unit of analysis for academic audits is usually whole institutions, but the assessment could work with individual programs or departments. Each institution is assessed on its own terms and reports are written with the institution in mind. Auditors deliberately avoid drawing comparisons among institutions. Current use of the academic audit is largely confined to higher education, although the principles could relate to training and professional development as well. In fact, the Teacher Education Accreditation Council (TEAC) is incorporating the use of the academic audit in the accreditation of teaching programs.

In the ISO 9000 and academic audit examples, the intermediary organization has a substantial amount of authority. Its judgment about the adequacy of the provider's assessment process carries some weight. In other cases, the intermediary using Model 1 does not possess such authority and does not actually make a judgment about the processes providers use for quality and productivity assessment. Instead, it provides recommendations for improving the assessment process, and suggests assessment tools, methods, and reasoning on which provider and stakeholders can draw. In this case, it can help promote quality by offering different types of assistance, but it cannot actually ensure quality.

The U.S. Department of Transportation (DOT) provides an example of this weaker version of Model 1. The DOT Learning and Development Program has developed a policy guide called the "Learning and Development Framework," which is designed for use by managers and supervisors in implementing the DOT's education and development policies and programs. The published framework provides recommendations for assessment of program activities as well, although the assessment is carried out at the operating administration level. In other words, the operating administrations determine for themselves whether their education and professional development activities are meeting the goals as defined by the Learning and Development Program. See Appendix F.1 for a fuller description of the DOT's Learning and Development Program.

Corporate learning organizations also often play this modified Model 1 role. Many serve as advisors to the business units that actually provide the training. They can be information clearinghouses, offering assistance on everything from curriculum development to assessment.

Model 2: Intermediary Conducts the Assessment

In Model 2, an intermediary conducts the actual assessment, including defining goals, measuring outcomes, and evaluating performance. Such an approach allows the intermediary to function as an independent check on quality. Except for corporate learning centers, most intermediaries are completely independent of the provider so that they can act as objective judges of quality. In this way, the model is well suited for the accountability function.

The independence of intermediaries also enables them to focus on system-level goals. State higher education coordinating and governing boards, for example, can manage the assessment process and choose performance measures that reflect state or system-level goals that might not be attended to by individual institutions. These issues, such as access and equity, are bigger than any individual institution and cut across schools. In this way, accountability systems provide states with leverage to influence institutions to focus on issues that they might otherwise overlook. In addition, some providers like having requirements imposed by external assessors because, for example, it allows them an opportunity to motivate their employees to undertake changes they might otherwise resist.

The independence of the intermediary, however, can also undermine the value of the assessment. Any approach imposed from an external organization runs the risk of focusing on inappropriate measures and failing to reflect institutional goals.

Organizations that use a Model 2 assessment approach include state higher education governing and coordinating boards, *U.S. News and World Report,* and traditional accreditation agencies. The Malcolm Baldrige National Quality Award program also fits into this mold. Each of these is described briefly below.

State Higher Education Governing and Coordinating Boards

State higher education boards work under the authority of the governor and legislature to ensure that postsecondary institutions operate collectively in ways that are aligned with state priorities and that serve the public interest (McGuinness, 1997). State boards include governing boards and coordinating boards, which differ in their responsibilities, influence, and level of authority.[5]

Most boards have created "accountability systems" to measure and ensure the quality of the institutions within their purview. Among the accountability systems in vogue today are performance indicators, report cards, and performance funding. Although accountability is the primary purpose of these systems, most states encourage institutions to use the data for self-improvement as well. However, report cards tend to be problematic in that they can enforce the lowest common denominator, rather than high quality or even quality improvement. Since the "cut scores" for passing or failing on report card types of assessments are typically set arbitrarily, it is likely that most institutions will "pass," thus eliminating incentives for improvement. Even those institutions that do not pass may only set their improvement goals on whatever the pass score is, regardless of the quality or level of improvement that meeting those scores entails.

Accountability systems differ in their level of collaboration among stakeholders, providers, and intermediaries. Some higher education boards are more directive than others. When governing boards determine assessment goals, measures, and evaluations without substantial input from providers, conflict and resentment often follow. Institutional leaders may feel that the state is imposing standards on them that do not reflect the institution's actual quality. Other state boards are more collaborative and ask institutions to play a substantial role in establishing assessment goals and methods. Although this approach leads to more acceptance of assessment by providers, it is time-consuming and costly.

The information gathered through these accountability systems is used in at least four ways, as described below.

- **Funding.** Some states link a percentage of funding to institutional performance. Tennessee awards 2–5 percent of its instructional budget based on assessment results. In theory, South Carolina awards 100 percent of funding based on performance, but in practice a much smaller percentage (about 5 percent) depends on assessment results (Schmidt, 1999).

---

[5]See Appendix B for a discussion of these differences.

- **Program Planning and Elimination.** Assessment results may contribute to decisionmaking about academic programs. For example, based on its review of assessment data, the Illinois Board of Higher Education in 1992 recommended the elimination, consolidation, or reduction of 190 programs at public universities, including 7 percent of all undergraduate programs, among other changes.
- **Comparisons.** In many states individual campuses are encouraged to use assessment results for self-improvement purposes. The degree to which this actually occurs is unknown.
- **Public Information.** Assessment results also provide a means of informing the public about its state's higher education system. Thus, some states publish report cards—for either the system as a whole or for individual institutions.

The effectiveness of state accountability systems is uneven. At best, the efforts may lead to quality improvements and better alignment between higher education and state policy goals. At worst, the efforts create dissension; force institutions to redirect resources away from other, arguably more valuable activities; and provide little insight into the performance of higher education institutions and systems.

See Appendices B, B.1, and B.2 for more detail about state higher education governing and coordinating boards in general, as well as two examples of such boards in Texas and Kentucky.

U.S. News and World Report

U.S. News and World Report publishes college rankings on a yearly basis. The company plays the role of an intermediary and sees itself as one potential source of information to the customers of higher education. The process does not encourage any formal collaboration among the stakeholders, providers, and the intermediary. *U.S. News and World Report* determines the assessment criteria, conducts the analysis, and provides the results to consumers. The rankings are based on quality measures determined by the publication, including, for example, reputation of the school, selectivity, faculty resources, and financial resources. The ranking formula weights the indicators by level of importance, imposing a model of what a "good college" or "good graduate program" is. In doing so, the *U.S. News and World Report* rankings system implicitly attributes goals to institutions and their stakeholders (see Appendix H.1 for more detail).

Accrediting Agencies

Accreditation is another example of intermediary assessment of provider organizations. Accreditation in U.S. higher education determines whether an institution or a program meets threshold quality criteria and therefore certifies to the public the existence of minimum educational standards. It is voluntary and is mostly carried out by eight regional commissions.[6] These commissions are responsible for accrediting whole institutions. In addition, there are dozens of national associations that offer recognized specialized and professional accreditation for programs or other academic units within an institution, or for freestanding single-purpose institutions.

Accreditation has primarily been about accountability, but there are efforts under way to make the process more flexible so that institutions can use the process for self-improvement. There are also signs that some accreditation commissions are working more collaboratively than others with the providers.

Accreditation is a multistep process. The program or institution first conducts a self-study, using guidelines from the accrediting agency. Following the self-study, the accrediting team conducts a site visit at the institution where the team meets with a range of institutional representatives. Based on the visit and the materials provided by the institution, the review team evaluates such measures as educational objectives, programs and curricula, degree programs, faculty, student services, student progress, admission policies and practices, student recruitment, and management. It submits a report to the accrediting agency, which provides a formal report to the program/institution. After the institution is given an opportunity to respond, the accrediting agency decides whether to grant accreditation. Although the result is made public, only the program and institution are provided the details that support the decision.

The accreditation process can be extremely expensive, particularly for major universities that go through the process multiple times for various specializations or programs, as well as institutional/regional accreditation. However, accrediting tends to be on a ten-year cycle, so institutions do not have to go through the process very often (the exception again being research universities with multiple departments going through specialized accreditation).

---

[6]There are only six accreditation *regions* in the United States: Middle States, New England, North Central, Northwest, Southern, and Western. Generally, there is a regional accreditation commission for each region. However, two of the regions (Western and New England) have two separate organizations: one in charge of accreditation for two-year colleges and one for four-year colleges. As a result, there are a total of eight regional *commissions*: MSA, NEASC (CIHE and CTCI), NCA, NWA, SACS, and WASC (Jr. and Sr).

See Appendix D for more on accreditation and Appendix D.1 for information on the Western Association of Schools and Colleges.

Malcolm Baldrige National Quality Award

The Malcolm Baldrige National Quality Award is another example of Model 2.[7] It differs from other Model 2 approaches in that providers must make an active choice to participate in the program—there is no direct or indirect requirement for them to do so. The program seeks to assess the overall performance management system of participating organizations and to recognize those that excel. The award criteria set standards for the level of assessment that institutions must undertake and evaluate them along specified dimensions related to quality. The Department of Commerce is responsible for the award, and the National Institute of Standards and Technology (NIST)[8] manages the program with assistance from the American Society for Quality. A Board of Overseers, made up of members from industry handpicked by the Secretary of Commerce, directs the award program and determines whether the evaluation process and requirements are adequate.

Organizations volunteer to participate in the program's assessment process because they view it as a means of self-improvement. Many organizations report having better employee relations and higher productivity and profitability as a result of their participation. Companies also report improved customer satisfaction after implementing Baldrige recommendations.

The Problem of Compliance

Intermediary assessors using a Model 2 approach are often caught off guard by institutional resistance (NCHEMS, 1996). For example, in state higher education systems, some state boards have proposed to assess graduation rates, while community college representatives argue that only one-third of their students aspire to graduate. In New Mexico, a report card requirement was dropped because of criticism from institutions that the diversity of institutions, missions, and students made institutional comparisons unreliable or only minimally indicative of institutional performance (Cole, Nettles, and Sharp, 1997). Negotiating such issues and reaching a compromise that satisfies both the assessor and the assessed can take tremendous time and effort.

---

[7]See Appendix I.1 for more information on the Baldrige Award.

[8]NIST is a U.S. Department of Commerce agency.

Even when assessors can agree on measures and overcome resistance, they are not necessarily certain that accountability-based initiatives will lead to institutional improvements (Boyer et al., 1987). Many suspect that accountability endeavors produce a compliance response that is divorced from improvement (Aper, Cuver, and Hinkle, 1990; Ewell, 1993; El-Khawas, 1995; Steele and Lutz, 1995). In the higher education sector, state initiatives that prescribe standardized measures may be less well accepted internally and thus less useful for informing institutional improvement than those that permit institutions to use locally developed assessment instruments (Ewell, 1987a; Jacobi, Astin, and Ayala, 1987; Ory, 1991; Terenzini, 1989).

Organizational theory posits that there are five strategies for responding to external requests or constraints: complying, compromising, avoiding, defying, and manipulating (Oliver, 1991). While complying may be the most ideal response, from the point of view of the organization asking for compliance, it is difficult to achieve. Even when institutions intend to comply, they may lack the know-how to do so effectively. In addition, avoidance can be masked by faked compliance. The organization may appear to comply with the request, but not actually follow through. In certain situations, the organization may defy the external request, such as when the perceived costs of resistance are low, when internal values diverge from external mandates, or when organizations believe they can demonstrate the rationality of their alternative conduct (Oliver, 1991). Finally, manipulation is an option, with organizations attempting to co-opt, influence, or control mandates. Manipulation is most often seen in cases where the external assessor's office is staffed by people who are close friends with those they are attempting to assess.

Organizations are most likely to comply in several circumstances: when they are highly dependent on the institution exerting the pressure;[9] when there is a legal or regulatory apparatus to enforce compliance; when the expectations are already very broadly diffused or supported or when the mandates do not impinge on the autonomy of core areas; and when the organization believes that complying will benefit it through conferring a positive reward such as resources or prestige, or reducing negative sanctions, such as censorious judgments (Oliver, 1991).

---

[9]Resource dependence theory (Pfeffer and Salancik, 1978; Greening and Gray, 1994; Heimovics, Herman, and Jurkiewicz Coughlin, 1993) also specifies that an organization will be less likely to resist external pressures when it is dependent on the sources of those pressures. An example of this theory is found in higher education state boards. Some of these boards control funding for new programs. Therefore, institutions are likely to comply with a board's vision, values, and mandates when creating new programs in order to secure funding.

There are many examples of assessors who do not have direct authority over the assessed, yet still achieve compliance. For example, to compete for the Baldrige Award (which is a voluntary choice), institutions acquiesce to the call for information because they can gain prestige from compliance. In this case, the institutions believe that they will benefit from complying (and they know that they will not be punished). Nursing, business, law, medical, and other professional schools comply with external assessments in the form of licensing and certifying examinations. Students must pass these exams to be able to work in their chosen industry. These providers comply with the assessment of their students in order to gain legitimacy. Students would not attend these institutions if they could not be certified to work in their field. Other organizations provide incentives to achieve compliance. The Kentucky Council on Postsecondary Education uses incentive funding to persuade higher education institutions to develop programs or services in line with its vision for higher education in the state.

Authority relationships influence not only compliance, but also what is done with the resulting assessment information. If there is no structure in place to sanction an institution that does not perform well or to demand that an institution improve, there is little likelihood that the assessment will have any impact. Of course, this is an issue regardless of the assessment model chosen. However, studies have shown that assessments that allow the provider more control over the process, as in Models 1 and 3, are more likely to lead to improvements (Aper and Hinkle, 1991; Ewell, 1991).

Model 3: Provider Conducts the Assessment

In our third model, providers conduct their own self-assessment to ensure quality and productivity without the involvement of any intermediary. Its purpose is improvement—a means of assuring customers they are getting what they need—rather than accountability. However, some of the most innovative approaches to provider assessment are building in greater versatility: They are multipurpose assessments designed to incorporate the perspectives of a range of stakeholders. The best examples of this model are higher education institutions or programs, both nonprofit and for-profit.

The University of Phoenix

The University of Phoenix[10] is a for-profit higher education institution that serves working adults with classes offered primarily on evenings and weekends. It serves 49,000 students at 65 campuses in 15 states, Puerto Rico, Vancouver, British Columbia, and via distance education. The curriculum is developed centrally for every program so that a certain required content is covered in the course and specific outcomes can be measured from a centralized perspective.

The University of Phoenix has a number of mechanisms in place for measuring quality, most of which were originally intended to demonstrate their quality to potential customers—both employers and learners—but are now used for program improvement as well. Their primary assessment tools are the following:

- **Student testing.** All students are tested at the beginning and end of each course to measure what they have learned. The test results are also used by the institution for self-improvement. If students do poorly on a certain section of the test at one campus, administrators work with that campus to improve instruction of the material. If students everywhere do poorly on a section, the university revises the course curriculum.
- **Surveys of customer and employer satisfaction.** Students are surveyed for their evaluation of the quality of teaching, curriculum, books, and supplemental materials. Alumni and employers are also regularly surveyed to determine whether University of Phoenix graduates have the right skills and are getting promoted. Beyond such surveys, students also participate in "exit interviews" to gauge their satisfaction. Results of such activities, along with information on other issues such as class size, are provided in quarterly (and sometimes monthly) reports that are sent to stakeholders. These reports are also used by campuses to improve their programs.
- **Reports on the quality and efficiency of business operations.** These reports compare the campuses in terms of their services and business operations. They assess such things as student numbers and whether learning centers are turning their paperwork in on time.

Like the corporate model of continuous process improvement, the university's ongoing evaluation of the data collected by these means encourages individual campuses to improve student learning. Although campuses are not penalized for poor performance, they are compared with one another. The university's

---

[10]See Appendix K.1 for more details on the University of Phoenix.

philosophy is managing by exception—it looks at outliers and then works with them to improve. It has also set up a buddy/mentorship program so schools that are not performing well in a particular area are matched with a campus that is doing well in that area.

The Urban Universities Portfolio Project

Public universities are increasingly being asked for more information about their practices: Legislators require information to justify funding levels for these institutions; potential students and their families require information about which schools offer the best education and best fit their needs; faculty require information to make sure their research and teaching is in line with school objectives and overall mission; accreditation agencies seek to better classify institutions according to services being offered. Increasingly, they must be able to demonstrate measurable progress toward clear goals.

It is becoming widely recognized, however, that a one-size-fits-all approach to assessment does not work. A group of urban public universities have come up with an innovative new method for communicating their difference from traditional public universities and assessing the quality and effectiveness of their institutions. Six universities—Indiana University–Purdue University Indianapolis, University of Illinois at Chicago, Portland State University, California State University at Sacramento, University of Massachusetts at Boston, and Georgia State University—participated in The Urban Universities Portfolio Project[11] funded by The Pew Charitable Trusts. All of these institutions serve primarily nontraditional students, many of whom are older than most college students and working full-time, and many of whom are first-generation, college-going students from diverse racial/ethnic backgrounds. Most of them attend classes on evenings and weekends or enroll in distance education courses. Aware of their special mandate, these universities collaborated to design an assessment method that would hold them accountable for making progress toward the goals they set themselves and provide them a tool for improving their educational practices. An additional objective of the project is to improve the understanding of the distinguishing features of urban public universities among both internal and external stakeholders.

The project calls for close collaboration with representative stakeholders. Two groups of external constituents have been established. Both the National Advisory Board (NAB) and the Institutional Review Board (IRB) are composed of

---

[11]See Appendix K.4 for more information on The Urban Universities Portfolio Project.

distinguished leaders from business, government, and education. The role of the National Advisory Board is to advise the project about its aims, practices, and progress by reviewing the evolving set of core goals, indicators, and measures and by keeping current on issues facing the urban public schools. Board members include key university officials and figures from higher education and accrediting organizations. The Institutional Review Board works closely with the participating urban universities advising on portfolio development. Members include college deans, directors of accrediting associations, professors, and provosts from a range of institutions.

Although each university is developing its own "portfolio" that will eventually be published on the web, all six of them will combine their efforts in order to define common objectives and outcome measures that reflect their similar missions. This process will help establish that urban public universities should not be judged by the same standards used for traditional universities. A common assessment approach will also allow students and policymakers to draw meaningful comparisons among urban public universities.

Model 4: Student Competencies Are Assessed

Model 4 represents a completely different approach to assessment, one that focuses attention on the student rather than the provider. The previous approaches, which focus on the provider, implicitly assume that if the institution is good, students who pass through the institution will learn what they need to learn. Indeed, information on student performance is an element in all assessments: Evidence of student performance, improvement, or achievement (e.g., pass rates on licensure exams) is considered a measure of an institution's success or failure. What makes Model 4 different is that the assessment essentially ignores the provider. In some cases, individuals need not attend an institution or take a course to achieve certification. Instead, they may learn skills or concepts on the job or through a CD-ROM, or they may be self-taught. The end result of the assessment accomplished through Model 4 is the certification of student competencies. Therefore, the Model 4 approach is often called "competency-based assessment."

In recent years, there has been increased attention focused on the concept of student competencies by business leaders and educators as an innovative approach to education and training, and assessment. The competency-based approach allows educators to organize courses and instruction around the gap between what students already know and what they should know in order to demonstrate a level of proficiency in a particular area.

There are several approaches to defining competencies. As discussed in the previous section, defining competencies can be a part of Phase One assessment for a system, as in the Air Force example. The most common method is to identify tasks that define competency in a certain domain and assess whether tasks are completed in order to conclude that proficiency has been achieved. Critics argue that this oversimplifies performance in the real world by ignoring the relationship between tasks and other factors that influence performance. Another approach looks only at general characteristics needed for effective job performance, such as critical thinking skills or communication skills. This method ignores the need for different skills in different domains and the need to transfer expertise from one area to another. A more integrated approach combines defined tasks as well as cross-cutting skills to identify the knowledge, skills, and abilities needed to perform effectively in particular domain areas. In this approach, "competence is conceived of as complex structuring of attributes needed for intelligent performance in specific situations" (Gonczi, 1994, p. 29). These competencies embody the goals of education and professional development.

Competency-based education and training is being used in government, private industry, and higher education as a way to meet the wide-ranging needs of a diverse group of learners. Examples highlighted below are Microsoft's technical certification programs, the Department of Labor's SCANS Initiative, and Western Governors University—a leader in the competency-based approach to higher education.

Microsoft's Technical Certification Programs

Microsoft has developed a well-known and widely recognized set of technical certification programs. According to its web site,

> Certification provides professionals with a valuable credential that recognizes their skills with the most advanced Microsoft technology. Certification also provides businesses with an objective way to identify individuals who can help them compete more successfully in their industry using Microsoft technology.[12]

Individuals can achieve technical certifications in one of several areas by taking a series of examinations. The Microsoft web site provides information on the exams required for each certification, skills being measured in a particular exam, ways to prepare for the exam (including official courses offered by Microsoft,

[12]Microsoft web site: www.microsoft.com/trainingandservices/default.asp?PageID =mcp&PageCall=certifications&SubSite=cert.

books, CD-ROMs, online content, and videos), and practice exams that measure technical proficiency and expertise in specific areas.

> As an industry leader in professional certification, Microsoft is at the forefront of testing methodology. Our exams and corresponding certifications are developed to validate mastery of critical competencies. Exams are developed with the input of professionals in the industry and reflect how Microsoft products are used in organizations throughout the world.

The examinations are offered by two independent companies at testing sites worldwide.

The Department of Labor's SCANS Initiative

The federal government has also recognized the benefits of conducting job analysis to identify the necessary competencies for certain jobs. The Department of Labor Secretary's Commission on Achieving Necessary Skills (SCANS) initiative was undertaken with the intent of linking competencies and skills needed by the business community and government to what is taught in schools. SCANS aims to "define the skills needed for employment, propose acceptable levels of proficiency, suggest effective ways to assess proficiency and develop a dissemination strategy" (U.S. Department of Labor, 1991, p. xv). While SCANS acknowledges that technical expertise varies among industries, it posits that the basic competencies, or "workplace know-how," are the same for all types of jobs. It identified five major categories of skills that are needed across the spectrum in all industries: resources, interpersonal, information, systems, and technology. In addition, according to SCANS, students need a three-part foundation consisting of basic skills, thinking skills, and personal qualities.

Western Governors University

The Western Governors University (WGU), established in 1997, has been a leader in higher education's competency-based approach to education. The university was created to address several challenges, including

> a wide geographic dispersion of students; non-traditional students, such as adults employed full time, seeking part-time enrollment; scarcity of workers in certain highly trained occupations; rising student costs of attaining higher education; existing and potential duplication of effort among states in developing courses and programs; failure of existing higher educational institutions to recognize and acknowledge skills and abilities which students already possess; and inadequate information to students about educational opportunities and choices (Testa, 1999, p. 3).

WGU differs from traditional institutions of higher education in that the degree and certificate programs[13] are defined by a set of competencies that students must demonstrate rather than a set of courses they must take. Thus, WGU's primary effort is directed toward defining an appropriate set of competencies, developing valid and reliable methods for measuring those competencies, and helping students identify learning opportunities that can help them acquire competencies they are lacking. The attainment of a degree or certificate is based not on credit hours but on the successful completion of a set of competency tests. In fact, students may earn a degree or certification without taking courses if they can demonstrate competency in a domain area (Testa, 1999).

WGU faculty play a key role in the design and development of programs and assessment instruments. Actual courses are delivered by distance learning providers, which are approved by WGU for providing education that fosters the development of specific competencies.

Competency-based education benefits students because it gives them recognition of past achievements, portability of course credits, and a system for lifelong learning (Paulson and Ewell, 1999). Institutions value competency-based education and training because they encourage stakeholders to closely examine what is important for students to know and instructors to teach as well as help in targeting scarce resources where they will be most effective (Mager, 1997).

Strengths and Weaknesses of the Four Approaches

Table 4.1 summarizes the strengths and weaknesses of all four models. One of the primary strengths of Model 1 is the flexibility achieved by its focus on process. Because the providers are allowed to conduct their own assessment, they can establish the goals and measures that best reflect their institutions. The review then focuses on whether the goals are reasonable, and whether the measures are valid and reliable indicators of achievement of these goals. This flexibility makes the model ideal for a heterogeneous system, where it can be difficult to define meaningful measures of quality that are appropriate for all institutions.

---

[13]WGU is currently a candidate for accreditation. Current degree programs offered include a general AA, an AAS in electronics manufacturing engineering, an AAS in information technology, and an MA in learning and technology. WGU is building a bachelor's degree in business.

Table 4.1

Strengths and Weaknesses of the Four Assessment Models

Model	Strengths	Weaknesses
Model 1 *Provider conducts the assessment, intermediary reviews provider's assessment process*	Flexibility of approach can accommodate diversity of institutions Approach promotes program improvement	Less suitable for the purpose of accountability Can serve to promote quality but not to ensure it
Model 2 *Intermediary designs the assessment process and conducts the assessment*	Independent check on quality Well suited for accountability Can focus on system-level goals	Its approach may be overly standardized and thus neglect differences among institutions Approach may be driven by goals that have little relation to the quality of education May lead to institutional resistance May have little effect on quality improvement
Model 3 *Provider designs the assessment process and conducts the assessment*	Flexibility accommodates differences among institutions Stimulus to self-improvement	Less suitable for accountability purposes Not useful for assessing system-level needs
Model 4 *Provider or intermediary assesses student competencies*	Focuses on measuring student learning Relates student learning to workplace competencies	Time-consuming and expensive process Difficult to measure competencies that are less defined and more abstract May be more suitable for professional education and training than traditional academic institutions

Although Model 1 is ideally suited for program improvement, it is less suited for accountability. One of the major drawbacks of this approach is that the intermediary does not assess actual educational or training outcomes. However, the assumption is that good internal processes for assessment will automatically lead to improved outcomes. Providers may choose to examine outcomes as part of their process.

Model 2, on the other hand, has the advantage of providing an independent perspective on quality and productivity. Because an intermediary conducts the assessment, the approach is well suited for accountability and can embrace systemwide issues, such as access and equity. The main disadvantage of this approach is that it fails to allow for important distinctions in mission and emphasis among provider institutions. It also imposes burdensome data collection requirements on institutions that cannot be used for the purposes of self-improvement. There is little evidence that state accountability systems, that use Model 2, have led to improvements in student learning. Moreover, Model 2 appears most likely to meet resistance from provider institutions.

Another potential challenge facing Model 2 is that intermediaries may pick the inappropriate goals and thus provide information that is misleading or irrelevant to customers and providers. For example, despite its popularity, *U.S. News and World Report* has been condemned for placing too much emphasis on reputation, for stifling diversity by using the same yardstick for all institutions, and for frequently changing the ranking methodology.

Even corporate learning organizations, the most "inside" of the intermediaries, are sometimes criticized by staff for being out of touch with the profit-making mission of the company. Accrediting agencies have come under attack for having a standard set of criteria that does not reflect the diversity of institutional missions and for focusing too heavily on inputs and not on educational outcomes.

In contrast to Model 2, the primary strength of Model 3 is the flexibility it leaves providers to define their own goals, assess their performance based on those goals, and learn from the process how they can best improve. However, the lack of external oversight or review of the provider's process implies that Model 3 cannot easily be used for accountability purposes. In addition, Model 3 provides no mechanism for assessing system-level needs.

Model 4 is appealing because, in the words of one commentator, it

> enables us to come closer than we have in the past to assessing what we want to assess—the capacity of the professional to integrate knowledge, values, attitudes and skills in the world of practice (Gonczi, 1994, p. 28).

But it is time-consuming and expensive to define relevant competencies, develop ways to measure them, and update the definitions and measures. Moreover, some competencies are easier to define than others. While it may be relatively easy to specify the competencies that a computer systems administrator must have, it is more difficult to specify the competencies that a plant manager needs to have. Many observers believe it is doubtful that a competency-based education approach will be embraced by the academic community (Carnevale, 2000).

This section has provided an overview of the approaches used by various organizations engaged in the assessment of education and professional development activities. We were not able to identify a single best model; each model has strengths and weaknesses described in this section. In the next section, we discuss some of the issues an assessor should consider in selecting among the different models.

5. Choosing the Right Model for Phase Two

This section discusses how to determine which model to select as an assessment approach in cases where one is free to choose an approach that is best suited to a certain education environment, as is the case of the new DoD Chancellor's office. New assessment processes should be created with care so that they fit logically into the network of assessors and reporting requirements that already exists. A single institution is often beholden to several assessment processes. A state university, for example, must be accredited as an institution, must have its preprofessional programs accredited separately, must be certified to receive Title IV funding, must be authorized by the state to offer degrees, and is probably subject to assessment by a state higher education governing board for accountability purposes. Multiple assessments are costly and time-consuming and often impose duplication of effort on institutions providing data to separate assessors.

Our analysis suggests that selecting an assessment approach should begin with a consideration of the purpose of the assessment and be founded on a clear understanding of the education system's characteristics, including the nature of the assessor's position within that system.

Purposes of Assessment

Any new assessor's office needs to first identify the problem it has been established to address and then articulate its mission in terms of that problem. According to Ewell (1999a, p. 155),

> considerable experience teaches us that we must be very clear about the nature of the particular problem we are trying to address through measurement, lest the measurement itself become the end of policy.

New assessment systems are usually established to address a problem that is not being monitored by existing assessors or that could be better addressed by an alternative approach or an agency with a distinctive competency. A newly established assessor needs to focus on this problem and develop a strategic vision for addressing it and a plan for implementing that vision (Levy et al., forthcoming). This process should help clarify whether the purpose of the assessment is primarily accountability or primarily improvement.

There are at least three contexts in which state higher education coordinating boards, a type of intermediary that is often interested in both improvement and accountability, typically favor accountability-based assessment over improvement-oriented assessment:

- When a system is moving from a centralized to a decentralized process for managing providers. States that relinquish control of program planning and curriculum design for their higher education institutions do so with the expectation that these institutions will demonstrate that they are maintaining quality.
- When resource allocations must be monitored. States become more concerned with accountability as they provide increased funding to higher education institutions. They want to ensure that these resources, which are scarce, are used effectively and efficiently by the recipient institutions (Stevens and Hamlett, 1983). Legislatures and the public in general often call for greater accountability without regard for improvement (Steele and Lutz, 1995).
- When there is a call for change. This type of assessment can be used to hold institutions accountable to meeting specific goals and therefore change behavior more quickly. In the 1980s it was used by external constituents for monitoring reforms within state higher education systems.[1]

Assessment for improvement purposes, on the other hand, is typically undertaken when quality improvement is the desired result and when there is no need for comparative data among different institutions. For example, several countries in Europe and Asia have instituted academic audits as their assessment process for their higher education institutions. Academic audits allow educational providers to conduct their own internal assessment, while an intermediary evaluates the process of this self-assessment. These countries are not interested in comparing their higher education institutions to each other, but do want to ensure that they are constantly focusing on internal improvement.

As we described in Section 4, the assessment process used for accountability differs from approaches devoted to quality improvement. In assessing for accountability, an external body controls the assessment, setting the goals against which performance will be assessed. A state board, for example, might hold an institution accountable for contributing to the state's economic development.

---

[1]Throughout the 1980s, a flurry of national reports argued both for substantial higher educational reform and greater accountability (e.g., Association of American Colleges Project on Redefining the Meaning and Purpose of Baccalaureate Degrees (1985); National Institute of Education (1984); and Bennett (1984)).

This goal may not have been a goal of the provider's, but since the assessment is for accountability purposes, an intermediary determines the goals. In assessment for accountability, an external evaluator also typically delineates the measures and evaluates the results. These results are used to judge the performance of the provider, often providing a reward or a sanction based on performance. This is the approach taken in Model 2.

In assessing for improvement purposes, the process is structured so that the provider can use the resulting information to make improvements. Typically, a provider, such as a college or a department within a university, delineates its own goals for improvement and conducts an assessment to determine how well it is meeting those goals. The measures used in such an assessment typically reflect input, process, output, and outcome variables, so that the assessor can understand what inputs and processes lead to what outcomes. Understanding these relationships allows a provider to identify the changes (to inputs, processes, or outputs) required to generate performance improvement within the organization. Models 1 and 3 are most suitable for this purpose. Model 4 may also contribute indirectly to provider improvement. In fact, an assessor need not commit to a single model for quality improvement assessments, but choose different models for different assessment tasks within the system.

Is it possible to design an approach that provides both accountability and program improvement? Many commentators hold that the two objectives are simply incompatible. They argue that what intermediaries typically need to hold providers accountable—i.e., uniform information that is easily communicable to external audiences—is not what the institutions being assessed need—i.e., information that links assessment results to specific institutional experiences (Cole, Nettles, and Sharp, 1997). Moreover, assessment data are gathered and reported much differently if the purpose is to reward and sanction rather than to identify opportunities for improvement. Institutions have incentives to package their data as positively as possible—even to provide misleading data—if they know they will be compared to others and that their results will be used in making summative decisions on funding or continued existence.

Other commentators believe that assessment for improvement and assessment for accountability need not be mutually exclusive (Palomba and Banta, 1999). Half of the existing state boards maintain that they have policies designed to both ensure quality and hold institutions accountable (Cole, Nettles, and Sharp, 1997). Palomba and Banta (1999) argue that it is possible, albeit challenging, to develop measurements that are meaningful both locally and to the "higher-ups." Ewell (1987b; 1990) approves of state initiatives that require institutions to report on improvements made based on information gathered for accountability assessments because they should promote greater institutional support for those assessments and lead to quality improvements.

Model 1 is the most promising approach for combining the two purposes. It has the potential to hold the provider accountable to at least a standard baseline of quality audit while assuring sound institutional processes for quality improvement. In addition, the intermediary can go beyond monitoring the process. Model 1 can be modified to include features that provide for accountability, such as minimum standards (Massy and French, 1999). It can require that the process contain a specific task, such as evaluating teacher quality, or it can set limits on the goals the institutions can have. For example, program faculty in institutions that are members of the Teacher Education Accreditation Council are required to accept the goal of preparing "competent, caring, and qualified teachers." Intermediaries could also require the provider to communicate the results of the assessments, even though these results would not be comparable to other institutional results (given the autonomy of each provider in establishing its own process). Finally, the intermediary can ask the provider to describe how the results of the process are used to make improvements, which could contribute toward both accountability and improvement.

Although Model 4 focuses on student competencies, it indirectly holds institutions accountable by withholding competency status from students who have not received the requisite education from specific providers. These providers must change to maintain their ability to attract students; in this way the assessment process stimulates improvement while indirectly holding providers accountable for change.

Level of Authority

Another key factor in considering an assessment model is the degree of authority the assessor has over provider institutions. Is there a formal reporting arrangement between the assessor and the providers? Does the assessor have the ability to offer incentives or impose sanctions to achieve compliance?

If the assessor has formal authority over providers and the power to offer rewards or impose sanctions for nonobservance, then any of the approaches to assessment could be successfully implemented. If, on the other hand, the assessor has limited authority over providers, the choices narrow. Since Models 1 and 3 provide more control to the providers, they are more likely to achieve their objectives without strong external incentives. Model 4 focuses on student competencies, so the issue of authority over providers is not relevant. Model 2, on the other hand, frequently elicits institutional resistance because it is imposed from the outside. Without a strong position of authority over providers in the system, that approach is less likely to succeed.

Authority relationships influence not only compliance but also impact. If there is no structure in place to either sanction an institution that does not perform well or demand that an institution improve, there is little likelihood that the assessment will have any effect. Of course, this is an issue regardless of the assessment model chosen. However, in Models 1 and 3, because the assessor allows the provider more control of the process, results of assessment tend to be used to make changes for improvement (Aper and Hinkle, 1991; Ewell, 1991).

Level of Resources

Available resources—including size of budget, staff, level of expertise, and credibility among key stakeholder groups—are another important consideration in choosing an assessment model. Assessment can be an extremely expensive endeavor, in many regards. Extensive information composes the base of any assessment task. Staff members are needed to gather information, forge relationships, and develop the assessment model. Expertise is needed in carrying out an assessment. Depending on the existing level of expertise, the assessor may need to hire additional (either permanent or temporary) staff or train existing ones. Conducting an assessment is not only labor-, but time- and energy-intensive as well. Credibility is another important resource for the assessor. Do key stakeholders believe that the assessor has the expertise required to design and implement the assessment and do they value the judgment of the assessor? Before choosing an assessment model, the assessor should consider whether the available resources are sufficient for the task.

Although it is obviously important to have enough resources to conduct high-quality assessment, it is difficult to say exactly how much is necessary. We were unable to find systematic information on the cost of implementing different types of assessment models, although we did get a general sense of the resources required through some of our case studies (e.g., the Western Association of Schools and Colleges, the Kentucky Council on Postsecondary Education, and the Texas Higher Education Coordinating Board). Models 2 and 4 are the more resource-intensive models for an intermediary. In Model 2, the intermediary is not only evaluating the results of assessment, but designing the assessment and typically the instruments that will be used to gather data as well. Although often ignored, substantial resources can also be required to overcome resistance to assessment on the part of providers. In Model 4, the intermediary is testing student competencies which also entails extensive resources for instrument design, data collection, and evaluations of the results. Moreover, the assessor's credibility will determine whether the certification is of any value to students.

While Model 1 may be less expensive, the intermediary still bears many costs. New staff may need to be hired and existing staff will likely need training. There will also be costs incurred in establishing relationships with providers, in developing guidelines for providers to use in monitoring quality, and in gathering information. While, for the intermediary, these costs should be less than those that would be expended under Model 2, the costs to the providers themselves may be more substantial under both Models 1 and 3. Because of the high cost to providers under these models, it may take more time and energy on the part of the intermediary to convince providers of the importance of conducting a Model 1– or Model 3–type assessment. If Model 3 is chosen, the costs to the intermediary are the lowest.

Centralization of Operations

The degree to which a system is centralized should also affect the choice of an assessment model. Specifically, the way in which a system has structured its information, policies, administration, and curriculum processes affects the efficacy of assessment under different models. Some systems, such as corporate learning centers or for-profit universities, are highly centralized in everything from curriculum development to data collection. At the University of Phoenix, a central office develops all of the course curricula, specifies intended course outcomes, and gathers data on both providers and customers into a central database. Therefore, much of the work of assessment (identifying the educational goals) is completed early in the process in a consistent manner. The central office that constructs the goals is also responsible for measuring attainment of those goals.

Other systems, however, are decentralized in their curriculum and delivery process but centralized in their data collection. In Texas, the Higher Education Coordinating Board oversees a heterogeneous and decentralized system of institutions, but has worked hard to ensure that they collect and manage extensive amounts of data. This board can track students across colleges or systems and into the workforce by linking Social Security numbers to Texas workforce commission data. As a result, institutions are aware of the paths taken by their graduates. Community colleges can track both transfer and graduation rates and all institutions can see where (and whether) their graduates end up working (as long as they stay in Texas). Having such centralized data can be instrumental to successful assessment endeavors.

In terms of the models, Model 2 works well in a system in which the intermediary controls the educational components of developing the curriculum and designing the delivery. In such a centralized system, the coordinating office or intermediary not only is involved in setting the initial educational goals, but is dealing with providers that are dependent on the expertise and guidance of the centralized entity. Such providers would tend to trust the judgment of and relinquish assessment authority to the centralized entity. Model 2 is also easier to implement if the intermediary has access to centralized databases. In systems without either centralized data or centralized curriculum processes, Models 1 and 3 may be a better fit. Under Model 4, information on students, rather than providers, needs to be centralized to some extent so that the assessor has a way of conveying whether the student has achieved the certification or not.

The most complicated environments for assessment are those in which both educational services and information gathering are decentralized. This is true of the DoD system of civilian education and professional development. The Chancellor's office does not control curriculum or delivery and has access to little centralized data. Therefore, it is necessarily dealing with providers who are independent and used to some degree of autonomy. All of these providers control their own curriculum and delivery systems, thus limiting the amount of knowledge the Chancellor has regarding their curriculum, delivery, and assessment processes. While gaining such knowledge is key to any assessment process, choosing Model 2 may lead to high degrees of resistance and, perhaps, an insurmountable learning curve for the Chancellor's staff.

System Heterogeneity

In choosing an assessment model, it is important to consider the heterogeneity of the educational providers within the system. Important dimensions of heterogeneity include size, geographic location, relationships to stakeholders, and organizational affiliation[2] of providers. Heterogeneity of mission is especially important. Within an educational system, providers may offer a wide variety of educational opportunities, ranging from an hour-long course to a doctoral degree program. The greater this variance, the more difficult it is to assess quality or productivity throughout the system using common indicators of quality for all the providers. An indicator of quality in a doctoral degree program, such as providing students with a context for analytical thinking, may

[2]Organizational affiliation can include whether the providers are part of the system being considered, or external to it. For example, the DoD civilian education and professional development system includes providers that are run by a DoD agency as well as providers run by external organizations.

not be a good quality indicator for a course in safety training, where the main objective may be to prevent accidents in the workplace.

State higher education boards are addressing this problem in a variety of ways. Some have chosen to cluster institutions with similar missions. In Tennessee, for example, institutions are divided into three categories: universities/doctoral institutions, two-year institutions, and technical colleges. With such groupings, the state developed indicators appropriate to each group so that institutions can compare themselves to similar institutions. Despite this ability to conduct comparisons, however, Tennessee provides funding by assessing how an institution's performance compares with its own performance in prior years rather than the performance of other institutions in its category. Other state higher education boards allow each institution to determine its own quality indicators. In Kentucky, the Council on Postsecondary Education, for example, concluded that there is no single definition of quality that would work for all the institutions in its system: two research universities, six comprehensive universities, and 28 community and technical colleges. Instead of clustering institutions, they decided to focus on individual "fitness for purpose" as a way for each institution to define its own purpose or mission. This allows for the assessment of quality to then focus on individual purposes unique to each institution. This focus is relatively new, and the success of this effort has not been measured.

While the Council on Postsecondary Education in Kentucky is mainly concerned with public education, it does attempt to ensure the quality of the state's private higher education institutions as well, even though the council does not exercise authority over them. This situation is analogous to the challenges faced by corporations and government agencies that are charged with assessing external contractors who provide educational opportunities for employees.

For systems with great heterogeneity, Model 1 provides the most flexibility to conduct systemwide assessment. Since Model 3 allows the provider to conduct its own assessment, it suits a heterogeneous system but does not include a role for an intermediary to make comparative or system-level assessments. Heterogeneity is not relevant to Model 4 since it focuses on assessing students. Model 2, on the other hand, which puts external organization in charge of the whole assessment process, is the most problematic approach for heterogeneous systems. As the experience of state boards in Kentucky and Tennessee suggest, accountability assessments must acknowledge that a single set of standards does not suit all institutions. Even accrediting agencies are modifying Model 2 so that institutions can develop their own indicators.

Providers of continuing and higher education to the civilian workforce at DoD are extremely heterogeneous. In fact, this system may be the most heterogeneous of any of the systems examined in this study. These providers vary not only in their mission, size, and geographic location, but in their placement inside or outside DoD. It is therefore important to take this heterogeneity into account when choosing an assessment model.

System Complexity

Within a system, individual providers can be more or less complex. While one provider may simply provide contracted courses, another provider might be offering courses, programs, and degrees. In these cases where different providers embody differing levels of complexity, it is difficult to determine how to measure the quality and productivity of the multipurpose providers and difficult to compare them to the providers who serve only one purpose.

This issue of complexity may be especially important to DoD. As Figure 2.3 illustrated in Section 2, the DoD civilian education and professional development system is highly complex. The network of providers alone (see Figure 2.2) is large and heterogeneous. Providers not only vary in internal complexity but some of them offer courses not only to DoD civilian workers, but also to military staff and students external to DoD. Since the goal of the Chancellor's office is to measure the quality and productivity offered to civilian workers, the realm of educational offerings under assessment can vary from one provider to the next. Some providers may target all of their educational offerings to DoD civilian workers, while others may only offer one course a year. The specific mission of the Chancellor's office, when combined with the heterogeneity and complexity of the providers within the system, presents a challenge in choosing a model for assessment.

Models 1 and 3 are well suited to a complex environment because they allow the provider institutions to determine the appropriate level and focus of assessment. Model 2 can work in a complex system, but requires a substantial amount of advance effort in defining the relevant unit of analysis for each assessment. This process is more challenging in large systems. Model 4 is somewhat immune to the level of complexity because students are assessed with little regard to their providers. Regardless of the model chosen, the Chancellor's office may want to spend time defining both the components and the levels of each of the providers that will be assessed.

Summary

Table 5.1 summarizes the applicability of different models to the factors discussed in this section. The table focuses on the purpose of assessment and constraining levels of other factors discussed in this section. By constraining levels, we mean levels at which certain models are more likely to succeed, such as low level of authority or high level of heterogeneity. When the level of these characteristics is not constraining (i.e., high level of authority or low heterogeneity), any of the models could be successful. The X's indicate those models most suited to that particular feature of the education system. An asterisk means that the model might work under these circumstances.

Table 5.1

Suitability of Assessment Models to Different Circumstances

Factors	Model 1	Model 2	Model 3	Model 4
Focus on accountability	*	X		*
Focus on improvement	X		X	*
Low level of authority	*		X	X
Constrained resources	*		X	
Little centralization of data, curriculum, etc.	X		X	X
High system heterogeneity	X	*	X	*
High system complexity	X	*	X	*

X: Model is likely to be successful.
*: Model may be successful.

Implications for the Chancellor's Office

Because the role of the Chancellor's office is still evolving, it is unclear how the office's situation matches some of the factors considered in this section. While there is evidence to support that the Chancellor's office has been charged with improving quality, it may also want to hold providers accountable, perhaps for addressing specific problems. The level and types of resources available to the Chancellor's office are unclear. Moreover, the Chancellor's office may be able to request additional resources to support a well-justified assessment activity. However, we do know that the Chancellor's office is operating within a system that is extremely heterogeneous and complex. It lacks both a centralized structure and a comprehensive information database. We also know that the Chancellor currently operates within this system with little formal authority. Given this context, we believe it would be extremely challenging to successfully implement a version of Model 2, in which the Chancellor's office would directly assess the quality of the providers. The other three models are better suited to the DoD-specific context.

It should be noted that the Chancellor does not need to adopt a single model for all purposes or all providers. Perhaps there are certain activities or job categories for which competencies could be defined and measured. This use of Model 4 could be combined with a version of Model 1 in which the Chancellor's office would evaluate the processes used by some providers to assess their own quality. With other providers, for example those that are already accredited by other intermediaries, the Chancellor may want them to conduct their own assessments and provide them with helpful information without attempting to evaluate their success.

6. Three Steps for Assessing Providers[1]

Regardless of the model chosen for Phase Two, there are three key steps involved in the assessment of the quality and productivity of providers of education and professional development: (1) identifying the goals that the education and professional development is designed to accomplish; (2) measuring performance related to those goals; and (3) evaluating performance measures in relation to the established goals.[2] The three steps used in the assessment of providers is part of Phase Two and is designed to answer the question: Are providers meeting the needs of their stakeholders?

The literature on education and training assessment is vast. Different sources often focus on only a single aspect or step of provider assessment. The information presented in this section synthesizes information on provider and, to a lesser extent, student assessment gathered through literature review, interviews, and conference attendance. Using this information, this section will describe ways in which various institutions set goals, determine measures, and evaluate those measures to ensure that the goals they have set are being met. This section summarizes important issues to consider at each step of the process of assessing providers. An important theme that emerged from the literature review is the need to integrate all three steps of the assessment process: identify goals, identify ways of measuring performance in relation to goals, and use the measures to evaluate performance relative to those goals. Although many organizations and assessment approaches provide useful examples of a single step of the process, such examples are often lacking on how to integrate the three steps. Therefore, after describing each of the three steps in detail, there is a subsection at the end of this section in which we describe the balanced scorecard process, which is a good example of how to integrate the three steps.

---

[1]Our review of the literature and current practices includes findings on assessment processes for measuring student competencies (i.e., Model 4). This section will contain some references to measuring student competencies, but the main focus is on measuring provider performance more directly, since this focus is most appropriate for the Chancellor's office.

[2]The literature on provider assessment is large, and we can summarize only a part of it in this section. We refer the reader to Palomba and Banta (1999) for a comprehensive discussion of provider assessment. Specific examples of measures used in particular contexts can be found in the appendices, which are structured so that a reader interested in a specific step of the assessment process can easily find information on that step and concrete examples of methods used. See Appendix A for an overview.

Step One: Identifying Goals

The first step in assessing providers is to identify the education and professional development goals against which the performance of the provider, or in the case of Model 4, the student, will be assessed. The goals should reflect the mission, vision, and values[3] of the assessor and address the question of what the education and professional development is trying to accomplish.

Goal Setting Guides the Assessment Process

Goal setting sets the stage for the entire assessment. It is important to establish goals before moving on to other assessment endeavors for at least two reasons. First, delineating goals ensures that all of the important aspects of the educational endeavor will be assessed. Second, this goal-setting process ensures that extraneous measures will not be created. Unfortunately, there is a tendency to ignore this first step and try to determine what can be measured without a framework of goals. Measures may then be chosen that are not necessarily reflective of a core value of the assessor. Unfortunately, then, people who must provide data to evaluate the measures will believe these measures to be important and thus time and effort and other resources may be spent on activities that are not reflective of core values. In addition, if assessors connect implications to performance measures, even greater incentives exist for the assessed to focus on performing well on the measure, even if the measure does not reflect the goal of either the assessor or the assessed. Goals and values are therefore inferred from the measures, yet they might not be the goals and values the assessor would have chosen.

How to Set Goals

Although the literature we reviewed and the practitioners we interviewed were clear on the importance of first establishing goals, there is no consensus on how to go about this process. Some entities develop goals in response to problems. For example, a state may develop a goal of guarding against fraud after discovering that institutions are misusing student loan funds. Other entities develop goals as part of a strategic planning process. These goals flow from their vision, mission, and values statement. The appendices provide examples of goals of varying entities that range in terms of their content and their level of

[3]For information on establishing a mission, vision, and values, please see Levy et. al, forthcoming.

specificity. Regardless of how the goals are chosen, there are two key points to keep in mind during the goal setting process. The first is to focus on a manageable number of goals. In undertaking the balanced scorecard approach to assessment, USC officials stressed that the process of limiting the number of their goals imposed discipline upon the committee and forced them to delineate their priorities. Limiting the number of goals keeps the assessment process focused on the values and priorities most important to the assessor. Keeping the number of goals limited also helps to reduce cost. There is no set number of goals that is touted as a "rule of thumb," but limiting them is a general best practice.

Level of Stakeholder Involvement

The second key point in the goal-setting process is to consider the level of involvement to accord to different stakeholders and the mechanisms for achieving such involvement. In deciding which stakeholders to include in the goal-setting process, the assessor should consider whom the assessment is intended to benefit. Intended beneficiaries should be involved in the goal-setting process. Many provider institutions hold town meetings or focus groups to gather important stakeholders, such as parents, community members, business owners, and government officials, to discern their goals for higher education. If stakeholders are not included in this goal-setting process, there is no guarantee that the assessment will benefit them. In cases where an intermediary organization controls the assessment process, goal identification becomes more complicated.[4] Most intermediaries operate at the system level, or even outside the system, so there can be tension between the goals that the providers and stakeholders articulate and what the intermediaries identify as the goals of the providers. For example, state higher education boards frequently mediate dramatic disconnects between system- and institution-level goals. At the state level, policymakers are concerned with issues such as access and equity for the state population as a whole. These concerns, however, may go against what institutional leaders desire for their campuses. An example of this could be a campus wanting to develop a new program, but the state deciding that the program would duplicate efforts at another campus.

There are different methods for dealing with this tension between intermediary goals and stakeholder/provider goals.[5] Some intermediaries set their own goals for the assessment without regard for the goals of stakeholders or providers. The

[4]When the assessor is part of a system, goal identification can overlap with Phase One assessment.

[5]Some of these tensions are addressed in Phase One activities.

U.S. News and World Report assessment process is the most extreme example of an intermediary that has identified goals with little input from either stakeholders or providers (see Appendix H.1). Not surprisingly, their rankings have been the object of criticism from providers and some customers for failing to account for important dimensions of performance. Nevertheless, *U.S. News and World Report* representatives are satisfied with their process.

Other intermediaries need to involve stakeholders and providers in the goal-setting process. This need typically arises from the need to ensure that the assessment meets the needs of the stakeholders. However, this need can also arise as a result of a lack of authority on the part of the intermediary (see Section 5 for a discussion on intermediary authority). If the intermediary has little authority, it may gain credibility by acting as a convener for stakeholders and a clearinghouse for their goals. If the intermediary does indeed want to gather stakeholder input during the goal-setting process, there are several examples from state boards, accrediting associations, and corporations of how to go about it.

Kentucky State Higher Education Board. In Kentucky, the current president of the Council on Postsecondary Education (CPE) visited each public higher education institution in the state when he was originally appointed. At the same time, the CPE president conducted focus groups with state citizens to understand their concerns about higher education. CPE and institutional leaders now meet monthly. The meetings keep CPE abreast of institutional concerns and innovations. They also illustrate the "vulnerabilities and alliances" of the institutional leaders. The CPE president uses the meetings to build consensus about institutional goals and priorities.

Western Association of Schools and Colleges Accrediting Agency. The Western Association of Schools and Colleges (WASC) is representative of a new direction in which some accrediting agencies are going. A new accrediting process is being developed that is based on the individual institutional mission. Therefore, goals on which the assessment process is based reflect each institution's mission, rather than a set of accreditation standards that are applied to every institution. In moving toward this new process, WASC has solicited feedback from several stakeholders. WASC has titled its efforts "Invitation to Dialogue," which aptly captures what it is trying to accomplish. There have been many different stakeholders involved throughout the "Dialogue" process, including a wide range of institutional representatives, plus other experts on higher education.

Corporate Learning Organizations. The approaches used by corporate learning organizations to identify goals for professional development and education display some common features. Typically, learning goals are based on the corporation's strategic plan, plus core competencies and other competencies taken as critical to the mission success of the enterprise's several lines of business. The learning goals therefore relate to business goals. Corporations use several methods for involving various constituents in defining these goals. For example, at Lucent, education and training activities are divided into 15 curriculum areas, such as software, wireless, diversity, and program management. Each curriculum area has a business performance council, which includes powerful people in the company (e.g., the software committee is headed by the vice president for software). There are over 160 people on these councils, including a dean and approximately 20 subject matter experts for each curriculum.

The business performance councils at Lucent are considered stakeholders in the education and training process, in that they are responsible for much more than education and training. They consider all strategic issues related to their particular area. They specifically consider education and training as part of the key strategic business issues, setting goals for the education and training that reflect their business needs.

Step Two: Selecting Measures

Once the goals for education and professional development activities have been identified, the next step is to develop measures of performance. These measures should be clearly linked to the goals identified in Step One. Linking measures to goals ensures both that all goals will be addressed and that extraneous measures will not be developed. Measures can focus on inputs, processes, or outcomes.

Input Measures

Inputs are any resources that are used in the education process, such as the learner's level of knowledge or ability upon enrollment; faculty, technology, or library resources; and dollars spent on curriculum development. Input measures are frequently used in the education, training, and professional development environment. The use of input measures is based on the assumption that more or better inputs generate more or better outcomes. Sometimes a correlation between inputs and outcomes can be established empirically. For example, the American Society for Training and Development (ASTD) benchmarking project found that training expenditures per employee are correlated with company performance; the amount of training expenditures per employee has thus gained credibility as a performance measure. Common input measures include education/training expenditures as a percentage of payroll, hours of training per employee per year, percentage of employees trained per year, education/training expenditures per learner, or employee and student characteristics (e.g., standardized test scores).

Process Measures

Process is the way in which the education and training is delivered or produced.[6] Process measures can include teaching methods, instructor characteristics, decisions about the content of materials, faculty-student contact, and the number of faculty per student. "Process" also includes more abstract concepts. Does a learning experience involve direct contact with tenured faculty? Does it require students to use critical thinking skills? Are asynchronous learning techniques used? All of these questions relate to the process of education and professional development.

Such process measures are also used frequently, particularly in higher education. There is growing interest in process measures due in part to the popularity of business models such as total quality management and continuous quality improvement that emphasize the role of production processes in generating better outcomes.

As with input measures, the use of process measures is based on the assumption that certain processes are associated with desired outcomes. In higher education a useful study linking process to outcomes, *Applying the Seven Principles for Good Practice in Undergraduate Education* (Chickering and Gamson, 1991), identifies processes that produce good student outcomes: student-faculty contact, cooperation among students, active learning, prompt feedback, time on task, high expectations, and respect for diverse talents. Cost per unit output, a typical productivity measure, is another process measure. When the output produced by the system is diverse (e.g., year-long courses as well as two-hour seminars), it is useful to use a method that can allow for the aggregation of such heterogeneity. For example, Lucent Technologies learning organization calculates cost per learner hour, which provides a common denominator that can

[6]We emphasize again that the use of the term "process" here differs from the use of the term in the description of Model 2. In Model 2, the intermediary is assessing the process used by providers to assess their own performance. Here, we refer to the process the provider uses to produce education and professional development.

allow for comparisons between very different types of learning activities (e.g., a week-long course and an hour-long tutorial).

Outcome Measures[7]

Outcomes reflect both what is produced by the education, such as the number of graduates, and the overall impact of the education and professional development. Outcomes typically relate closely to the goals of the education and professional development process. Outcomes can include the impact of the learning experience on the learner's job performance or lifetime income, or the acquisition of a specific skill or level of knowledge. Outcome measures are attractive because they can be directly related to goals. Examples of outcome measures used in higher education include passing rate of graduates on licensure exams (by discipline or field), scores on a senior exit exam, employment outcomes, job performance evaluations, and evidence of skills acquired.

As opposed to inputs and processes, which typically describe characteristics of the institution, outcome measures are desirable in that they examine the impact of the institution. Such impacts are typically similar to the institution's goals. For example, an outcome measure (and an institutional goal) may be to graduate a higher percentage of students. Examining outcomes by themselves can provide a good diagnostic tool identifying problems with the education and professional development, but outcome measures alone are limited in their usefulness for proposing solutions to deficiencies. To find such solutions, outcomes should be measured in relation to both inputs and processes, so that the assessor can understand the processes that affect outcomes. For example, if pass rates on a specific examination are low, the assessor should relate these rates to the level of preparation of the students upon entry (inputs) and the classes they take and other experiences they have during the educational process (processes).

---

[7]The assessment literature formerly emphasized a distinction between outputs and outcomes. Outputs reflect what is produced by the education activity, whereas outcomes reflect the overall impact of the education and professional development and relate more closely to the goals of the education and professional development process. Outputs are normally stated in terms of numbers: the number of students served, the number of graduates, etc. Outcomes are much more general and can include the impact of the learning experience on the learner's job performance or lifetime income. The literature now tends to refer to both outputs and outcomes as outcomes because both are closely related to goals and can be understood as outcomes of the educational process. We have adopted that convention in the text of this report.

Choosing Measures

In choosing measures, it is important to keep five key points in mind. The first is to attempt to develop a mix of input, process, and outcome measures. Although input measures are frequently used as measures of quality in the education, training, and professional development setting, the systems we examined (corporations, states, government agencies) are increasingly emphasizing the use of all three types of measures (input, process, and outcome measures). The emphasis stems from a desire for valid and reliable (see discussion below) evidence of progress toward desired goals. Banta and Borden (1994, p. 99) compiled a list of specific measures used by institutions of higher education across the country. They found that

> input or resource indicators originally received most attention because they were easiest to measure. . . . The 1980s saw a groundswell of interest in the other side of the ledger: outcomes. Following the advent of performance funding in Tennessee, three-quarters of the states adopted policies that caused public colleges and universities to collect and report some kind of outcome information. . . . More recently, Deming and others have caused us to turn our attention to the intervening processes that use resources to produce outcomes. Measuring an outcome will not, in and of itself, result in improvement, they say. We need to examine carefully the processes that lead to outcomes if we hope to improve them.

The second key point is to go beyond readily available measures. In examining measures commonly used to assess higher education at the state level, Richardson (1994) found that states tend to focus on readily available measures. Most states measure enrollment, retention rates, progression rates, and graduation rates. While collecting these data may indeed allow the states to measure whether they are meeting their goals, it is likely that there are additional goals that cannot be measured without gathering more extensive data.

- Recognizing that readily available measures fail to account for important goals, many providers or assessors are undertaking major projects to gather information for alternative measures. The Texas Higher Education Coordinating Board has developed the Academic Performance Indicator System. This information system contains longitudinal data on students (demographic information, unique identifiers, courses enrollments, and completions), courses (including how many students began and completed the course), and student outcomes (graduation, employment). Students can be tracked across colleges or systems, and even into the workforce by linking Social Security numbers to Texas Workforce Commission data. As a result, schools can get a picture of how their graduates do. These data are instrumental in determining whether Texas institutions are meeting goals of student achievement both while in college and after graduation.

- The University of Phoenix staff has developed its own assessment tools to measure whether it is meeting its goals. For example, the Cognitive Outcomes Comprehensive Assessment (COCA) and the Adult Learning Outcomes Assessment (ALOA) are curriculum-specific tests administered to students at the beginning and end of each course to measure what they have learned. The COCA is a cognitive assessment tool while the ALOA is an affective/behavioral assessment. All the students take the COCA and ALOA as a matriculation and graduation requirement. Examining the scores on these tests allows university staff to determine if the institution is meeting its goals regarding student achievement, including whether students are learning the skills deemed important in the course objectives. The University of Phoenix also conducts regular surveys of alumni and employers to ensure that it is meeting its goals of preparing alumni for the workforce (for more information, see Appendix K.1).
- The Kirkpatrick model is used in corporate and government settings to assess the quality and productivity of professional development and education. This model recommends the use of several measures for each of four levels described by the model. In the first level, learner satisfaction is measured through the use of course evaluations, satisfaction surveys, and other tools. At the second level, course mastery is assessed through such measures as skill tests, observations, and passing rates. In the third level, job application of the learning is measured through such tools as interviews, focus groups, and manager ratings of students. Finally, at the fourth level, impact on the organization is measured through the use of such tools as customer satisfaction surveys, customer retention, and continued demand for the education or training. Obviously, much time and effort goes toward developing measures when organizations choose to follow the Kirkpatrick model (for more information on the Kirkpatrick model, please see Appendix G).

A third key point in choosing measures is that although it is important to go beyond readily available measures, developing measures can be expensive, so it is necessary to keep value for cost in mind. A choice faced by assessors in all contexts we examined is how much effort to expend on data collection for the purposes of constructing performance measures. Ultimately, each assessor must grapple with the trade-off between higher cost and better information on how well the provider is meeting the desired goals. For the University of Phoenix, the costs to develop its homegrown instruments are substantial. The university would like to utilize externally developed tests, so that it could compare its students to national norms, but good tests are not available in most of the subject areas the university needs. Therefore, it has decided to spend the money for developing its own tests.

The fourth and fifth key points in terms of choosing measures will be fleshed out in the subsection on validity and reliability. The fourth point is that it is important to get feedback from stakeholders on measures if stakeholders will be involved in either gathering or evaluating the measures. One method of getting this feedback is to pilot the measures with a subset of the population. Piloting is typically an effective and efficient way to obtain feedback. Fifth, as again will be described in the validity and reliability subsection, it is important to develop multiple measures for each goal. Such redundancy helps to ensure that the goal will be validly and reliably measured.

Step Three: Evaluate Performance Using Measures

In the course of our research, we identified four basic methods used to evaluate performance in the education and professional development context. Each method is based on a comparison involving the measured performance of the provider or student; the methods differ in the basis against which the comparison is made. There are four bases of comparison: (1) the performance of external peers, (2) preset performance standards, (3) the performance of internal peers, and (4) prior performance of the provider or student. Of course, these methods of evaluation are not mutually exclusive; an assessor may combine them for a more comprehensive interpretation of the results. In our review of the literature, we found no evidence supporting the notion that one evaluation method is better than the others. Each evaluation method has its own strengths and weaknesses, depending on the circumstances, available data, and the existence of internal or external peers. In general, organizations make use of several evaluation methods. There can be overlap between the four basic evaluation approaches. In particular, evaluation can be based on objective standards and still involve a comparison with internal or external peers, or even with past performance. This often occurs, for example, with performance budgeting.

Comparison with External Peers

One approach to evaluating outcomes is to compare the performance of a provider or a student with the performance of similar external providers or students on the same measures. External benchmarking, as it is commonly called, is a traditional method of evaluation in the case of providers assessing themselves for program improvement and intermediaries assessing education systems for accountability. For example, many state higher education coordinating boards identify peer institutions for each of the institutions in their state and compare performance on that basis. In other cases, institutions themselves identify a set of peer institutions and compare their performance with those peers, normally to promote program improvement. In The Urban Universities Portfolio Project, a group of urban institutions rallied together to form a set of measures that are relevant to their own unique mission and student bodies. In Kentucky, the state as a whole compares itself to other states on some high-level performance measures such as *Kids Count* rankings (which ranks states in terms of how well they foster the welfare of children) and higher education participation rates.

To evaluate measures via comparisons with external peers, three conditions should be met. First, appropriate peer groups must be available. Second, these peers must provide the necessary data. Some organizations rely on third-party entities to collect data on providers that can then be used by the providers themselves for benchmarking purposes. For example, the American Society for Training and Development collects input and process measures associated with performance improvements from a group of organizations known for their best practices. Availability of data is an important factor in determining the feasibility of external benchmarking, since it requires providers or third-party groups to consistently and honestly report information on the criteria of interest; which brings us to the third point—assessors must be able to trust the data provided by peers. *U.S. News and World Report* rankings, a clear example of the use of external benchmarking for evaluation, has faced criticism regarding the reliability of information (particularly the self-report information) used to develop the rankings (see Appendix H.1). As the rankings have grown more popular in the public eye, institutions have a greater incentive to provide erroneous information.

Comparison with Preset Standards

A second evaluation method is to compare performance to preset standards. Some state higher education coordinating boards use this evaluation approach in preparing "report cards" on each institution that rank how well the institution has done in comparison to preset standards, such as rates for enrollment, retention, and graduation. The report cards can also include measures of student learning, academic programs (i.e., program accreditation), faculty productivity, and financial accountability. The Tennessee and South Carolina report card systems set specific performance targets for different types of institutions. Indeed, as discussed in Section 5, a challenge that assessors face as they try to evaluate a heterogeneous group of providers is setting standards appropriate to different types of providers.

One limitation of using preset criteria is that they can stifle any incentive to perform at a level above the criteria. Also, if the result of such an evaluation is simply whether or not the institution met the criteria, then this approach will not allow stakeholders to distinguish among providers. This is a criticism levied against the accreditation process, which traditionally compares an institution's performance measures to preset criteria required for accreditation.

Comparison with Internal Peers

Another method for evaluating measures is to compare performance with that of internal peers. This approach is used in education in situations where internal peers are available, such as within a multi-campus institution or a multi-institution system. For example, as part of its assessment process, the University of Phoenix benchmarks the performance of 65 different sites against one another. The university uses a broad portfolio of assessment practices that enables it to compare both the quality of curriculum as well as the quality of administrative practices among the different sites. Campuses are not graded or penalized for poor performance, but they are compared to one another, and the incentive structure attempts to link rewards to outcomes.

Comparison with Past Performance

Lastly, organizations can compare themselves with their prior performances. This method is referred to as historical benchmarking. In such cases, organizations generate baseline data and compare past to present performance—where were we in terms of quality and productivity, and where are we now? Normally, the evaluation centers on whether performance is improving.

This method is extremely common because it does not require the entity to identify peers or to gather external data. It is relatively easy to collect and track the same information on a single provider or student over time, especially as organizations install suitable information systems. For example, the Learning and Development unit at Lucent Technologies closely tracks the cost per learner hour and compares it with past performance on that dimension. The unit has reduced that cost by 50 percent and views it as a major success.

An important limitation of historical benchmarking is that it lacks an external perspective. Performance may be improving, but was the baseline bad or good? Is the improvement occurring quickly enough? For this reason, historical benchmarking is often paired with external benchmarking.

Measurement Validity and Reliability

In establishing goals, choosing measures, and evaluating these measures, it is important to consider issues of validity and reliability. In other words, does the assessment process accurately capture what it intends to capture? In this subsection, we briefly review applications of the literature on validity and reliability to assessment.[8] Validity and reliability concern whether measures, as designed and administered, provide good estimates of the concept under investigation. Most of the literature in this area relates to valid and reliable measures of learning. In other words, researchers are interested in whether the tests used to ascertain student learning are valid and reliable. However, the concepts of and challenges to validity and reliability discussed here also pertain to other types of measures. Although the issues of measurement validity and reliability appear to relate primarily to Step Two of the assessment process (selecting measures), they are, in fact, important concepts to consider in all three steps.

Validity

Validity can be defined as a judgment of the degree to which empirical evidence and theoretical rationales support the adequacy of interpretations of measures (Messick, 1989; cf. Cook and Campbell, 1979). In other words, does the measurement used truly measure what it purports to measure? Validity is not a property of the measurement technique per se. Rather, it is a property of the meaning attributed to the measure (Messick, 1996; Cronbach, 1971). Validity has to do with whether measures can be interpreted as good indicators of the constructs they are intended to represent. A construct is the activity, performance, or entity that is being assessed.[9] There are obviously many measures (e.g., grade point average, test scores, retention, completion, graduation, etc.) that could be used to assess this construct.

---

[8]We do not attempt to review the classical literature on validity and reliability (see, for example, American Psychological Association, 1985; Campbell and Fiske, 1959: Campbell and Stanley, 1966; Cook and Campbell, 1979; Cronbach and Gleser, 1965; Messick, 1989; Messick, 1975; Snow, 1974; Thorndike, 1971; Winer, 1971).

[9]For example, "student achievement" is a construct.

Face validity (Babbie, 1992) refers simply to the subjective judgment that, on the face of it, a measure agrees with our common understanding of the construct the measure is intended to represent (Singleton, Straits, and Miller Straits, 1993; Babbie, 1992). Face validity is usually the first test of acceptability of a proposed measure, established by having domain experts examine it and agree that it "looks right, reads right, feels right" (Light, Singer, and Willett, 1990). However, for most assessment purposes, face validity alone is generally not acceptable; rather, objective validation of measures is needed as well. More objective validation can be achieved through considering both internal and external (Campbell and Stanley, 1966) validity.

Internal Validity. Internal validity refers to the relationship between the measure and the underlying construct of interest. The two most common types of internal validity are content validity and construct validity.

Content validity has to do with the content relevance and the technical quality of measures. In other words, is the terminology used throughout the measure accurate and relevant? Is the problem statement realistic and relevant? It is usually the concern that dominates initial measurement development.

Construct validity refers to the likelihood that measures represent the underlying processes to which they are being applied. Construct validity usually involves two kinds of concerns—substantive and structural.

- Substantive construct validity concerns the extent to which a particular measure reflects the constructs it is designed to capture. "Think-aloud" protocols, for instance, would be an appropriate procedure for getting at whether test problems are engaging the intended types of problem solving (Tannenbaum and Yukl, 1992; Messick, 1989). Substantive construct validity is usually threatened in one of two ways. Construct "underrepresentation" occurs when an evaluation omits something critical to the construct, for instance, by including too few tasks to represent it adequately (Phillips, 1996). Construct overrepresentation, in contrast, refers to inclusion in the evaluation of material irrelevant to the construct. Richly contextualized simulations or hypothetical problems, for instance, may present details that do not represent the construct of interest but that nevertheless act as performance cues or miscues (Dickinson and Hedge, 1989; Messick, 1996).
- Structural construct validity refers to the relationships among items within a measure. Structural construct validity is usually established by statistical tests designed to determine, for instance, whether a competency is uni- or multi-dimensional, whether a set of skills can be ordered hierarchically, and whether other relational properties of the measures model what is known

about the internal structure of the construct domain. A common validity problem is that evaluations often implicitly assume uni-dimensionality of competencies and hierarchies of skills without ever corroborating these relationships empirically. In other words, a measure may assume that the test taker can perform a "higher level" task, such as synthesizing, if that same test taker performs well on a "lower-level" task, such as summarizing. This assumption may not always be accurate.

External Validity. External validity has to do with the *generalizability* of inferences based on outcome measures to and across populations of persons, settings, and tasks (Cook and Campbell, 1979; Brennan, 1996). *Predictive validity* is perhaps the most important form of external validity. It has to do with whether measures are good indicators of future real world performance in the domain of interest. For example, if a person does well on a test intended to measure writing skills, will the person do well in a writing-intensive job? Are the results of the test generalizable to a realistic setting? It is generally recognized that standardized paper-and-pencil tests lack predictive validity; that is, they tend to predict how examinees will perform on another test but not how they will perform outside of test situations later on (Jaeger et al., 1996).

Reliability

Reliability is a necessary but insufficient condition for validity. Reliability is construed as the consistency of a measure (Cole et al., 1984). In other words, if a test or survey is given to many different individuals, will they all interpret it as asking for the same information? Reliability is represented by measurement stability and jeopardized by random measurement error (Cole et al., 1984). If measures are not reasonably reliable, they provide poor estimates.

There are several well-developed procedures for empirically determining the reliability of measures, including the alternate forms method, the test-retest method, the subdivided (split-half) method, and the internal consistency method (e.g., Nunnally, 1970; Winer, 1971). These methods generally depend on using a number of measures representing the constructs of interest and gathering scores from a sizable population that exhibits substantial individual variation. That is to say, most of these standard procedures for reliability analysis have been developed for norm-referenced measurement approaches. Norm-referenced approaches require obtaining a representative sample of persons from some population of interest (Hambleton and Novick, 1973). Professional licensing and certification examinations are generally norm-referenced (Cole et al., 1984).

There are adjustments to most standard reliability analysis procedures—including the four listed above—that make them suitable for use with criterion-referenced measures (Cole et al., 1984; Maratuza, 1977; Nunnally, 1970). On the basis of a review of existing performance standard setting methods, Jaeger et al. (1996) recommend two approaches to setting criteria. In one method, called an "iterative, judgmental policy capturing procedure," panelists respond independently to graphic profiles of performance for hypothetical learners, making judgments about whether the performance or profile should be considered deficient, competent, accomplished, or highly accomplished. Model-fitting methods are then used to capture the panelists' standard-setting policies from their reactions to the sample performances presented to them. A second method is termed a "multi-stage dominant profile procedure." Using this approach, a variety of interactive procedures are used to get panelists to formulate explicitly their standard-setting policies. The procedure differs from the previous one in that panelists' standards are generated directly through discussion of presented hypothetical profiles and performances rather than inferred from panelist ratings.

Implications

There are several techniques used in attempts to ensure both validity and reliability. Four of these techniques are presented here and all are relevant to assessment steps one through three. The techniques include: (1) the continued solicitation of expert feedback (for examples of such solicitation, see the discussion of course objectives and associated competencies in the U.S. Department of Transportation case, Appendix F.1, and the U.S. Air Force Education and Training case, Appendix F.2); (2) extensive piloting of the measures with members of the target population before use; (3) use of multiple measures to evaluate the underlying construct; and (4) comparing results of measures used to results of other measures and tests for similar groups over time.

During Step One, as goals are defined, feedback should be solicited from appropriate stakeholders, including those who will be involved in judging whether the objectives are met. During Step Two, as measures are chosen, again, feedback should be solicited from stakeholders to assure that objectives have been realistically represented. In developing these measures, the assessor should ensure that there are multiple measures used for each goal. Once measures have been developed, they should be piloted with a subset of the intended population. In Step Three, when these measures are evaluated, they should not only be evaluated as stand-alone measures, but they should be compared, to the extent possible, with other preexisting measures. These actions may not ensure validity and reliability, but are good steps in that direction.

Bringing It All Together: Integrating All Three Steps

While the literature review and case studies provide concrete information on each step, there are few examples for guiding an intermediary in integrating all three steps. The balanced scorecard provides a useful framework for such integration. The balanced scorecard framework has been adopted as a strategic management system by a wide range of organizations including corporations, universities, nonprofit organizations, and government agencies.[10] The balanced scorecard is a framework designed to help organizations translate their vision and mission statements into performance goals, while taking into account multiple perspectives, including those of customers, internal constituents, and providers of the education or training. The balanced scorecard is used primarily by provider organizations to identify goals and then translate those goals into operational performance measures.

The balanced scorecard approach is based on four main processes: translating the vision, communication and alignment, business planning, and feedback and learning. All four processes aim to create consistency and integration of priorities across the organization and to determine the right performance measures. The translation of the vision is meant to create an understanding of the organization's vision through an "integrated set of objectives and measures, agreed upon by all senior executives, that describe the long-term drivers of success" (Kaplan and Norton, 1996, p. 76). The vision and strategy should then be communicated throughout the organization to ensure that departmental and individual employee goals are properly aligned with the long-term strategic vision. The business planning aspect links the budget to strategic planning and performance measurement, allowing decisionmakers to direct resources appropriately. Finally, the feedback and learning mechanism provides an opportunity for decisionmakers to review performance results and assess the validity of the organization's strategy and performance measures. The balanced scorecard approach places a heavy emphasis on continually updating strategy and measures to accurately reflect the changing operating environment.

The balanced scorecard allows the provider to include as many stakeholders as necessary in the goal determination process. The scope and number of goals are flexible in that they can change as the operating environment of the institution

---

[10]See Appendix K.3 for more-detailed information on the balanced scorecard.

changes, although it is suggested that the number of goals in each perspective area be limited to a handful. According to University of Southern California officials, the process of limiting the number of their goals imposed discipline upon the committee and forced them to delineate their priorities. Furthermore, the balanced scorecard framework encourages institutions to identify a limited number of measures that relate to the goals they have established.

In this process, evaluation of the measures relies on the comparison of performance with that of external peers (benchmarking). Indeed, the need to benchmark and the availability of such benchmarking information influences the choice of performance measures. The purpose of the balanced scorecard approach is for managers to select indicators that can help them monitor progress toward a few key goals. Table 6.1 provides examples of the University of Southern California's goals, measures, and benchmarks used in its balanced scorecard assessment process.

Table 6.1

University of Southern California's Goals, Measures, and Benchmarks

Goal	Measure	Benchmark
Quality of academic programs	Ranking in the *U.S. News and World Report* Teaching effectiveness	Ascend to the top 10 schools of education Equal average of top 5 of USC Schools
Student-centeredness	Quality of student services is measured by student satisfaction with advisement, career development, job placement, course offerings, financial aid, etc. School climate for special-population students, e.g., international, minority, and women	
Quality of faculty	Publications Research funding	Exceed average of publications per USC tenure-track faculty member Equal average of top 11–20 in *U.S. News and World Report*
Value for money	Retention Reduced time-to-degree Return on student investment	Equal average of top 5 of USC graduate programs Reduce time by 20 percent Break even
Alumni satisfaction	To be developed	
Employer satisfaction	Quality of elementary and secondary school teachers	

SOURCE: O'Neil et al., 1999, p. 37. Reprinted by permission.

Relevance of the Three Assessment Steps for the Chancellor's Office

Our description of the three principal steps of assessment highlights several points that have particular relevance to the Chancellor's office. The first is that the steps should be followed in order. In particular, it is crucial to avoid selecting measures *before or without* defining goals. Practitioners in higher education, corporate, and government agency settings stressed the tendency of individuals to value or emphasize what is measured and divert attention toward it. Therefore, it is important for any assessor to be sure that the measures they are examining are tightly related to key goals.

In determining goals, it is important to reach consensus on a manageable number of goals. In addition, the Chancellor's office should consider which stakeholders and providers to include in this consensus-reaching process for determining goals. The Chancellor's office should include all the stakeholders and providers who are intended to benefit from the assessment. In other words, if a stakeholder such as a functional sponsor is intended to benefit from the assessment, this sponsor should be included in the goal-setting process for the assessment. Including such stakeholders should have the added benefit of increasing the legitimacy of the role of the Chancellor's office. There are several ways to solicit such input, including meetings, visits, focus groups, and establishing boards or committees.

In terms of selecting measures, the Chancellor's office should ensure that the measures flow from the chosen goals. Within this constraint, the Chancellor's office should ensure that the measures chosen reflect input, process, and outcome measures, going beyond readily available measures to ensure that there are valid and reliable measures for each goal. Choosing multiple measures for each goal helps to ensure reliability and validity. Throughout this process, the Chancellor needs to continue to consider value for cost, since much of this work is quite expensive. Finally, when multiple measures reflecting inputs, processes, and outcomes have been chosen for each goal, the Chancellor's office should pilot these measures with a subset of the institution's population to ensure that they will work for the institution's purposes.

In evaluating the measures, the Chancellor's office has four methods to choose from: comparing measure performance to (1) external peers, (2) preset standards, (3) internal peers, and (4) prior performance. All of these evaluation techniques should be considered for each measure, and combining more than one technique is encouraged. Multiple methods of evaluation help to ensure the reliability and validity of the measures. Opportunities for using each of these techniques, as well as their strengths and weaknesses, have been covered in this section.

One final lesson from this section is that many organizations continually reconsider each of the three steps in the assessment process on a regular basis. Establishing a regular cycle and process for determining goals helps to ensure that goals reflect current needs. This process can be formal or informal, and the appendices contain examples of how other organizations conduct it.

7. Conclusions and Recommendations

This report has provided a broad overview of the variety of approaches used within different systems to assess the quality and productivity of education, training, and professional development. Such an overview should be useful to any organization that is developing from scratch or refining an educational assessment activity, particularly the DoD Office of the Chancellor for Education and Professional Development. In presenting this overview, we have developed a scheme for classifying assessment approaches, which distinguishes different stages of the process and distills common features among seemingly different assessment activities.

First, we distinguish between the high-level assessment of whether the set of educational providers is meeting the needs of the system as a whole (Phase One) and the more narrow assessment of whether providers are meeting the needs of their current stakeholders (Phase Two). We subsequently categorized the approaches of Phase Two assessment into four types (Models 1–4) and described the strengths and weaknesses of those models. Within this structure, we considered key lessons for the DoD's civilian education and professional development system.

Phase One: DoD Should Devote Attention to the First Phase of Assessment

Education and professional development systems, as we have defined them in this report, are normally part of larger systems with a mission that goes well beyond education and training. A clear trend in each of these "larger" systems we considered (states, corporations, and government agencies) is the development of a learning organization of some sort that is responsible for more than just the assessment of existing providers. Rather, these organizations play a key role in promoting communication among stakeholders and developing a clear link between education, training, and professional development on the one hand and the basic mission of the system on the other. Corporate learning organizations describe this as "becoming a strategic partner" in the corporation. Part of this function is often to convince customer organizations that learning is important.

Levy et al. (forthcoming) emphasizes that the DoD civilian education and professional development system has multiple stakeholders; that there is loose integration between workforce planning, education, and personnel reward systems; and that there is an uneven commitment on the part of customer organizations to education and professional development. These characteristics suggest that DoD could benefit from the focused, high-level, integrated attention to workforce education and training issues that results from the "strategic partnership" model.

The Chancellor's office should consider assuming the role of primary advocate for the development of a central learning organization, modeled after a corporate learning organization or a state higher education coordinating board, which would institutionalize high-level consideration of workforce education and training issues from a broad base of stakeholders. Over the long run, this could have an important and far-reaching effect on the quality and productivity of civilian education and professional development.

We are not advocating that the Chancellor's office become that organization; a substantial amount of thought and input from various stakeholders would need to go into the development of such an organization. Other organizations within DoD, particularly those responsible for workforce planning and personnel policy, would have an important role to play in such a learning organization. In corporations, successful learning organizations command the attention of the CEO, and in states, successful boards command the attention of the governor. By analogy, in DoD, the success of such an effort would depend on high-level support from the Secretary of Defense.

Phase Two: Recommendations

In this report, we present four models for Phase Two assessment. We found no clear evidence that one assessment approach is unequivocally more effective than others. Each model has strengths and weaknesses, many of which depend on the specific context of the system and of the organization in charge of the assessment. We emphasize that the Chancellor's office does not need to choose a single model for all purposes or providers. For example, Model 4 might be useful for specific groups of learners who are acquiring well-defined, job-related competencies. Model 3 might be useful for DoD institutions that are already accredited by regional accrediting agencies. Model 1 or 2 might be useful for DoD institutions that are not otherwise accredited and for external providers.

Consider the Purpose of Assessment

What is the purpose of DoD's assessment efforts? Is it to promote improvement within provider institutions? Is it to hold institutions accountable to stakeholder needs? Is it to fix a specific, perceived problem? As this report discussed in Section 5, different assessment models have relative strengths and weaknesses related to the purpose of assessment. If accountability is an important purpose, then Model 2 is the most effective approach, and Models 1 and 4 could also work. On the other hand, if improvement is the aim, then Models 1 and 3 are most likely to succeed. Model 1 appears to have the best chance of promoting both improvement and accountability.

Consider Constraints Within the DoD Education and Professional Development System

Levy et al. (forthcoming) emphasizes that the provider organizations in the DoD system are extremely heterogeneous and complex, and that the Chancellor's office currently has minimal authority over the provider organizations. Under these circumstances, as discussed in Section 5, Model 1 offers clear advantages for the second phase of assessment. Model 1 delegates to the provider organizations the task of defining goals, measuring outcomes, and evaluating outcomes. As a result, Model 1 can be more easily applied to diverse providers in a system with a low level of authority and little centralization. The primary disadvantage of Model 1 is that it does not, on the face of it, provide accountability. However, the implementation of the academic audit, an example of Model 1, suggests that the model is flexible and could be easily modified to provide for accountability. For example, the Chancellor's office could develop an audit process that places restrictions on the goals that are deemed appropriate and the type of evidence that can be used to support claims of quality and productivity. The audit process could also be modified to explicitly request certain information.

If the Chancellor's office were to adopt Model 1, it would need to design the auditing process, disseminating results (including best practice reports), and modify the process over time. The Chancellor's office could audit not only DoD institutions, but also programs and contractor-provided education and professional development. The audits themselves could be conducted by internal staff or by committees made up of external experts. Again, effort would be required to design and implement a governance structure for assessment. The design of an audit procedure would require some knowledge of existing assessment efforts within institutions and programs.

Integrate the Three Assessment Steps

In terms of the process used to assess providers, this report has emphasized that there are three key steps involved in that process: identifying goals, measuring outcomes, and evaluating outcomes in relation to goals. Linking measures and evaluation to goals is a clear best practice used by all sorts of providers in many contexts. The balanced scorecard approach (Appendix K.3) provides a useful framework for linking the three steps.

Our literature review also suggests the importance of (1) limiting the number of goals driving the assessment process; (2) selecting process and outcome measures, in addition to input measures; and (3) going beyond readily available measures and choosing multiple measures to ensure that there are valid and reliable measures for each goal.

In evaluating the measures, the Chancellor's office has four methods to choose from: Compare performance measures to (1) those of external peers, (2) preset standards, (3) those of internal peers, and (4) prior performance. All of these evaluation techniques should be considered for each measure and combining more than one technique is encouraged. Multiple methods of evaluation also help to ensure the reliability and validity of the measures.

Appendix

A. Overview of Appendices

There are 20 appendices, in addition to this overview, each of which provides more-detailed information on the organizations we studied in the course of this research. Like the main report, the information in the appendices is drawn from our literature review, site visits, and interviews. Organizations where we conducted interviews and site visits had the opportunity to review the relevant appendices before publication.

Six of the appendices begin with a description of a general type of organization (Appendices B, C, D, E, G, and J). They are followed by specific examples of that type of organization (in B.1, B.2, C.1, D.1, etc.). Appendix B, for example, presents an overview of the assessment approaches used by state higher education coordinating boards and is followed by descriptions of two examples of that type of organization: the Texas Higher Education Coordinating Board (B.1) and the Kentucky Council on Postsecondary Education (B.2). The other appendices have no overview section. Appendix F on government agencies, for example, has no general description of government agencies, since there is no general literature on education and training in government agencies; that appendix consists of a set of three case studies of government agencies (F.1, F.2, and F.3). Table A.1 provides a guide to the appendices.

Table A.2 helps to map the appendices to the topics discussed in the report. Because the distinctions we draw between Phase One and Phase Two and the three steps in Phase Two are a synthesis of everything we reviewed, no single appendix contains information on both phases and on each step of Phase Two. Different appendices are good examples of certain topics, but not others. Some of the appendices provide clear examples of one of the four models, but some appendices (e.g., Accrediting Agencies) discuss groups of organizations that use more than one assessment model. For this reason, we provide Table A.2 to help readers locate material in the appendices that relates to a topic of interest.

Table A.1

Overview of Appendices

Organizational Type	Appendix	Specific Organizations	Appendix
State Higher Education Boards	B	Texas Higher Education Coordinating Board	B.1
		Kentucky Council on Postsecondary Education	B.2
Process Auditors—Academic Audit	C	International Organization for Standardization (ISO)	C.1
Accrediting Agency	D	Western Association of Schools and Colleges	D.1
Professional Societies	E	none	
Government Agencies	none	U.S. Department of Transportation	F.1
		U.S. Air Force	F.2
		U.S. Navy	F.3
Corporations and Corporate Learning Organizations	G	Lucent Technologies	G.1
Ranking Systems Sponsor	none	*U.S. News and World Report*	H.1
Voluntary Quality Award Sponsor	none	Baldrige Quality Award	I.1
Certifiers of Student Competencies	J	Western Governors University	Included in J
Provider	none	University of Phoenix	K.1
		U.S. Air Force Academy, Department of Management	K.2
		Balanced Scorecard	K.3
		The Urban Universities Portfolio Project	K.4

Table A.2

Map of Appendices

Appendix	Involvement in Assessment Process		Phase One	Phase Two: Model Emphasis				Phase Two: Assessment Steps		
	Provider	*Intermediary*		*1*	*2*	*3*	*4*	*One*	*Two*	*Three*
B. State Higher Education Boards	Medium	High	High		High			High	High	High
B.1. Texas Higher Education Coordinating Board	Medium	High	High		High			High	High	High
B.2. Kentucky Council on Postsecondary Education	Medium	High	High		High			High	High	High
C. Process Auditors (Academic Audit)	High	High		High				High	High	High
C.1. International Standards Organization (ISO)		High		High				High	High	High
D. Accrediting Agencies		High		Medium	High			High	High	High
D.1. Western Association of Schools and Colleges		High		Medium	High			High	Medium	High
E. Professional Societies		Medium	Medium		Medium		Medium			
F.1. U.S. Department of Transportation		High	High	High				High	High	High
F.2. U.S. Air Force		High	High							
F.3. U.S. Navy	Medium	High	High		High			Medium	High	High
G. Corporations		High	High	Medium	High	Medium		High	High	High
G.1. Lucent Technologies	Medium	High	High	High				High	High	High
H.1. Ranking Systems—*U.S. News and World Report*		High			High			Medium	High	High
I.1. Baldrige Quality Award		High			High			Medium	High	High
J. Certifiers of Student Competencies	Medium	Medium	Medium				High	High	Medium	High
K.1. University of Phoenix	High					High		Medium	High	Medium
K.2. USAFA, Department of Management	High				Medium	High		Medium	High	High
K.3. Balanced Scorecard	High					High		High	High	High
K.4. The Urban Universities Portfolio Project	High		Medium			High		High	Medium	High

Key

■	High
▒	Medium
□	None

B. State Higher Education Boards

Overview

State higher education boards work under the authority of the governor and legislature, with the purpose of ensuring a constructive relationship between postsecondary institutions and the state. Boards vary in their responsibilities, influence, and level of authority over higher education institutions. Three examples of state boards include consolidated governing boards, coordinating boards, and planning boards. Governing boards, as implied by their name, govern individual higher education institutions through planning, problem resolution, program review, budget and policy development, personnel appointment, and resource allocation. Coordinating boards do not govern individual institutions. They instead tend to focus on planning for the statewide system as a whole. These boards may review and even approve both budget requests and academic programs. They do not, however, appoint personnel or develop policies for individual institutions. Planning boards typically are voluntary, rather than statutory. These boards facilitate communications between individual institutions and states, but do no governing or coordinating activities.

In response to mandates from state legislators or governors, most boards have created "accountability systems," or structured efforts to measure and ensure the quality of the institutions within their purview. Among the accountability systems in vogue today are performance indicators, report cards, and performance funding. Although accountability is the primary purpose of these systems, most states encourage institutions to use the data for self-improvement as well.

Accountability systems differ in the level of collaboration among stakeholders, providers, and intermediaries. Some higher education boards are more directive than others. When governing boards determine assessment goals, measures, and evaluations without substantial input from providers, conflict and resentment often follow. Institutional leaders may feel that the state is imposing standards on them that do not reflect the institution's actual quality. Other state boards are more collaborative and ask institutions to play a substantial role in establishing assessment goals and methods. Although this approach leads to more acceptance of assessment by providers, it is time-consuming and costly.

The information gathered through these accountability systems is used in at least four ways, as described below.

- **Funding.** Some states link a percentage of funding to institutional performance. Tennessee awards 2–5 percent of its instructional budget based on assessment results. In theory, South Carolina awards 100 percent of funding based on performance, but in practice a much smaller percentage (probably about 5 percent) depends on assessment results (Schmidt, 1999).
- **Program Planning and Elimination.** Assessment results may contribute to decisionmaking about academic programs. For example, based on its review of assessment data, the Illinois Boards of Higher Education in 1992 recommended the elimination, consolidation, or reduction of 190 programs at public universities, including 7 percent of all undergraduate programs, among other changes.
- **Comparisons.** In many states individual campuses are encouraged to use assessment results for self-improvement purposes. The degree to which this actually occurs is unknown.
- **Public Information.** Assessment results also provide a means of informing the public about their state's higher education system. Thus, some states publish report cards—for either the system as a whole or for individual institutions.

The effectiveness of state accountability systems is uneven. At best, the efforts may lead to quality improvements and better alignment between higher education and state policy goals. At worst, the efforts create dissension; force institutions to redirect resources away from other, arguably more valuable activities; and provide little insight into the performance of higher education institutions and systems.

Phase One

Most state boards are involved in coordinating their statewide systems of higher education. Such coordination ensures that postsecondary institutions operate collectively in ways that are aligned with state priorities and that serve the public interest (McGuinness, 1997). Coordinating efforts can be achieved through both long-range or master planning and focused research studies. A detailed example of Phase One assessment at the state level will be provided in Appendix B.1.

Phase Two

State-level accountability and assessment systems most resemble Model 2. Whether conducted under the guise of performance indicators, performance funding, or report card programs, state boards choose the goals upon which the assessment is to be based and then collect information from institutions and make judgments on this information. However, there are states that tend to use a version of Model 1. Appendix B.2 describes how the Kentucky board allows higher education institutions to determine their own "fitness for purpose" upon which assessments are based. In addition, some other states use a version of Model 4. Florida, for example, has a statewide rising junior exam for college students at the sophomore level. Legislation passed in 1995 limited the use of this exam, called the "College Level Academic Skills Test" (CLAST) so that students can bypass the test if they score well on the Scholastic Aptitude Test (SAT) or if they perform well in specific courses. Nonetheless, use of the CLAST is an example of Model 4 assessment. Even Model 3 may be relevant to some state boards. While Model 3 involves a higher education institution conducting its own assessment, state boards can provide information to help institutions assess themselves or incentive funding to induce institutions to conduct specific assessments. Uses of Model 3 were in vogue in many states in the early 1980s (Ewell, 1999a).

Identify Goals for Education and Training

State accountability systems focus on goals linked to the state's overall higher education mission (reflecting the needs of the general public and of corporate, civic, and political leaders), rather than individual institutions' missions. Typically, the goals address such issues as educational access and affordability, quality and effectiveness, diversity and equity, efficiency and productivity, contribution to state needs, and connection to other education sectors (e.g., K–12). Goals may relate to inputs, processes, outputs, and outcomes. Goals may be established by the state legislature, governor, or the coordinating/governing board.

Develop Measures of Quality and Productivity

In some cases, states mandate measures with little input from the institutions. In other states, the selection of measures is the result of extended discussion and negotiation between institutions and governing/coordinating boards. The measures that constitute state accountability systems vary on several dimensions.

- **The number of measures.** Although institutions generally want more measures included in an assessment program, to maximize the likelihood of high performance on at least some measures, this approach also increases costs. Thus, the costs of assessment are less in Tennessee, with 15 measures, than in South Carolina, with 37.
- **The level of control exercised by the state.** Some states, such as Colorado, encourage institutions to select measures that satisfy internal institutional improvement needs. Others, such as South Carolina, prescribe the measures. Most states are plagued by ambiguity in operational definitions and measurement methodology. For example, student-faculty ratios can be calculated in different ways, leading to significantly different results.
- **The unit of analysis.** Whole institutions are the typical unit of analysis for accountability systems. Within this unit of analysis, politicians seem to be most interested in student-related variables, such as institutional retention rates and pass rates on licensing examinations.
- **Data sources.** In most cases, measures are culled from major institutional databases, from such areas as admissions, registration, and finance. Other measures are based on unit-level data, such as library-use statistics. Still others, such as satisfaction surveys, require new data collection, often at substantial cost. Some states, such as Texas and Virginia, have developed large centralized databases that provide the state board direct access to a wide range of data for assessment. Most, however, rely on institutions to report the results of requested analyses.
- **Measurement focus.** Accountability systems, starting in the 1980s, tend to emphasize outcomes. Scholars are stressing, however, that assessment systems should place equal emphasis on the processes that lead to outcomes so decisionmakers will understand what changes they need to make to have an effect on outcomes (Banta and Borden, 1994).
- **Measurement variation.** Some states apply the same measures to a wide range of institutional types. Other states use different measures for different types of institutions.

Typical accountability measures, or indicators, address admission standards, characteristics of incoming students, admissions "yield" rates, enrollment, total student credit hours, transfer rates, retention and graduation rates, student time to degree, degrees awarded, professional licensure exam pass rates, results of satisfaction surveys (by students, alumni, and employers), faculty teaching workload, and extramural or sponsored research funds.

Tennessee's accountability system, now over 20 years old, was developed in response to the implementation of performance-based funding in the 1970s. The accountability system has undergone a number of changes—most recently, the state started issuing report cards for each institution. Table B.1 displays the indicators used in the report card. South Carolina has also developed a strong accountability system, the major elements of which are displayed in Table B.2.

Evaluate Quality and Productivity Using Measures

Generally, the coordinating or governing board carries out an evaluation process using data submitted by institutions. Institutional performance may be compared to state-set standards (e.g., South Carolina), peer group performance, or past performance (e.g., Tennessee).

Table B.1

Report Card Indicators Used in Tennessee

Categories	Indicators
Student learning	Licensure examination pass-rates Job placement (percentage) Student satisfaction (satisfaction survey responses) Alumni satisfaction (survey responses) Core knowledge and skills (performance on national tests) Graduation rates Degree granted
Academic programs	Program accreditation (percentage eligible accredited) External peer review (number meeting standards)
Faculty productivity	Hours of instruction Students per class
Financial accountability	Tuition and fees Staffing (number full-time) Expenditures (by function) Private giving Financial aid (percentage of students receiving aid)

Table B.2

Performance Measures Used in South Carolina

Categories	Indicators
Mission focus	Expenditures to achieve mission Curricula offered to achieve mission Approval of a mission statement Adoption of strategic plan Attainment of strategic plan goals
Quality of faculty	Academic and other faculty credentials Performance review (to include student and peer evaluation) Posttenure review Compensation Faculty availability to students outside class Community and public service
Instructional quality	Class size and student-teacher ratio Number of credit hours taught by faculty Ratio of full-time faculty as compared with other full-time employees Accreditation of degree-granting programs Institutional emphasis on teacher education quality and reform
Institutional cooperation and collaboration	Sharing and use of technology and other resources internally and with external partners Collaboration with private industry
Administrative efficiency	Administrative and academic cost comparisons Use of best management practices Elimination of waste and duplication General overhead costs per FTE student
Entrance requirements	SAT and ACT scores of student body High school standing, GPA, and student activities Nonacademic achievements of students In-state student enrollment
Graduates' achievements	Graduation rate Employment rate for graduates Employer feedback on graduates Scores on professional exams Graduates continuing education in state Credit hours earned of graduates
User-friendliness of institution	Credit transfer to and from institution Continuing education units Accessibility of institution to state citizens
Research funding	Grants for teacher education Public and private sector grants

NOTES: FTE is full-time equivalent. ACT is American College Testing. GPA is grade point average.

B.1. Texas Higher Education Coordinating Board

Overview

The Texas Higher Education Coordinating Board was established in 1965 by the state legislature. Its overall objective is to promote quality and efficiency in the higher education system. The coordinating board serves as an intermediary between the state legislature and the institutions and its responsibilities fall into three major areas:

- **Coordination:** The coordinating board works with the legislature, governor, and institutional governing boards to coordinate Texas higher education to expand access, improve equality, and promote efficiency through such actions as developing higher education plans and reviewing and approving degree programs and construction of major facilities.
- **Information:** The coordinating board provides information on higher education to state policymakers and citizens.
- **Administration:** The coordinating board administers state and federal programs.

The Texas system consists of 120 public and private institutions—three-quarters are four-year, and one-quarter are technical or community colleges. Fifty-four percent of students are enrolled in the four-year institutions, and 46 percent are enrolled in community or technical colleges. There are 966,840 students in all of postsecondary higher education in Texas. The state expects enrollment in public institutions to continue increasing over the next five years.

In terms of assessing higher education's quality and productivity, the coordinating board's main tool is its authority to approve[1] and/or close programs. The coordinating board conducts two types of reviews at the program level:

1. Initial reviews of programs that institutions would like to offer. Approval by the board is required for the program to be eligible for state funding.
2. Ongoing reviews of programs that have been approved by the board.

---

[1]More specifically, approve the programs for state funding according to an established formula.

Programs must be approved by the board to be eligible for state funding. Programs can lose their approval in the ongoing review, although that rarely happens. Coordinating board staff members know that they will approve some programs that are not worthwhile (about 10 percent will be bad investments); it is impossible to avoid such mistakes. It is important, however, to constantly reevaluate the need for existing programs so as to minimize the effects of mistakes.

In addition to approving and reviewing programs, the board evaluates the effectiveness of the community and technical colleges in the state. The "institutional effectiveness process" is a "comprehensive approach for verifying the effectiveness of Texas' community and technical colleges in achieving their local and statutory missions."[2] Extensive information is gathered from community colleges to evaluate their effectiveness. These data are maintained in a longitudinal database that allows for a strong tracking capability. Every fall, the coordinating board creates an incoming cohort and tracks them as a group for seven years. Students can be tracked across colleges or systems, or even into the workforce by linking Social Security numbers to Texas workforce commission data. As a result, institutions know where their graduates go and can answer such questions as: Do community college graduates go on to a four-year college? If so, do they eventually graduate? Do graduates get jobs in the State of Texas?

Although these data are collected annually, overall institutional effectiveness is measured through a peer-review process with a site visit every four years. This site visit accomplishes both the institutional effectiveness review and the individual program-level review.

The purpose of initial program review and ongoing reviews is both accountability (ensuring that the institutions are spending state money for useful purposes) and program improvement. Similarly, the purpose of the institutional effectiveness process is to hold the community and technical colleges accountable to meeting their missions and to help them improve. The assessment processes are intended to benefit various stakeholders, including legislators, the public, and students, and to assist the institutions in their quests for improvement.

All of these assessment efforts are controlled by the coordinating board, acting as an intermediary. The initial program review includes a market assessment that encourages collaboration between providers and stakeholders. Ongoing reviews at the community and technical colleges also involve an advisory board that

---

[2] *State-Level Institutional Effectiveness Process for Texas Community and Technical Colleges,* Texas Higher Education Coordinating Board, Community and Technical Colleges Division, Austin, Texas, September 2000, p. 1.

includes people from outside the institution, suggesting that stakeholder involvement is promoted during this process.

Initially, colleges were resistant to the coordinating board's role as the main information resource. Resistance diminished as the institutions came to see value in the published reports and online data. In the past, many colleges did not have the capability to provide the data required by the Southern Association of Colleges and Schools and did not have the resources to manipulate any existing data. Currently, the coordinating board not only analyzes the data it receives from institutions, but it packages the information for redistribution to colleges and other interested organizations. Due partly to these efforts, the response by colleges to the coordinating board's assessment efforts has been very positive.

Phase One

The coordinating board engages in statewide higher education planning processes. One of these planning efforts involved developing the Workforce Education Course Manual, which is "the state community and technical college inventory of workforce education courses."[3] Developing this manual was a substantial and ambitious effort. To develop the manual, the coordinating board gathered experts and faculty together and got them to agree on a set of courses, an appropriate content description, and a range of "contact" hours for courses in particular sequences. This process was in response to excessive program duplication and insufficient transferability of courses from one institution to the next. The manual is an attempt at eliminating both of these roadblocks. During this manual development process, course duplications were uncovered and remedied. For example, the number of welding courses was reduced from 900 to 96. Now, every college that offers introductory welding calls it the same name (e.g., Welding 101). The course involves the same number of contact hours regardless of where it is delivered. Now, a person can take Welding 101 in Del Rio, and then be ready to take Welding 102 in San Antonio. Overall, the number of courses offered throughout the state by the community and technical colleges went from over 30,000 to approximately 6,000.

There have been two effects of this manual: (1) businesses know that programs are the same in each college, and (2) students can transfer credits from one institution to the next without difficulty. The Workforce Education Course Manual effort took approximately four years and cost approximately $150,000 per year.

---

[3]See www.thecb.state.tx.us/divisions/ctc/ip/WECM2000/about.htm.

Phase Two

The assessment process used in Texas most closely resembles Model 2. The intermediary decides the criteria upon which the assessments are conducted. This intermediary (the coordinating board) then collects data and judges whether the program under review is worthy of either initial or continued funding.

Identify Goals for Education and Training

Underlying goals are evident in the initial program approval process. This process is based on five criteria. The criteria are not literally goals, but guiding principles for evaluation. The coordinating board has used the following criteria since its inception:

1. **Need:** Does the state need this program at this institution?
2. **Quality:** Are new programs of good quality (thus protecting student interests)?
3. **Cost:** Is the program worth the cost?
4. **Duplication:** Does the program duplicate existing programs?
5. **Mission:** Does the program fall within the scope of the institution's mission?

In addition to these five goals for program approval, there are seven standards of program and institutional quality that must be adhered to by the community and technical colleges. Institutions must

- fulfill their statutory mandate and meet the unique needs of their service area
- use Perkins[4] resources effectively
- provide sufficient access and effective student services
- ensure student achievement
- provide quality continuing education
- provide quality academic programs and services
- provide quality workforce education programs.

Develop Measures of Quality and Productivity

The measures of quality and productivity used differ for initial program approvals, ongoing reviews at universities, and ongoing reviews at two-year

[4]As mandated by the federal Perkins Act.

colleges. In general, the initial program approval process uses similar measures at universities and two-year colleges.

Initial Program Approval. Measures are categorized according to the goals to which they relate:

1. The need criterion looks at student and job demand. Does the state need this program at this institution? Different types of data collection methods are used to answer this question, including surveys, national data on doctoral programs, occupational handbooks for job demand projections in particular sectors, the link to the Texas economy, and the relative number of programs in Texas with respect to other states in the country. At the technical and community college level, the program under consideration must have a business advisory board.
2. The quality criterion is based on the rationale of protecting students' interests. The quality indicator focuses on faculty and resources (i.e., whether engineering programs have adequate labs and facilities). It also considers things like whether there are enough faculty members to staff the program. For example, there is an informal standard of a minimum of four FTE faculty members for doctoral programs. One coordinating board member said, "We want planned programs that have a national reputation." In addition, the quality assessment considers Southern Association of Colleges and Schools accreditation and qualification of faculty.

   At community and technical colleges, the coordinating board also looks at whether the institution has started any relevant external accreditation process where such a quality assessment process is available (e.g., programs for dental assistants). The coordinating board also looks at how the college is doing in other programs. If the college is not meeting standards in other areas, it may be prevented from starting a new program.
3. The cost criterion examines the projection of the cost to the state. The state wants to know whether or not programs will be self-supporting after they have been initiated. Programs with high cost and low funding or demand do not make sense. The coordinating board asks for detailed accounts of how the proposed program will be funded during the start-up phase. Since enrollment-based funding is based on enrollment from previous years, a new program will not generate revenues in real time.
4. The duplication criterion looks at whether higher education institutions within a given geographic area have similar programs.
5. The mission criterion simply looks at whether the program falls within an institution's mission.

Ongoing Program Review—Universities. In reviewing existing programs at universities, the coordinating board relies to a large extent on accreditation; programs should meet Southern Association of Colleges and Schools and program-specific accrediting agency standards. Other than this measure, the coordinating board does not systematically examine the quality of programs, except in the area of teacher education. The legislature has been focused on teacher education and is concerned about the quality of graduates from teacher education programs. The coordinating board has imposed additional requirements on teacher education programs, including more interdisciplinary studies, a larger number of required math courses, and the elimination of math and science courses designed just for students in the education programs. In other words, the board is directly intervening in the process by instituting specific curricular requirements. The board also collects and reports information on the pass rates of licensing exams for graduates of professional programs.

In addition to examining ongoing program quality at the four-year institutions, the coordinating board is involved in ongoing productivity reviews. Publications are available on classroom utilization, research expenditures, and research funding per faculty member. In addition, programs must graduate at least three Ph.D.s within a five-year period to be considered productive.

Ongoing Review—Two-Year Colleges. The measurement of performance of two-year colleges by the coordinating board is more involved than it is for the universities. This review is conducted through an on-site peer review process. This process, conducted every four years, not only serves as a program review process, but as a method for evaluating institutional effectiveness. Therefore, the coordinating board asks for data on both program-level assessment and the meeting of the seven statewide goals mentioned above. A committee of college presidents, faculty, students, and industry representatives identified 66 different measures to be collected from each two-year institution to meet these seven goals. The state legislature's budget board passed a law requiring all two-year colleges in the state to collect these data. Table B.1.1 displays some examples of the measures the coordinating board uses to determine whether these goals have been achieved. This table is not an exhaustive list; each goal typically has five to ten measures. For the most part, information is provided by the institutions, but some information is available from external sources. Approximately $530,000 is used to support this data collection effort annually.

Table B.1.1

Examples of Measures for Texas Two-Year Colleges

Goals	Examples of Measures
Fulfill their statutory mandate and meet the unique needs of their service area	Published mission statement addresses all statutory requirements
Use Perkins resources effectively	Current funds must be expended on allowable costs
Provide sufficient access and effective student services	Proportion of women and minorities in all workforce education enrollment is comparable (±5 percent) to overall college enrollment or shows improvement compared with overall college enrollment
Ensure student achievement	30 percent of full-time, first-time-in-college students not receiving remediation receive a degree or certificate or transfer within three years
Provide quality continuing education	College shows documented evidence of serving literacy needs in the college district (either through college efforts or collaboration with other entities) offering certain programs[a]
Provide quality academic programs and services	The college has incorporated a core curriculum of at least 42 semester credit hours into each academic degree plan, unless a smaller core curriculum component is specified in a statewide field of study curriculum
Provide quality workforce education programs	Program must have had 15 graduates over last three years

[a] Adult basic education, general equivalency diploma, English-as-second-language, and Workforce Literacy programs.

Evaluate Quality and Productivity Using Measures

In approving new programs, the coordinating board compares institutional data on the new program with the existing five criteria. In reviewing existing programs, the process is much more involved for the community and technical colleges. For the four-year institutions, the coordinating board basically ensures that the program is accredited, although it does examine the teacher preparation programs in greater detail. These examinations are, again, made in reference to existing standards. For the community and technical colleges, institutional data are again compared with existing standards. However, the board's general philosophy is to allow colleges to draw their own conclusions and make their own decisions based on the reports provided. So colleges use reports to facilitate decisionmaking, while the coordinating board plays a supportive role and assists the colleges where needed.

B.2. Kentucky Council on Postsecondary Education

Overview

The Kentucky system of higher education consists of two research universities (The University of Louisville and The University of Kentucky), The Kentucky Commonwealth Virtual University, six comprehensive regional universities, and a system of 28 community and technical colleges. These institutions serve approximately 47,000 credit and 144,000 noncredit students each year.

The Kentucky governor has made higher education a defining issue of his administration. In 1996, the Kentucky General Assembly adopted Senate Concurrent Resolution 93, which created the Task Force on Postsecondary Education. This task force commissioned a review of postsecondary education in Kentucky and published the results in March 1997. This report spurred further legislation, which established five goals for the state to achieve by 2020, called *2020 Vision: An Agenda for Kentucky's System of Postsecondary Education.*

This same legislation mandated the mission for the Kentucky Council on Postsecondary Education (CPE), which is Kentucky's coordinating board for their higher education system.[1] The purpose of the CPE, an intermediary in this system,[2] is to provide factual information to state political leaders, to adopt a statewide agenda that provides direction to the system, and to eliminate duplication and wasteful competition. The CPE is charged with leading the reform efforts envisioned by state policy leaders. Council members have pledged reduced bureaucracy, staunch advocacy, decisive management, and effective stewardship to achieve six results:

- Public support for the value of postsecondary education.
- Information that is helpful to students and their families in making educational decisions.
- An educational system that is well coordinated and efficient.

---

[1]See Education Commission of the States (1997) or Appendix B for a complete description of the distinction between coordinating and governing boards.

[2]Each university and community or technical college in the state has its own governing board.

- Incentives that stimulate change and prompt institutions to redesign programs and services, realign resources for priorities to improve productivity, and generate new resources.
- Information that shows the public how the system and its institutions are performing.
- Data and research that help policymakers make good decisions.

CPE has 50 employees—half support and half professional. Under guidance of its mission, the CPE's work involves coordinating the improvement of Kentucky postsecondary education. Some of what CPE does is regulatory (approval of new academic programs, for instance), and some is advisory (such as budget recommendations to the governor and the general assembly). State legislation also gave CPE control over the allocation of incentive funds. In addition, CPE licenses the private institutions in the state. Finally, CPE was specifically assigned with developing and implementing a strategic agenda, as well as performance indicators to track the progress of the five goals listed in *2020 Vision,* which is the mechanism the state uses to assess its higher education system.

This assessment process is intended to promote improvement within institutions and the system as a whole and to hold institutions accountable to the state and its citizens. The assessment is stakeholder-driven, because it is motivated and guided by the governor and the legislature. The assessment process is designed to benefit all stakeholders, including legislators, the governor, students, graduates, business owners, and all citizens. The assessment process is an important tool allowing the governor and the legislature to monitor the progress of individual institutions and the higher education system as a whole.

Each year, CPE produces a status report for the governor and the legislature discussing progress toward the *2020 Vision* goals. Information from the assessment process, including comparisons to national standards, influences funding.

Phase One

Creating the Task Force on Postsecondary Education in 1996 was a first step in Phase One assessment in the state of Kentucky. Task force members completed a basic needs analysis of higher education throughout the state. They found low participation in postsecondary education and below-average per-capita income that was, in their opinion, creating a vicious cycle. The task force concluded that postsecondary education was the key to prosperity—for their citizens, their businesses, their communities, and their children. Therefore, in the broadest sense, the mission of the Kentucky system of postsecondary education became economic development. The task force concluded that a responsive and flexible system of postsecondary education needed to become a key tool in helping Kentucky flourish in the early decades of the 21st century. Greater economic prosperity could be achieved by making it possible for all Kentuckians to participate in lifelong learning. These Phase One activities culminated in *2020 Vision,* the goals for higher education in the state.

Phase One activities continue through the Strategic Committee on Postsecondary Education, which brings together state policy leaders in a forum to exchange ideas about the future of postsecondary education in Kentucky. Its members (including the governor, legislative leaders, the CPE members and president, and other representatives) play a pivotal role in assuring that the efforts of the postsecondary education system have the long-term support of policymakers and are tied to statewide needs and economic well-being.

Phase Two

The assessment process used in Kentucky most closely resembles Model 2. The legislature has defined the goals and an intermediary collects information on whether the individual institutions are meeting the goals through gathering data from the institutions. However, measures for whether the institutions are meeting the goals were developed through extensive collaboration with diverse stakeholders. The intermediary then determines the extent to which each institution has met the state's goals.

Identify Goals for Education and Training

The five goals for the assessment process were delineated in the 1997 legislation that created *2020 Vision.* The intent is to achieve these goals by the year 2020. The following text is from *2020 Vision:*

> We ask you to envision a Kentucky in the year 2020 recognized throughout the nation and across the world for having:
>
> - Educated citizens who want advanced knowledge and skills and know how to acquire them; and who are good parents, good citizens, and economically self-sufficient workers.
>
> - Globally competitive businesses and industries respected for their highly knowledgeable employees and the technological sophistication of their products and services.

- Vibrant communities offering a standard of living unsurpassed by those in other states and nations.
- Scholars and practitioners who are among the best in the world, dedicated to creating new ideas, technologies, and knowledge.
- An integrated system of elementary and secondary schools and providers of postsecondary education, committed to meeting the needs of students and the Commonwealth, and acclaimed for excellence, innovation, collaboration, and responsiveness.

The primary purpose of these goals is to bring Kentucky up to the national average in terms of quality-of-life indicators. While the scope of these goals go beyond the traditional scope of higher education institutions, these institutions will play specific roles to move the state toward achieving the goals. The Kentucky Community and Technical College System will be the primary provider of two-year transfer and technical programs, workforce training for existing and new businesses and industries, and remedial and continuing education to improve the quality of life and employability of the citizens of the Commonwealth. The regional universities[3] will work cooperatively to assure statewide access to appropriate, high-quality baccalaureate and master's degree programs. Each university will develop at least one program of national distinction. The University of Louisville will be a premier, nationally recognized metropolitan research university. The University of Kentucky will be a major comprehensive research institution ranked nationally among the top 20 public universities.

In addition to these specific roles, CPE needs to identify goals for educational quality that incorporate the views of all stakeholders. Because of the challenges involved in understanding the views of certain stakeholders, CPE has hired a consulting company to conduct focus groups with students, alumni, parents, and employers to determine what they think a "quality education" entails.

Develop Measures of Quality and Productivity

CPE, in conjunction with individual college leaders, wrote an action agenda that addresses how it will implement *2020 Vision* goals over the next four years. In writing this agenda, CPE also got feedback from a range of Kentuckians through teleconferences, radio shows, meetings, telephone interviews, and focus groups. These activities targeted involvement of campus administrators, faculty senate

---

[3]Eastern Kentucky University, Kentucky State University, Morehead State University, Murray State University, Northern Kentucky University, and Western Kentucky University.

leaders, legislators, teachers, principals, superintendents, students, alumni, parents, employers, and business and civic leaders.

These efforts helped in developing measures for the five goals included in *2020 Vision*. CPE has developed measures relating to students on such issues as access, enrollment, college readiness, retention, time to graduation, graduation rates, lifelong learning, postcollege quality of life, postcollege career success, and postcollege civic and social roles. Other measures are institution-focused and include research dollar obtainment, space usage, employer satisfaction, position in rankings, and continuing education opportunities. An example of these measures on space utilization is the average weekly use of classroom and lab space and percentage occupancy per session.

While most of these measures have been fairly easy to develop, it is more difficult to measure the achievement of broader social goals. Furthermore, there has been disagreement within CPE about how to measure higher education quality. It is not easy to define the concept of quality in absolute terms, and CPE has not come to any agreement. Some elements of quality can be measured through the use of nationally normed tests. CPE is interested in using the concept of value-added, which considers the characteristics, skills, and values of students upon entry, not just absolute outcomes. CPE is also interested in "fitness for purpose," since there is not one single definition of quality that will work for all institutions. The search continues for measures both of quality and of the broader social goals contained in *2020 Vision*.

Evaluate Quality and Productivity Using Measures

CPE measures the progress of the Kentucky higher education system against national averages and against similar information from other states. The council has a benchmark list of comparison institutions from throughout the country for each university. Comparison with other states is the primary type of evaluation. Kentucky has expanded the list of states it compares its institutions to; the state wants to look beyond its traditional comparison states, such as Mississippi, Alabama, and Arkansas, to a group of states that includes North Carolina, Ohio, and Virginia. In addition, the evaluation also occurs through a self-comparison over time; Kentucky wants to see improvement on each measure over time.

C. Process Auditors—Academic Audit[1]

Overview

The academic audit is a relatively new approach to quality assessment that has been implemented abroad—in Hong Kong, Scandinavia, Great Britain, Australia, New Zealand, and the Association of European Universities (CRE)—and has begun to receive attention from U.S. accrediting organizations, such as the Western Association of Colleges and Schools. The academic audit is an external peer review of institutional quality assessment and improvement systems at a particular provider institution. The focus of the audit is on an institution's own processes for measuring and improving academic quality.

The academic audit originated in 1990 in the UK, when the government became increasingly interested in ensuring that sufficient attention was paid to teaching in the face of rapid growth in higher education. There was a threat that Her Majesty's Inspector (HMI) would undertake an audit of colleges and universities. Instead,

> the Academic Standards Group of the Committee of Vice Chancellors and Principals recommended the creation of an Academic Audit Unit (AAU) to provide external and independent assurance that UK universities had adequate and effective mechanisms and structures for monitoring, maintaining, and improving the quality of their teaching (Dill, 2000a, p. 189).

Implementing the audit process precluded an evaluation from HMI.

The emergence of the academic audit is related in part to the changing global market for education, which is increasing pressure on higher education worldwide. Particularly in Europe, where higher education has traditionally been state run, the issue facing education policymakers is how to create markets. In the United States, market forces have been at work for many years. This market pressure has induced institutions to maintain or improve quality. Dill suggests that the academic audit has caught on in other countries first because

[1]This appendix is based on a literature review and a personal conversation with David Dill, April 20, 2000. Dill, Professor of Public Policy Analysis and Education at the University of North Carolina, Chapel Hill, has written extensively on the academic audit. See his web site for additional information, including reviews of other countries that have implemented the process, manuals, and review instruments: www.unc.edu/courses/acaudit.

they are more seriously looking for something, beyond market forces, that can help with quality improvement.

Academic audits normally are conducted by an intermediary organization, not a customer or the provider. The team of auditors typically includes generalists, not subject experts, although audit teams usually include faculty members experienced in teaching and academic work. The exact size and composition of audit teams vary across countries. In Hong Kong, audits are carried out by the University Grants Committee (UGC), which is a nonstatutory advisory body whose members include distinguished overseas academics, prominent local professionals and business people, and senior, locally based academics (see Massy and French, 1997). This committee includes local academics to "encourage mutual learning and acceptance of the process locally" (Massy and French, 1997). According to the perspective of outside evaluators, the academic audit appears to encourage collaboration among the stakeholders, providers, and the intermediary.

An academic audit typically involves three steps: (1) the inspection of documents supplied by the university under review/self-assessment, (2) a visit by a team of auditors to examine things in situ, and (3) the writing of a report (by the auditors). In Hong Kong, the institution prepares a 20-page report describing its quality improvement and assurance measures. The review team assesses the documentation, visits the institution, and compiles a report. The steps in the UK audit are similar to those used in Hong Kong, as well as to the process for accreditation in the United States: Institutions submit materials to the review team, the review team conducts a site visit to the institution, and then the review team issues a report. After going through the materials sent by the provider, the audit team typically visits the institution for several days and interviews dozens of representatives including senior administrators, quality assurance committee members, department and/or program heads, and students. The team's findings are then documented in a report that should focus on processes as opposed to individuals.

The unit of analysis for academic audits is usually whole institutions, but the assessment could work with individual programs or departments. In fact, the audit of an institution usually involves a review of a sample of programs. It is difficult to audit all departments at one time. Dill suggests sampling departments randomly, rather than relying on volunteers since volunteers will likely be an unrepresentative sample of the quality processes in an institution.

The objective of an academic audit is to ensure that institutions have processes in place for measuring their own quality and thus can engage in ongoing self-improvement. Each institution is treated on its own terms, and audit reports are written principally with the institution in mind. Auditors do not compare institutions. It is this self-assessment that ultimately leads to quality improvement. The audit process usually includes a publicly available report that serves as a form of accountability. Publicizing the report both motivates the institution to take the process more seriously and enables the public to verify that institutions have processes in place to ensure quality. Furthermore, in Hong Kong, there have been discussions of using the report to inform funding decisions.

The academic audit is related to total quality management (TQM), continuous quality improvement (CQI), the Baldrige Award, and the process-oriented tradition. These techniques are informed by the business literature. To the extent that the Baldrige Award, TQM, and other business-oriented quality processes have been used in higher education, it has been in the operating (and other nonacademic) departments. The academic audit has been more successful in permeating higher education because it is less adversarial and more "academic." Dill believes that academics have resisted a direct application of business techniques as foreign, hostile, and not in synch with the university culture. Academics view the academic audit as less alien because this process originated in the academic community and is based on a research orientation that builds evidence to support quality assertions.

According to Dill, academic audits are efficient forms of assessment relative to alternatives such as accreditation, subject review, and program review. Subject reviews are very in-depth and can result in a high level of accountability for a specific area. However, they are also very costly. The cost/benefit ratio tends to be very low. Audits are much more efficient.

Identification and analysis of "best practices" can follow from an academic audit. Although the audits are general and open ended, experience shows that good departments employ certain types of quality assessment practices. For example, the quality assurance agency in the UK has generated two *Learning from Audit* reports on best practices. Best practices have also emerged from the Hong Kong and CRE efforts (Dill, 2000a). The CRE holds an annual conference for the institutions that were audited that year. This conference provides audited schools an opportunity to share what they learned from the experience and the best practices that emerged. Over time, such a review of best practices might help an intermediary develop minimum standards for an audit process.

Implementation of academic audit processes has generally been incremental and collegial, with substantial input from the schools themselves. Providers spent a lot of time looking at how other institutions implemented the academic audit. Some countries piloted the academic audit process to obtain gradual buy-in. In the UK, and to some extent in Scandinavia and Australia, there is formal training available for those who conduct academic audits. There are also audit manuals and audit visit protocols available from some of these countries. Organizations interested in the academic audit typically visit and learn from the organizations that have already implemented it. The audit teams in Hong Kong included experts from other countries. Although organizations do learn from one another, they tend not to implement the academic audit exactly as another organization or country has done. Rather, they mold it to fit their own circumstances.

The academic audit method assumes that good people working with sufficient resources and following good processes will produce good results, while deficient processes will make it difficult for even good people with ample resources to produce optimal outcomes. In addition, the audit assumes that quality processes can be identified and articulated through the self-study process and verified by an outside team through interviews with faculty and staff.

Dill points out that the academic audit may be a transitional process that will fizzle out as market generated assessment tools (e.g., *U.S. News and World Report*, industry certifications) become more prominent overseas. There is a question of the long-term viability of the academic audit. Thus far, the countries that have completed one audit cycle have found it to be useful, have modified it, and are signing on for another cycle. Whether this process will continue is unclear.

Phase One

Academic audits are designed for use with individual provider institutions. The intermediaries who conduct the audits are not, therefore, interested in assessing the needs of the larger system, although they may insert system-level goals into the audit process. Phase One activities are therefore not relevant to the academic audit process.

Phase Two

The academic audit is an example of Model 1. In an academic audit, the provider institution assesses itself, and an intermediary evaluates this self-assessment. The intermediary may prescribe the process and may dictate a limited number of goals, but the provider, for the most part, is in control of its own assessment. The intermediary then certifies the assessment process.

Identify Goals for Education and Training

As mentioned above, the premise behind the academic audit is that the intermediary (auditing organization) assesses the internal quality process of the provider institution. Although the auditor may establish certain parameters for acceptable goals, the institutions are generally responsible for setting their own goals for the education activities in which they are engaged. According to Dill, goals for the audit process were unclear when audits were first implemented but are becoming clearer over time. In other words, as institutions become familiar with the audit process, they tend to focus on similar goals. Currently, there are three common goals typically used as a base for an academic audit.

> Auditors review and verify the effectiveness of an institution's basic processes of academic quality assurance and improvement by: 1) how an institution designs, monitors, and evaluates academic programs and degrees; 2) how an institution assesses, evaluates, and improves teaching and student learning; and 3) how an institution takes account of the views of external stakeholders in improving teaching and student learning (Dill, 2000b).

Additional goals should reflect the individual culture and mission of the institution being reviewed.

In the UK, auditors determine whether institutions have processes in place for assuring quality in relation to mission, institutional policies, strategies and operational procedures, institutional resources and organization, staff and student recruitment and development, institutional leadership, research, design of courses and degree programs, teaching methods, involvement of stakeholders, teacher evaluation, and assessing learning outcomes. The academic audit visit itself consists of an extensive investigation of three to four processes that the audit team selects based on what was submitted by the institution.

Develop Measures of Quality and Productivity

The academic audit approach to assessment delegates the selection and development of measures to the provider. The auditing agency may submit broad guidelines to the institution to help it select performance measures, but it generally gives institutions flexibility over the data they submit. Massy and French (1999) caution against system-level performance measures: "'One size fits all' performance measures should be viewed with suspicion." They believe that in an academic audit process, performance measures should be developed at the program or institution level.

Because it emphasizes process, the academic audit has been criticized for a lack of attention to inputs and outcomes. However, the academic audit does not so much ignore outcomes as delegate responsibility for assessing outcomes to the provider. In fact, Dill stressed that audits are increasingly focusing on outcome measures, pressing the institutions to examine their measures and how they know that the measures are reliable and valid indicators of what they are trying to accomplish.

In the UK, the AAU suggests materials that institutions might submit as part of the academic audit, including formal publications (such as annual reports), codes of practice, official policies, internal handbooks, external examiner reports, new course approval documents, and meeting minutes. Other supporting documentation may include mechanisms for monitoring academic quality and means of providing support for academic quality improvement.

Evaluate Quality and Productivity Using Measures

Intermediaries typically do not prescribe a specific template or model against which quality processes will be measured. Each institution is treated on its own terms, and audit reports are written principally with the institution in mind. Results are not compared with other institutions' academic audits. Neither are there set standards against which to compare results. The academic audit, therefore, is sensitive to the different roles, missions, and characteristics of institutions. As a result, it is particularly useful for systems with a diverse set of providers.

C.1. International Organization for Standardization

Overview

In 1947, the International Organization for Standardization (ISO) developed common international product standards to enhance international commerce. Forty years later, the ISO created a management strategy referred to as "ISO 9000," as well as ISO 9001, 9002, 9003, and 9004. The ISO 9000 and 9004[1] are guidelines, whereas ISO 9001, 9002, and 9003 are three separate contractual standards used to certify an organization as ISO compliant (Mendel, 2000). Together, these guidelines and standards are designed to ensure that standardized quality production is being implemented and adhered to by an organization.

The ISO 9000 system is a set of guidelines and standards designed to ensure that high-quality production processes are being implemented and adhered to by an organization. ISO 9000 registration does not guarantee that an organization's system of production is a good one, but serves as evidence that the organization is strictly adhering to its own internal quality production standards. In some cases, the ISO standards are used for internal review to improve the quality of products or services. However, in other cases, the ISO standards are implemented in hopes of bringing more credibility to the organization. In many industries, customers even require suppliers to have ISO certification.

For ISO 9000 standards to be successful, leaders within an organization must explicitly define and document its policy for quality, which ultimately becomes a "quality manual." The adopted policy should not only be a standard of quality within the organization, but also a standard of quality that can be verified and certified by a third party. Because evaluation is an essential part of the ISO 9000 philosophy, it is crucial that workers keep up-to-date documentation that can be used by external auditors to certify[2] the organization as an ISO organization. However, it should be emphasized that an ISO 9000 registration does not mean that finished products have been evaluated or that the organization has a "great"

[1]ISO 9000 is generally used to guide an organization to the choice of standards it should use, whereas ISO 9004 provides information about implementation and using the guidelines.

[2]Also referred to as being registered.

system of production. Rather, it assures, through third-party verification and internal audits, that an organization systematically adheres to a "quality system" (Mendel, 2000). To become certified, a third-party organization must serve as an objective evaluator of the organization's adherence to its quality manual.[3] In theory, once an organization is certified, it is recognized around the world as having a quality system that is fully and consistently utilized.[4]

Each of the ISO standards (9001, 9002, 9003) has a specific role in developing quality assurance and is used for different purposes. ISO 9001 is the most comprehensive of the three and is used to demonstrate an organization's capabilities in designing or developing products or services (Izadi, Ali, and Stadt, 1996). ISO 9002 is identical to ISO 9001, except that the organization utilizing ISO 9002 is not responsible for the design or development of the product or service yet still wants to demonstrate its capabilities for production, installation, and servicing. ISO 9003 is the least comprehensive of the three standards and is utilized to ensure the quality of a product or service in a final inspection or test. Collectively, these standards are designed to ensure quality to an organization's customers and to reduce production costs.

Recently, ISO standards and guidelines have become more popular within the service industries. One exception to this trend is in higher education. This resistance can be partially explained by the presence of certain thoroughly entrenched traditions of measuring quality in higher education (Izadi, Ali, and Stadt, 1996). However, some researchers argue that ISO 9000, along with TQM strategies, can be used to enhance customer satisfaction, reduce attrition, and improve graduation rates while reducing costs (Vandenberge, 1995; Spanbauer 1992). In fact, the American Society for Quality Control Standards (ASQC) Committee notes that other countries are beginning to use ISO 9002 as a mechanism to ensure quality and consistency (ASQC Committee, 1996).

As in other service organizations, education and training provide an intangible, rather than a physical, product and therefore, production is often difficult to assess. However, administrators can use the ISO system to ensure that instruction is provided consistently. One mechanism for employing the ISO philosophy is a guideline document referred to as the ANSI/ASQC Z1.11.[5] Z1.11 incorporates generic quality system requirements of Q9001 and Q9002 to help design, develop, deliver, and assess instruction, including specified learning

[3]The Registrar Accreditation Board (RAB), an affiliate of the American Society for Quality Control, regulates the external audits for certification.

[4]The certification lasts three years.

[5]ASQC also suggests that an organization follow the guidelines outlined in ANSI/ISO/ASQC Q9004-1-1994.

objectives for each instructional course.[6] These goals are a function of not only specific administrative practices of the organization, but also the stakeholders involved. For example, an organization can have multiple stakeholders, including the organization providing instruction, the students, and in some cases, employers of the students.

Ultimately, part of the objective for Z1.11 is to ensure that

> (1) the customer requirements are properly defined; (2) discrepancies between the customer and supplier (i.e., the organization) are resolved; (3) the supplier is capable of satisfying contractual requirements; and (4) proper records are maintained (Hutchins, 1993, pp. 75–76).

Based on this description, the Z1.11 system is a highly interactive system in which feedback from multiple stakeholders, including customers, is greatly encouraged. An example of this is at Carnegie Mellon University (CMU) (Izadi, Ali, and Stadt, 1996). CMU has set up experimental classes in which the students, as the customers, participate in planning the courses, designing the syllabi, and even assigning grades.

Phase One

ISO 9000 is concerned with organization-level quality issues, not system-level assessment. As a result, Phase One does not apply.

Phase Two

ISO 9000 exemplifies Model 1 in Phase Two where the intermediary is responsible for assessing the provider's quality assurance process and the provider is responsible for implementing that process to actually assess its quality and productivity.

Identify Goals for Education and Training

The main objective of ISO 9000 is to provide a standard of production to which the organization systematically adheres. As part of this process, the organization must define and document its goals in a quality manual. These goals should be

[6]While it can be difficult to assess product quality in educational institutions, Z1.11, much like the ISO 9000 system, suggests that quality control mechanisms should be implemented to ensure that each instructor is consistently using a process to prevent root causes of "deficient administrative or instructional practices" that would lead to unsatisfactory student performance (ASQC Committee, 1996, p. vii).

closely linked to the organization's mission. For example, in education, administrative and instructional practices are monitored to achieve the best possible student performance (ASQC Committee, 1996). When developing goals, process goals rather than outcome goals should be the main focus. It should also be noted that ISO 9000 requires the organization to define quality and process goals across different dimensions. For instance, ISO 9000 requires the organization not only to define goals for the quality of its products but also to specify mechanisms to achieve quality standards.

ISO 9000 supporting documentation highlights a process of establishing goals. The first step is to identify goals the organization or institution wants to achieve. As part of the process, the organization should identify what others (including customers, suppliers, employees, shareholders, and society) expect from the organization. Second, the organization should evaluate its current status, which could come from self-assessment, customer feedback, or an assessment by an external organization. Third, following the guidelines provided by the ISO standards, the organization could improve the quality of production and its final product or service by developing a quality manual as a guideline for production or providing services. Fourth, to ensure quality to the organization's customers, ISO certification can be obtained through an external audit.[7]

Develop Measures of Quality and Productivity

ISO 9000 requires that measures be developed for assessing a process. However, in certain organizations, it is difficult to precisely measure it. Therefore, the quality control system selected is influenced by the different objectives or administrative practices of the organization. For instance, an institution of learning that is designed to provide physical skills rather cognitive skills may have a different quality control system and a different form of assessment from more-traditional institutions. The specific techniques used to measure performance will differ according to the purpose of the organization. As a result, it is not possible to simply require that every organization collect a common set of data. Because the measures of quality and productivity vary from institution to institution, the evaluation process can be time consuming.

---

[7] *Selection and Use of the ISO 9000*, www.isonet.com, 2000.

Evaluate Quality and Productivity Using Measures

ISO 9000 requires that the leaders of the organization explicitly define its quality standards for producing products or services that meet the standards of ISO 9001, 9002, or 9003. The organizational standards should be stated principally in terms of performance. Once the standards are established, the organization should work toward these standards as goals for improving quality. Eventually, an organization can invite an accredited external auditor to evaluate its effectiveness in meeting these standards. If the auditor provides confirmation that the organization's standard is effectively being adhered to, then the organization can be certified as an ISO 9000 organization. This certification can be a helpful tool for customers choosing between providers.

D. Accrediting Agencies

Overview

Accreditation is a form of nongovernmental, self-regulation; the process determines whether an institution or a program meets threshold quality criteria and therefore certifies to the public the existence of minimum educational standards. Accreditation in U.S. higher education is voluntary. Institutional accreditation is mostly carried out by eight regional commissions.[1] These commissions are responsible for accrediting whole (generally undergraduate) institutions. In addition, there are dozens of national associations that offer recognized specialized and professional accreditation for programs or other academic units within an institution, or for freestanding single-purpose institutions (e.g., the Accrediting Commission of Career Schools and Colleges of Technology). Overseeing all of this is the Council for Higher Education Accreditation (CHEA). However, there are some accrediting agencies that operate outside the aegis of CHEA.

In theory, accreditation is intended to serve the dual purposes of accountability and self-improvement. However, there is an inherent tension between these aims. Accreditation has primarily been about accountability, but there are efforts under way to make the process more flexible so that institutions can tailor the process to reflect their own mission and purpose.

Accreditation is based on a number of assumptions. The primary assumption is that a group of peers can ensure quality through a periodic review. It also assumes that inputs and resources are a good proxy for quality, and that if an institution has the "right" resources then it will provide good education. Accreditation also assumes that one set of standards can be applied to widely differing programs and institutions.

Historically, accreditation commissions have not encouraged the participation of institutions or other stakeholders in the development of the criteria by which a

[1]There are only six accreditation *regions* in the United States: Middle States, New England, North Central, Northwest, Southern, and Western. Generally, there is a regional accreditation commission for each region. However, two of the regions (Western and New England) have two separate organizations: one in charge of accreditation for two-year colleges and one for four-year colleges. As a result, sometimes there are references to eight regional *commissions*: MSA, NEASC (CIHE and CTCI), NCA, NWA, SACS, and WASC (Jr. and Sr.).

particular institution will be assessed. However, several of the regional accrediting agencies are working with a number of institutions on an experimental basis that could result in more-collaborative relationships.

At the highest level, the accreditation process and the resulting stamp of approval benefit many stakeholders:

- The stamp of approval from accrediting agencies enables student consumers to know that the institution or program meets a minimal set of criteria.
- The process provides education providers evidence for determining whether to accept/recognize credit for courses taken outside their institution.
- The federal government uses accreditation status to determine an institution's eligibility for federal student financial aid. It only awards federal financial aid to students enrolled at accredited institutions, or at institutions that are candidates for accreditation.
- Most professional societies will license students only if they have completed their studies at an accredited institution (see Appendix E).

Phase One

Accrediting agencies do not serve a contained, identifiable group of customers. Therefore, these agencies do not engage in Phase One assessment.

Phase Two

To help illustrate how the agencies conduct Phase Two assessment, we have included summaries (Tables D.1 through D.6 at the conclusion of this appendix) describing the goals and measures used by the eight regional accrediting agencies.[2] While the range of topics addressed is fairly consistent across the agencies, the way the measures are written leaves open the possibility of some interpretation—they are written broadly enough that the review team members can use their best judgment to determine whether a particular institution is meeting the criteria. In addition, the agencies differ in how they structure the measures. Finally, each of the agencies also has a set of initial eligibility criteria that must be met to even become a candidate for accreditation (the eligibility criteria are not described here).

---

[2]Much of the language in the summaries is taken verbatim from the agency web sites and printed documents.

For an example of goals and measures from a nonregional accrediting agency, see Table D.7, which shows details from the Accrediting Commission of Career Schools and Colleges of Technology (ACCSCT).[3] ACCSCT is one of the specialized/professional accrediting agencies, and as its name suggests, it accredits career and technical schools.

The traditional accreditation process is typical of Model 2 assessment. Accrediting agencies are intermediaries that determine whether institutions or programs are meeting threshold quality criteria, which are developed by the accrediting agency (not the providers). However, as will be described more fully here and in Appendix D.1, several of the accrediting agencies are starting to incorporate features of Model 1 assessment. Some agencies are shifting away from the emphasis being on only accountability to also valuing institutional self-improvement efforts.

Identify Goals for Education and Training

The goals of the accreditation process currently do not necessarily reflect specific institutional mission or goals, but there is discussion and experimentation under way to better link the process with institutional needs. So, while historically accrediting agencies have determined the goals that drive the assessment process, some agencies are now working to make the goal-setting process more inclusive. Agency goals tend to address educational objectives, programs and curricula, degree programs, faculty, student services, student progress, admission policies and practices, student recruitment, and management.

In this document, RAND has used the term "goal" in a specific way, and the language used by accrediting agencies is not consistent with RAND's usage. So, when accrediting agencies refer to standards or topic areas, they are generally referring to what RAND terms "goals"—these are the agency's expectations for what a school should be doing, and these are often abstract ideas.

Topic areas addressed by the standards tend to be similar across the various accrediting agencies. Most of the standards have been in place for several decades and reflect commonly accepted ideas about what is important in higher education. A number of agencies are rethinking their measures. In doing so, they are soliciting input from a wide range of stakeholders as they go through

[3]We are showing their standards because they are some of the most detailed ones we found in our informal search of the web. This is due, in part, to ACCSCT being a specialized accrediting agency. As such, it has a more narrow focus and can therefore have more narrowly defined criteria and measures.

the change process. As part of the North Central Association of Colleges and Schools Commission on Institutions of Higher Education (NCA) Mission Project, for example, the agency is asking for input from anyone who would like to contribute. As part of a more formal process they have set up "R-Groups"—R stands for Read, Reflect, and Respond. These external and internal groups consist of presidents, North Central Association Consultant-Evaluators, self-study coordinators, business, industry, government, members of the Commission's Academic Quality Improvement Project, as well as other current and recently retired NCA trustees and staff. The groups provide "commentary, analysis, and/or reaction" throughout the project. In addition, NCA is utilizing focus groups consisting of institutional chief officers, trustees, other NCA decisionmakers, and staff to provide feedback plus draft ideas for the NCA board (www.ncacihe.org/mission/index.html).

According to the New England Association of Schools and Colleges, Inc., Standards for Accreditation (www.neasc.org/cihe/stancihe.htm),

> The Standards for Accreditation were developed through a lengthy participatory process which involved each member institution as well as the public. The Commission continually evaluates the effectiveness of its standards and its processes for applying them, and makes changes as conditions warrant.

Develop Measures of Quality and Productivity

As with the term goals, there is a disconnect between what RAND calls "measures" and how agencies refer to the same concept. RAND defines measures as the specific elements (i.e., policies, procedures, or other kinds of evidence) that are recorded or looked at to help determine whether goals are being met. Some agencies have their own terminology for these elements, such as "patterns of evidence" (MSA) or "criteria for review" (WASC).

Measures used in accreditation span a broad range in terms of level of abstraction and content. Examples are provided in Tables D.1 through D.7.

Evaluate Quality and Productivity Using Measures

The institutions are evaluated against a set of specific goals, but these goals are generally written so that they can be open to interpretation. The regional accrediting agencies rarely quantify the goals and measures and explicitly say that the measures should not be considered checklists that must be met point by point, but rather they are guidelines for institutions and review teams. Thus, the accreditation process is subjective, and the review teams have discretion in interpreting how many and in what ways the goals and measures are met.

Accreditation is a multistep process. The program or institution first conducts a self-study using guidelines from the accrediting agency. Following the self-study, the accrediting agency team will conduct a site visit to the institution during which the team meets with a range of institutional representatives. Afterwards, the review team prepares a report based on the visit, which is then vetted by the accrediting agency. Once the agency issues its formal report, the program/institution has an opportunity to respond. The accrediting agency then makes a final judgment as to whether an institution meets the standards for accreditation.

During the site visit, institutions submit many different types of data to the accrediting agencies. Data range from the number of books in the library, to student/faculty ratios, to the number of Ph.D.s on the faculty.

The overall process is very consistent across accrediting agencies with the basic steps of self-study, a site visit by the review team and the issuance of a report by the agency. However, as noted previously, a number of accrediting agencies are actively experimenting with new procedures. The North Central Association of Colleges and Schools (NCA) recently introduced a new process for accreditation. NCA institutions will now have the option of choosing the traditional method or the new Academic Quality Improvement Project (AQIP). AQIP will involve more frequent evaluations but will be based on an institution setting its own goals for the accreditation process. According to the agency the new process will replace "the current 'one-size-fits-all' approach with one that can be tailored to respond to an institution's distinctive needs and aspirations" (www.AQIP.org). Institutions will establish their goals and ways of measuring progress toward those goals every three to five years. And every seven years NCA will reaccredit institutions based on annual reporting from the schools. WASC is also modifying its evaluation process to make the process more streamlined and less burdensome (which will be described in more detail in Appendix D.1).

The accrediting process can be extremely expensive, particularly for major universities that go through the process multiple times for various specializations or programs in addition to institutional/regional accreditation. However, accrediting tends to be on a ten-year cycle, so each entity (whether a program or institution) does not have to go through the process very often.

At the conclusion of the review process, accreditation can be revoked or recommendations can be made about specific areas that need improvement. The overall final result is made public, but only the program and institution being reviewed see the details. Over the years, accrediting agencies have been criticized for not being tough enough on low performers.

Reformers hope that the "new" processes and resulting findings will lead to greater institutional self-improvement than took place under the old system. With the influence of the academic audit in particular, there may be more effort to publicly share findings throughout the process and not just publish the final outcome.

Examples of Goals and Measures

The following tables include examples of goal statements and measures from the eight regional accrediting agencies and from ACCSCT. This is just a random selection to illustrate the range in how the goal statements are phrased and in the types of measures suggested by the agencies. The agencies typically refer to goal statements as standards and use different terms for measures. Much of this text is taken verbatim from the agency documents describing their respective "standards" (goals) for accreditation.

Middle States Association of Colleges and Schools

The Middle States Association of Colleges and Schools stresses that these are qualitative, not quantitative descriptions, since each institution will implement the principles in a way that makes sense for their particular mission and goals. The manner in which the text is written makes it hard to separate the goals from the measures since both are described in fairly abstract terms. Their goals address 14 topic areas.

New England Association of Schools and Colleges

The New England Association of Schools and Colleges has two commissions: the Commission on Institutions of Higher Education and the Commission for Technical and Career Institutions. The seven goals for the higher education institutions are meant to represent key areas of institutional activity. The goals are considered to be qualitative criteria that can encompass a wide range of institutions—ones that differ in purpose, size, organization, scope of program, clientele served, support, and control.

Table D.1

Examples of Goals and Measures Used by the Middle States Association of Colleges and Schools

Topic Area/ Goal Statement	Examples of Measures/Evidence/ Criteria for Review
Integrity in the institution's conduct of all its activities through humane and equitable policies dealing with students, faculty, staff, and other constituencies.	The requirements for degrees must be specified and maintained. Policies and procedures by which requirements are established and performance evaluated must be examined carefully if their effectiveness is to be assessed meaningfully.
Clearly stated mission and goals appropriate to the institution's resources and the needs of its constituents.	Well-defined goals and objectives include the following: clear, expressed in simple terms appropriate to higher education, and suitably broad in scope; identifiable with the particular institution; honest in describing the institution's plans and programs; stated in terms of results sought and the means by which they are attained.
Clearly stated admissions and other student policies appropriate to the mission, goals, programs, and resources of the institution. Student services appropriate to the educational, personal, and career needs of the students.	Support of students requires a well-organized program of student services, which may include but are not limited to admissions, financial aid, registration, orientation, advising, counseling, tutoring, discipline, health, housing, placement, student organizations and activities, and security. The admissions program must provide accurate, comprehensive, and realistic information about curricula, student development services, campus housing, tuition, fees, etc.

Table D.2

Examples of Goals and Measures Used by the New England Association of Schools and Colleges

Topic Area/ Goal Statement	Examples of Measures/Evidence/ Criteria for Review
Each institution must have a mission and purposes appropriate to higher education, although they can vary across institutions.	Mission and purposes should be realistic, concrete, etc. and communicated in a concise statement. They should be accepted and understood by stakeholders and reassessed over time with the results of the assessment being used to make changes.
The institution does appropriate planning and evaluation—systematic, broad based, etc.	Many stakeholders should be involved in short- and long-term planning, and it should be a well-resourced process. Use data collected to support planning. Data support accomplishment of mission.
The governance system supports its purposes, mission, teaching, learning, scholarship, etc.	Roles and responsibilities are described in the constitution, by-laws, etc. People understand these and they are regularly communicated. The governing board has ultimate responsibility. There is a Chief Executive Officer whose power and authority is delegated by the board. The CEO manages resources and is responsive to stakeholders.

North Central Association of Colleges and Schools

The North Central Association of Colleges and Schools has five criteria for accreditation. Each criterion includes "patterns of evidence," which are typical areas of institutional activity or concern that can be used to demonstrate achievement of the criterion. NCA emphasizes that these are broad descriptions, not checklists.

Table D.3

Examples of Goals and Measures Used by the North Central Association of Colleges and Schools

Topic Area/ Goal Statement	Examples of Measures/Evidence/ Criteria for Review
The institution has clear and publicly stated purposes consistent with its mission and appropriate to an institution of higher education.	Short- and long-range goals; inclusive processes for evaluating purposes; appropriate decisionmaking processes; constituents understand purposes and are kept informed of goals; support for freedom of inquiry.
The institution has effectively organized the human, financial, and physical resources necessary to accomplish its purposes.	Governance by a board that follows policy and has integrity; well-defined and understood governance structure; adequate faculty credentials.
The institution is accomplishing its educational and other purposes.	Educational programs appropriate to higher education (well defined, coherent, stimulating, use scholarship, intellectual interaction between faculty and students); assessment of student achievement (proficiency, coherent course, mastery for degree, faculty control of assessment process).

Northwest Association of Schools and Colleges

The Northwest Association of Schools and Colleges (NWA) has nine goal "groups." The groups are typically divided into multiple subtopic areas and often also include references to supporting documentation that is either required or suggested. Several also include references to policies on specific subtopic areas. For example, under the major category Educational Program and Its Effectiveness, there are eight subtopic areas and six policy areas (such as Policy on General Education/Related Instruction Requirements). The NWA goals are more exhaustive than those of the other regional accrediting agencies, addressing many more topic areas than the others.

Table D.4

Examples of Goals and Measures Used by the Northwest Association of Schools and Colleges

Topic Area/ Goal Statement	Examples of Measures/Evidence/ Criteria for Review
The institution's mission and goals define the institution, including its educational activities, its student body, and its role within the higher education community.	Mission and goals are derived from, or are widely understood by, the campus community, are adopted by the governing board, and are periodically reexamined. The mission, as adopted by the governing board, appears in appropriate institutional publications, including the catalog.
The institution engages in ongoing planning to achieve its mission and goals.	The institution clearly defines its evaluation and planning processes. It develops and implements procedures to evaluate the extent to which it achieves its institutional goals.
Student programs and services support the achievement of the institution's mission and goals by contributing to the educational development of its students.	The organization of student services is effective in providing adequate services consistent with the mission and goals of the institution. Student services and programs are staffed by qualified individuals whose academic preparation and/or experience are appropriate to their assignments.

Southern Association of Colleges and Schools

The Southern Association of Colleges and Schools goals are grouped into four broad categories and described in varying levels of detail. The documentation is written in the style of a legal document with each line numbered for easy reference. It also includes many "must" statements—institutions *must* do this and institutions *must* do that, which is not the case in any of the other agency documents. Each section has an introduction and various (sometimes many) subheadings.

Table D.5

Examples of Goals and Measures Used by the Southern Association of Colleges and Schools

Topic Area/ Goal Statement	Examples of Measures/Evidence/ Criteria for Review
Planning and evaluation activities must be systematic, broad based, interrelated, and appropriate to the institution.	Must develop guidelines and procedures to evaluate educational effectiveness. Must gather and analyze both quantitative and qualitative data that demonstrate student achievement. Measures may include the following: evaluation of instructional delivery; adequacy of facilities and equipment; standardized tests; analysis of theses, portfolios, and recitals; completion rates; results of admissions tests for students applying to graduate or professional school.
Institutional research must be an integral part of the institution's planning and evaluation process.	The research should include the following activities: ongoing timely data collection, analysis, and dissemination; use of external studies and reports; design and implementation of internal studies related to students, personnel, facilities, equipment, programs, services, and fiscal resources; development of databases suitable for longitudinal studies and statistical analyses, etc.
An institution must provide evidence that it has employed faculty members qualified to accomplish its purpose.	Institutions are encouraged to recruit and select faculty with the highest degrees earned from a broad representation of institutions. Recruitment and appointment procedures must be described in the faculty handbook or other published documents. Institutions must ensure that each faculty member employed is proficient in oral and written communication in the language in which assigned courses will be taught.

Western Association of Schools and Colleges

The Western Association of Schools and Colleges has two commissions: the Senior College Commission and the Accrediting Commission for Community and Junior Colleges. The examples below are taken from the Senior College Commission goals. There are four goal areas, each of which is fairly broad. WASC has recently revised its process and standards, and these standards reflect three priorities: reduced burden during the accreditation process, a change in emphasis away from compliance to collaboration, and greater focus on educational effectiveness and student learning.

Table D.6

Examples of Goals and Measures Used by the Western Association of Schools and Colleges

Topic Area/ Goal Statement	Examples of Measures/Evidence/ Criteria for Review
Through its purposes and educational objectives, the institution dedicates itself to higher learning, the search for truth, and the dissemination of knowledge.	The institution's formally approved statements of purpose and operational practices are appropriate for an institution of higher education and clearly define its essential values and character. Educational objectives are clearly recognized throughout the institution and are consistent with stated purposes.
The institution achieves its institutional purposes and attains its educational objectives through teaching and learning, scholarship and creative activity, and support for student learning.	The institution's educational programs are appropriate in content, standards, and nomenclature for the degree level awarded, regardless of mode of delivery, and are staffed by sufficient numbers of faculty qualified for the kind and level of curriculum offered.
The institution sustains its operations and supports the achievement of its educational objectives through its investment in human, physical, fiscal, and information resources and through an appropriate and effective set of organization and decisionmaking structures.	The institution demonstrates that it employs a faculty with substantial and continuing commitment to the institution sufficient in number, professional qualifications, and diversity to achieve its educational objectives, to establish and oversee academic policies, and to ensure the integrity and continuity of its academic programs wherever and however delivered.

Accrediting Commission of Career Schools and Colleges of Technology

ACCSCT is the accrediting agency responsible for schools and colleges that offer technology-related programs. Many of its standards are similar to those of the regional accrediting agencies and focus on the qualifications of instructors, financial stability, condition of facilities, etc. However, given the emphasis of the agency, several of its standards relate to more employer-specific issues, such as job placement rates of students and employer satisfaction.

Table D.7

Examples of Goals and Measures Used by the Accrediting Commission of Career Schools and Colleges of Technology

Topic Area/ Goal Statement	Examples of Measures/Evidence/ Criteria for Review
Instructional Materials and Equipment	Instructional materials are sufficiently comprehensive and reflect current occupational knowledge and practice. And instructional equipment is similar to that found in common occupational practice and includes teaching devices and supplemental instructional aids appropriate to the subject.
Program Advisory Committee	Each accredited school shall have a Program Advisory Committee for each program or each group of related programs. The majority of the membership, more than 50 percent, of each Program Advisory Committee must be employers representing the major occupation or occupations for which training is provided. At least two regularly scheduled meetings must be conducted annually, one of which must be held at the school, and written minutes of each meeting must be maintained.

D.1. Western Association of Schools and Colleges

Overview

The Western Association of Schools and Colleges is one of the eight U.S. regional accreditation associations. It evaluates and accredits schools, colleges, and universities in California, Hawaii, American Samoa, Guam, the Commonwealth of the Northern Marianas, the Republic of the Marshall Islands, the Federated States of Micronesia, and the Republic of Palau. WASC currently serves 146 accredited and candidate institutions throughout the region. This is a diverse group of institutions with even more diverse student bodies. WASC functions through a board of directors and three accrediting commissions: the Accrediting Commission for Senior Colleges and Universities, the Accrediting Commission for Community and Junior Colleges, and the Accrediting Commission for Schools. The WASC board of directors consists of nine members; each accrediting commission selects three members. This discussion will focus on the senior colleges and universities commission.

In 1996, WASC initiated a redesign of its accreditation procedures. In 1998, WASC published *An Invitation to Dialogue,* which outlined six principles for a new process. It then embarked on a lengthy process of meetings and "concept development sessions" in which it solicited input from hundreds of stakeholders (including regional and national institutional representatives as well as experts on higher education). At the same time, it began a series of experimental site visits with a range of institutions. Through these experiences, WASC generated ideas for "new models of self-study and visits that focus on student learning and educational effectiveness." These new ideas were published in *Invitation to Dialogue II* in the spring of 1999. WASC ultimately published its revised standards in the *Handbook of Accreditation,* 2001.[1]

WASC was motivated to change the process as a result of the changing nature of higher education. Given the increasingly diverse nature of students and institutions, a single definition of quality based on resources and reputation was no longer adequate. WASC decided that it needed multiple models of quality to

---

[1]The WASC web site is continually updated to reflect progress on the "Invitation to Dialogue" process.

reflect the diversity of institutional models. In the past, higher education institutions developed masters of information, but now they focus on developing learning skills, and accreditation should reflect that change.

The new forms of accreditation being experimented with do encourage collaboration between WASC and the institutions being reviewed, whereas the old methods did not. As noted, WASC is currently working closely with many institutions to design more-appropriate measures for those schools. In addition, a number of focus groups (with institutional representation) have been utilized to gather feedback on some of the proposals under consideration.

The shift to a new review process means that WASC will have to train its review team members. This is a major issue that the agency still needs to work through. Also, while WASC is extremely enthusiastic about the new direction it is taking, it realizes that holding institutions accountable for high standards is harder than simply ensuring that institutions are meeting a minimum set of externally established standards.

Phase One

The institutions that make up the western region are not a system per se, so WASC does not engage in Phase One assessment.

Phase Two

WASC, like the other accrediting agencies, is an intermediary assessor that applies a set of goals and measures that it established, so it is an example of Model 2. However, as will be discussed further below, the association is working on giving institutions more control over the assessment process. This will include institutions identifying a subset of goals and measures that are relevant to their mission and purpose and changing the steps and timing of the review process to better suit institutional needs. As these changes are made, the assessment process could more closely resemble Model 1. Even with these changes, however, institutions will operate within parameters set by WASC.

Identify Goals for Education and Training

Some of the assumptions underlying the traditional processes are now open for consideration in the context of the redesign. For example, in the past one set of standards was applied to multiple types of institutions. Now, institutions are going to have more flexibility in selecting the standards that will be used to evaluate them. In addition, in the past most of the measures were inputs, and today, WASC is moving away from the assumption that if an institution has the right resources then it will provide a quality education. Instead, WASC will, as the first phase, focus on whether the institutions are operating with integrity and have the resources to do what they have promised. The second phase will involve WASC determining whether the institution is operating at high standards. This will be done, in the words of Ralph Wolff, Executive Director of WASC, "through dialogue, collaboration, and stimulation."[2] The focus has to be on learning, and while there are a number of ways to measure learning, it is difficult to come up with the right configuration of assessment techniques for each institution. It is important to avoid mechanical test-oriented processes for measurement, but rather develop a more robust way of measuring student learning.

The committee working on redesigning the accreditation process had six goals, or "guiding principles" (WASC, 1998). These goals reflect a shift away from ensuring compliance with minimum standards toward helping institutions focus on improvement.

1. Significant changes are needed to make the content and the process of accreditation more relevant both to institutions and to the public.
2. The WASC process needs to be demonstrably value adding and cost effective.
3. Greater emphasis is needed on evidence of educational effectiveness and student learning.
4. The accreditation process needs to shift from an "in or out of compliance" stance on every issue to a recognition that many aspects of quality are best addressed on a continuum.
5. More-efficient means are needed to enable institutions to establish that they meet basic resource and integrity standards.
6. WASC needs to maintain a posture of experimentation in the years ahead, leading to the institutionalization of a more adaptive and responsive process of accreditation.

In a presentation at the annual CHEA (Council for Higher Education Accreditation) Conference in January 2000, Ralph Wolff shared a one-page handout that summarized the changes this way (Wolff, 2000):

---

[2]Personal communication with Ralph Wolff, May 17, 2000.

- From regulatory to capacity building
- From policeman to partner
- From standards-based to context-based
- From compliance to inquiry and engagement
- From "we can evaluate it all" to development of our core competencies
- From "we know how to do it" to creation of a learning community where we learn together
- From monopoly to acting in a free market
- From old to new model of accountability.

In summary, in the past it was assumed that a standard set of measures could be applied to many different types of institutions. In the future, the assumption will be that institutional mission matters, so that evaluation criteria will reflect what each institution is trying to achieve. And the purpose of WASC will be to serve as a guide and stimulator of dialogue at the campus. Furthermore, WASC is trying to model the behavior that they would like to see adopted at the campus level.

Current WASC documentation states that WASC accreditation is "framed around two 'core commitments'—Institutional Capacity and Educational Effectiveness" (WASC, 2001, p. 15). The goals (what WASC refers to as standards) are broken down into four categories:

1. Defining institutional purposes and ensuring educational objectives (institutional purposes and integrity).
2. Achieving educational objectives through core functions (teaching and learning, scholarship and creative activity, support for student learning).
3. Developing and applying resources and organizational structures to ensure sustainability (faculty and staff; fiscal, physical, and information resources; organizational structures and decisionmaking processes).
4. Creating an organization committed to learning and improvement (strategic thinking and planning, commitment to learning and improvement).

Accompanying each goal is "criteria for review," guidelines, and a set of "questions for institutional engagement." The following are some examples of statements that support WASC's goals (see WASC, 2001, pp. 17, 20, 22, and 26):

- Institutional Purposes. Criteria for review: *The institution's formally approved statements of purpose and operational practices are appropriate for an institution of higher education and clearly define its essential values and character.* Guideline: *The institution has a published mission statement that clearly describes its purposes.*

The institution's purposes fall within recognized academic areas and/or disciplines, or are subject to peer review within the framework of generally recognized academic disciplines or areas of practice.

- Teaching and Learning. Criteria for review: *The institution's educational programs are appropriate in content, standards, and nomenclature for the degree level awarded, regardless of mode of delivery, and are staffed by sufficient numbers of faculty qualified for the kind and level of curriculum offered.* Guideline: *The content, length, and standards of the institution's academic programs conform to recognized disciplinary or professional standards and are subject to peer review.*
- Scholarship and Creative Activity. Criteria for review: *(1) The institution actively values and promotes scholarship, curricular and instructional innovation, and creative activity, as well as their dissemination at levels and of the kinds appropriate to the institution's purposes and character. (2) The institution recognizes and promotes appropriate linkages among scholarship, teaching, student learning, and service.*
- Fiscal and Physical Resources. Criteria for review: *Fiscal and physical resources are effectively aligned with institutional purposes and educational objectives, and are sufficiently developed to support and maintain the level and kind of educational programs offered both now and for the foreseeable future.* Guideline: *The institution has a history of financial stability, appropriate independent audits, and realistic plans to eliminate any accumulated deficits and to build sufficient reserves to support long-term viability.*

Develop Measures of Quality and Productivity

The institutions will have more say in how the process works for their schools and in the specific criteria considered. WASC will, however, provide feedback and help guide the process. In the past, the link was stronger between measures and WASC's goals, rather than institutional goals. Since the institutions will have a role in identifying which of the WASC standards to apply, the proposed changes will strengthen the link between the institution's goals and the basis of how they are evaluated.

The campuses submit data to the WASC review team. Larger institutions typically have institutional research offices with staff who work on accreditation. The cost of the process can be quite high, but it only happens every ten years. There is going to be more emphasis on ongoing data collection, rather than only collecting data every seven to ten years.

Specifics about data collection under the new process are still open for discussion, but the goal is for the data to better reflect institutional mission, and to be more useful to institutions above and beyond the accreditation process. The use of data portfolios is being experimented with, and thus far the portfolios appear to have longer-term value to the institutions than did traditional forms of data collection. The content of data portfolios is determined by the institution being reviewed. After identifying several core competencies, the institution then compiles data to reflect its progress on those specific competencies. For this reason, data portfolios consist of data more relevant to the institution than the traditional data collection. Also, the content of portfolios will vary across institutions since each one selects its own particular core competencies and data that serve as evidence.

Evaluate Quality and Productivity Using Measures

Accreditation is a multistep process. The program or institution conducts a self-study; the accrediting team conducts a site visit at the institution; the program/institution responds to the report issued by the review team (following the site visit). But as has been discussed, WASC is changing both the process and the content of the visit (see Table D.1.1 for the proposed timeline). The first step will be for the school to submit a proposal, which should include its goals.[3] About two years later, the first review, of core capacity, will take place. At this stage, the institution will submit a data portfolio and brief analytical essays. WASC will ensure that the data are accurate and that the institution is at or above the threshold around the core capacity; WASC will also assess and assist with the institution's ability to thoughtfully reflect on its educational effectiveness. A year later, educational effectiveness will be assessed more formally, and the institution will identify themes as the focus of the assessment. Educational effectiveness includes outcomes and educational design. Institutions then have seven years "off." In year eight, the institution will submit a proposal for the next cycle. While the institution will have the seven-year interim period, it will still have three opportunities to get feedback from WASC. WASC can take action (such as sanctions) after the preparatory review and after the educational effectiveness review.

---

[3]While it considered moving to a 12-year cycle, WASC appears to now be settled on keeping the ten-year process.

Table D.1.1

Proposed Timeline

Year	Activity
–2	Submit proposal
0	Core capacity review (preparatory review)
1	Educational effectiveness review
8	Next proposal

Accreditation can be revoked or recommendations can be made on specific areas that need improvement. Accreditation status affects an institution's ability to access federal funds and desirability to some potential consumers. The overall final result of the evaluation is made public, but only the program and institution being reviewed see the details. This aspect of WASC's role will continue—WASC will make suggestions to institutions about how to improve, and WASC can certainly revoke the accreditation of a poor performer, although most institutions are above the line.

E. Professional Societies

Overview

Professional societies and the accreditation associations that oversee the education standards for specific professional groups act as intermediary agents between the customers and the providers of education and training.

Playing a different type of intermediary role, the state boards of different professions are responsible for licensing of individuals. Professional associations may operate alone or work in partnership with others in establishing and managing education standards. Consequently, they play different roles in the process.

One approach is for a professional association to partner or affiliate with a smaller entity that develops and maintains education standards. The association exerts its influence over the smaller entity, but the latter has control in decisionmaking. An example of this model would be the American Medical Association (AMA); in partnership with the Association of American Medical Colleges, AMA founded the Liaison Committee on Medical Education that still maintains standards and accredits all the medical schools in the United States including the Uniformed Services University of the Health Sciences (USUHS). Also, AMA is affiliated closely with the Accreditation Council for Graduate Medical Education, which accredits residency programs, and with the Accreditation Council on Continuing Medical Education, which certifies providers of continuing medical education in the field.

Another approach is for several professional societies in the field (with different specializations) to combine energies to form an accreditation body to oversee the education standards for the field as a whole. An example of this system is the Accreditation Board of Engineering and Technology (ABET) and the 28 professional associations in all the engineering disciplines that founded it. Representatives from these societies, who are practicing professionals from industry and academe, form the body of ABET through its board of directors and its accrediting commissions. Program criteria are developed by ABET, or at the request of the commissions, or by other societies or groups having appropriate expertise.

A third approach is for a single association to control education guidelines and licensing requirements. Typically, an internal department is created to develop and manage the guidelines and to accredit the programs that meet those standards. An example of this approach is the American Bar Association (ABA); it has created the Council of the Section of Legal Education and Admissions to the Bar to take on the responsibility of administering ABA's accreditation process.

Phase One

Professional societies cover a diverse landscape. Many of these organizations share the following common goals:

- Advance the profession by establishing a code of ethics and conduct, or by disseminating information.
- Increase public awareness through information dissemination.
- Improve knowledge by organizing forums or conferences to discuss current issues in the field, or by publishing.
- Encourage participation, especially of minority groups.
- Offer awards of excellence.

Some societies may also work with government on policy, maintain databases that include technical information or maintain lists of experts, and/or accredit programs. However, one must keep in mind the following two important distinctions.

First, not all associations seek to certify or license professionals either through testing or continuing education. Second, some associations exert influence over a very small geographic region and can operate somewhat independently at the local level.

Most large associations work closely with

- state professional boards that license professionals and that may oversee continuing education
- other national associations that partake in the development of educational guidelines
- other state or local associations that comply with guidelines to provide education to professionals.

Phase Two

Professional societies typically use some combination of Models 4 and 2 for Phase Two assessment in a manner that is fully described in other appendices. The Model 4 approach is evident in professions that require individuals to pass an examination to become an official member of the profession. When requiring such examinations, professional societies act as certifiers of student competencies and engage in the Phase Two activities described in Appendix J. Such examinations can be created and administered by a state agency—as is often the case for teaching, nursing, and medical certification examinations—or by a branch of the professional association, such as the state bar associations. Even when the professional societies do not create and administer the examinations, they are often involved in the certification process. For example, they might create the criteria for eligibility to take a licensing examination.

Instead of or in addition to requiring members of a profession to have passed an examination, professional societies often require members to have graduated from a school or program accredited by the professional society. Thus, some professional societies function as an accrediting agency and engage in the Phase Two efforts described in Appendix D.

F.1. U.S. Department of Transportation

Overview

The U.S. Department of Transportation (DOT) education and professional development policy is coordinated through the Learning and Development (L&D) Program in the Office of Human Resource Management. The office provides policy guidance and recommendations to the operating administrations (OAs) through a collaborative effort with the OA representatives who serve on an L&D council. Members of the human resources department from each OA represent their respective agencies on the council and provide input and feedback on education and development policies for the department as a whole.

Each OA in DOT is responsible for

> assessing, planning, budgeting, and providing for the learning and development needs of the employees within their organizational units and for delegating responsibilities to the headquarters and/or regional managers as appropriate (DOT, 1997a).

Implementation of education and professional development activities takes place at the OA level, and the L&D Program has no direct control or authority over what is carried out. OA training offices do not report to the L&D Program, nor does the L&D Program have any control over training budgets. The senior-level officials in the OA are charged with seeing that their training offices carry out the administration of education and development policies. Training offices provide resources and guidance to managers/supervisors and employees for their training needs, and they are responsible for developing and administering assessment of training. Managers, supervisors, and employees are responsible for identifying individual-level training needs and taking advantage of the appropriate training and development resources. They are also responsible for assessment of training courses.[1]

The majority of DOT programs and courses are provided by outside vendors, with the exception of a few centers, academies, and institutes run by individual operating administrations, specifically by the Federal Aviation Administration

[1]It is unclear how the responsibility for assessment of training programs is divided between the training offices and managers/ supervisors. The framework document assigns the responsibility to the training offices, but the "evaluation guide" appended to the framework says that the guide is intended for managers/supervisors' assessment efforts.

(FAA), Coast Guard (USCG), and the Federal Highway Administration (FHWA) (see Figure F.1.1).

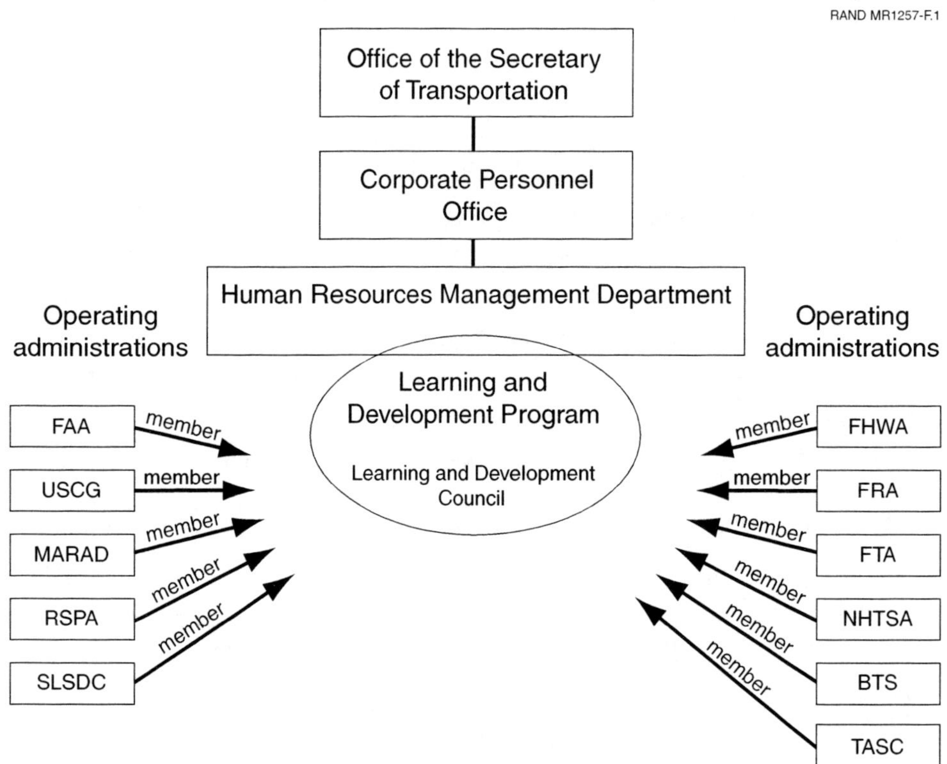

Figure F.1.1—DOT Learning and Professional Development System

Phase One

Despite its limited authority, the L&D Program is responsible for Phase One activities, which include guiding the education and professional development activities at the system level and "ensuring that these activities are results-oriented, comprehensive, integrated, cost-effective, recorded appropriately, and responsive to the needs of employees and departmental management" for the department as a whole (DOT, 1997a). The L&D Program has developed a policy guide called the "Learning and Development Framework," which is designed to be used by managers and supervisors in implementing the department's education and development policies and programs. The framework provides recommendations for assessment of L&D activities as well, although the assessment is carried out at the OA level.

The goal of the L&D Program is to "enhance the operation of the Department in accomplishing its mission by investing in the development and utilization of its human resources" (DOT, 1997a). The L&D Program goal is linked to DOT's overall management strategy, ONE DOT, which is designed to develop an integrated and unified department, where intermodal collaboration and partnership between the operating administrations will provide the highest-quality transportation system for the country. Building on the ONE DOT concept, the department has identified 60 flagship goals based on the department strategic goals, which unify the operating administrations in vision for ONE DOT success over the next two years. Included in these flagship goals are workforce planning and employee development, which are both high-priority initiatives across the department. The workforce planning flagship goal is to "identify workforce needs through 2003, emphasize continuous learning, and expand workforce planning to key occupations" (DOT, www.dot.gov/onedot/ flagcms.htm, 1999). The employee development flagship is to

> ensure a continuous learning environment required of all high-performing organizations by implementing policies, providing resources and opportunities, which enable all DOT employees to build the job competencies, computer technology capabilities, work management skills, flexibility and organizational knowledge required to achieve the Department's strategic goals (DOT, 1997b, p. 62).

The L&D Program is charged with coordinating learning and professional development activities toward these goals.

A problem identified by the L&D Program is that the department does not learn as "ONE DOT." There are areas where OAs overlap in their mission ("intermodalism") and where it would be possible to get together and learn from and with each other. Another challenge is that DOT currently provides very little education outside the technical training realm (e.g., air traffic control, safety inspection versus managerial learning).

The OAs can conduct their own Phase One assessment on issues specific to their business areas. FHWA has been working on developing an Intelligent Transportation Systems (ITS) Professional Capacity Building Program over the past few years. This effort is motivated by a belief that the transportation industry is changing dramatically because of technological advances, and that as a result, the workforce needs of FHWA have changed. The FHWA effort reflects an instance where the customer of education and professional development is taking the lead in professional development efforts (including assessment) with substantial input from an intermediary, in this case the L&D unit. We should stress that the ITS Professional Capacity Building Program is a broad effort, with the ultimate goal of improving the quality of the workforce. It integrates the workforce planning function, the education delivery function, and the education assessment function. However, the effort is in the initial stages and has not yet addressed the issue of assessment in any detail.

Phase Two

DOT's L&D Program uses a modified version of Model 1, where the intermediary does not actually review the process that education and professional development providers are using for assessment, but rather provides guidance and recommendations for assessment. The L&D framework encourages the OAs to assess the extent to which courses are meeting their stated objectives to determine success or failure of the course. The assessment process allows the OAs to determine whether their education and professional development activities are meeting their L&D goals and objectives. According to the framework's evaluation guide,

> there are two main reasons to evaluate learning and development activities: to gain information on how to improve the activity and to decide whether to continue, expand or eliminate the activity (DOT, 1997a).

Identify Goals for Education and Training

OAs are responsible for developing their L&D goals and objectives. The L&D Program collaborates with the OAs through the L&D Council to develop assessment policy and practice guidance, but the OAs are ultimately only responsible to themselves for L&D activities and assessment.

Develop Measures of Quality and Productivity

DOT spends less than 2 percent of payroll costs on fees for learning and development activities. The L&D Program is attempting to sell the program as an investment and emphasizes that there are consequences for not investing. The goal is to have every OA investing at least 2 percent of payroll on these activities (a ten-year-old standard). The 2 percent standard was set as an early target with a view to stretching it later on—it is low for private industry but will be perceived as high by DOT, so L&D expects resistance to increasing it. The percentage of payroll spent on learning and development activities was chosen because ASTD recommends it as a benchmarking measure.

The *Learning and Development Framework* recommends the use of certain assessment criteria, but it is up to the OAs to determine what assessment measures they will employ. OAs are only *required* to keep records of individual training records, payments made, special programs attended, etc. Currently there is no central system for reporting or tracking learning and development activities, although the L&D Program is trying to develop a "human resources information system," which would include this information linked with other relevant data. Every few years, the idea of developing a broad human resources information system surfaces, but it has not yet been built.

The framework recommends that in their records, OAs also consider the questions developed by the American Society for Training and Development Benchmarking Forum, which would serve as input and output measures for the OA learning and development goals. These questions are presented in Table F.1.1.

Table F.1.1

Performance Measures Proposed by L&D Program

Area	Candidate Measures
Financial	How much did the agency spend on training? (Average amount/employee; internal vs. external training costs; sources of funding.)
Staffing	Who provides the training? (How agency decides to develop or buy training.)
Organizational structure	How is training structured and operated? (Types of programs offered; centralized or decentralized.)
Delivery systems	How is formal training delivered?
Measurement and evaluation	What difference does the training make? (Indicate at what of the four Kirkpatrick levels courses are being evaluated.)
Demographics	Who gets the training? (By occupational category and subject matter; who gets internal vs. external training.)
Customer requirements and satisfaction	How does training organization know if customers are satisfied? (Use of student evaluations, feedback from program sponsors or managers, etc.)

At the student level, the L&D Program recommends that OAs use the Kirkpatrick model of assessment and provides guidance on selecting the appropriate level. If adopted, the Kirkpatrick model of assessment measures input, output, and outcome and is based on participant ratings at all four levels. In addition, at levels 3 and 4, ratings by supervisors and observations of employee behavior are also included. The unit of analysis is the course being taken.

In a study on DOT training conducted by Arthur Andersen, recommended targets were set for the percentage of DOT L&D courses that should be evaluated at each level. Arthur Andersen advised that 100 percent of courses should be evaluated at level 1, 50 percent at level 2, 30 percent at level 3, and 10 percent should be evaluated at level 4.

The L&D Program hopes to convince DOT to view training and education as an investment. Although it is unclear how the value of investment can be evaluated, the Kirkpatrick model is useful in addressing this. They are concentrating on measuring return on expectation rather than return on investment.

Evaluate Quality and Productivity Using Measures

The L&D Program encourages the OAs to use measures that are based on information collected by the American Society for Training and Development Benchmarking Forum so that they can use external benchmarking as a method of evaluation. The L&D Program sees a clear need for partnership between OA management and the L&D Program in designing and assessing training. The L&D Program emphasizes that the closer you get to assessment of organizational impact, the more the managers get involved (individual employee opinion or reaction to the courses is the most common form of assessment).

F.2. U.S. Air Force Training and Education

Overview

Training and Education in the Air Force is divided between (1) individual education and training programs, which include initial skill training, officer training, advanced and supplemental training; and (2) unit training programs. The Air Education and Training Command (AETC) oversees individual education and training programs and reports directly to the U.S. Air Force Chief of Staff. By contrast, unit training is overseen by the Director of Air and Space Operations and is conducted by the major commands. This summary will address the assessment of individual programs only.

Phase One

In developing training programs, the AETC relies mainly on the Instructional System Development (ISD) process.

> The goal of ISD is to increase effectiveness and cost-efficiency of education by developing instruction on job performance requirements, eliminating irrelevant skills and knowledge instruction from courses and ensuring that the graduates acquire the necessary skills and knowledge to do the job.[1]

As a result, ISD is a total quality process[2] that provides a system approach to training programs. A cyclical process in nature, ISD helps in identifying knowledge needs of the student, in developing curriculum based on those needs, in defining the skills learned upon completion of training, in determining whether the skills learned match the needs, and in using assessment to improve curriculum and instruction. The process uses the following approach:

- Analyze and determine what instruction is needed.
- Identify requirements or what the student needs to know.
- Define objectives or what the student should know.
- Test or develop measures that meet the objectives.
- Design instruction to meet the need.

---

[1] Air Force Instruction 36-2201 (1998). *Training Evaluation.* Department of the Air Force.

[2] AF Handbook 36-2235 (1993). *Information for Designers of Instructional Systems.* Department of the Air Force.

- Develop instructional materials to support system requirements.
- Implement the instructional system.
- Evaluate: Evaluation takes place in each of the phases. Quality is evaluated constantly so that each phase is measured against the job requirements.

An important implication of the ISD model is that there is a strong link between military requirements, training, and job performance. The Air Force uses the Career Field Education and Training Plan as a tool to identify job requirements for every field and develop training for career progression. Capability and requirements analyses for career fields are also conducted and reviewed periodically to ensure Air Force readiness.

To make the ISD model successful, all stakeholders are involved in the assessment process, and commanders at different levels identify training requirements and priorities. AETC is the primary agency responsible for training development and Phase Two assessment. The major commands identify mission demands and training/personnel needs. The Air Force Deputy Chiefs of Staff oversee the management and policies for training. All of these entities, along with the training managers, supervisors, and students, provide input into the quality assessment process.

The first part of the process described above is viewed as a key element in ensuring quality and productivity of the training activities and is conducted by the Air Force Occupational Measurement Squadron (AFOMS). The office was founded in 1970. During the 1970s the Air Force was going through a large downsizing, and AFOMS conducted occupational analyses to identify functions that were no longer being done, and thus no longer needed to be trained.

Each AFOMS analysis focuses on one occupational specialty, defined by an Air Force Specialty Code (AFSC). Every military and civilian job in the Air Force is associated with a functional AFSC, which is in turn part of a career field. Each career field has a high level manager—a person in charge of the enlisted, officer, and civilian workforce in that functional area. Among other things, that individual is responsible for the training and education of individuals in that career field. The career field manager is in the Pentagon (functional headquarters) or in a specific command (when the specialty is confined to one major command).

The Air Force's goal is to be well prepared for all missions. The ISD model, the training goals, and all instructions serve that purpose. Several stakeholders are involved in the goal determination process including the Air Force Deputy Chief of Staff for Personnel, major commands, career field managers, and AETC.[3]

The Air Force education and training program should provide

- the best trained individuals, units, and forces possible for DoD
- increased readiness and military effectiveness through quality programs
- job-oriented training in the skills and knowledge required to perform effectively
- life-cycle education and training programs using the continuous learning concept
- rigorous evaluation, feedback, and improvement to ensure training and education programs to prepare the forces to meet the challenges of the future.[4]

In addition, the Air Force is interested in ensuring that the training establishment provides the training efficiently. The activities of AFOMS provide the information necessary for Air Force managers to determine whether the appropriate training needs are being addressed. However, AFOMS does not address individual job performance or the quality of the training provided.

AFOMS collects data about the work done in every specialty in every career field.[5] It typically analyzes each specialty on a three-year cycle. AFOMS prepares an inventory of the tasks associated with every occupational specialty (except for musicians, whom the Air Force does not train).[6] The office then builds a questionnaire about each specialty and surveys each person assigned to that specialty to find out what he or she does on a day-to-day basis. If there are 3,000 people or fewer in the specialty, AFOMS surveys everyone. If there are 3,000 or more, a stratified random sample is surveyed. It conducts differential analysis and looks at the breadth of skills across levels and ranks. Surveys are

---

[3]Technical training takes place at four Air Force bases, although the Air Force also uses Army and Navy training sites. The training centers are under AETC, but the wing commander of the base at which the center is located runs the center. The functional community controls the content of staff training.

[4]Air Force Instruction 36-2201 (1997). *Developing, Managing and Conducting Training.* Department of the Air Force.

[5]The AFOMS surveys regularly look at the functions performed by enlisted personnel, but sometimes also include officers and civilian personnel. The career field manager determines whether officers and civilians will be included. At this time, about 20 percent of civilian workers are included in the surveying.

[6]AFOMS identifies tasks by meeting with people at the schools and with operational people in the field.

distributed to 130 locations around the globe, and AFOMS generally gets about a 70 percent response rate.[7]

Once AFOMS gets the completed surveys, it uploads the data into the Comprehensive Occupational Data Analysis Program, a software system for occupational analysis that allows for clustering, sorting, and comparisons.

It takes AFOMS about one year to complete a project on a specialty. It takes two months to build the inventory. Creating and fielding the inventory takes one week to three months (depending on the format). Data collection takes one week to four months. Uploading the data takes one week. Then it takes about four months to do analysis, write reports, and prepare briefings.

AFOMS staff total 150. About 50 are devoted to promotion test development. The staff for occupational analysis consist of 76 people. Ten people develop inventories, twenty people do analysis, and five interface with the occupational analysis software, which is pre-Windows. Their budget includes approximately $200,000 for travel, and $100,000 for printing. The total annual expenditures are likely between $1 and $2 million. The staff spend about $650,000 to bring the subject matter experts (SMEs) together to write the promotional tests.

The staff have a standard set of analyses for all specialties. The analysis enables AFOMS staff to identify different jobs that make up a specialty and different tasks that make up a job. They also can identify who does those jobs and at what point in their careers. They look at task responses by skill level, compare domestic and abroad, and compare guard, reserve, and active airmen. A task breakdown of each occupation identifies the skills, knowledge, resources, and equipment needed to perform an occupation effectively.

Concurrent with the AFOMS survey and analysis, personnel are assessed on their current knowledge level in a given occupation to determine knowledge gaps between past and revised occupational standards. These analyses may culminate in the elimination and/or creation of new tasks within an occupation or new occupations altogether. In addition, education curriculum is being evaluated continuously during the design, development, and implementation stages at the provider institutions.

AFOMS activities play an important role in this process. The final report from AFOMS is delivered to the training establishments. Following the report, there is a utilization and training workshop that involves all the stakeholders: the career field manager, the training community, policy-level people (who are responsible

---

[7]The survey is mailed in hard copy or on disc, e-mailed, or made available on a web site.

for deciding the future direction of the field), the operational community, and occupational analysts. These workshop participants will rewrite classification documents and determine training for the future. The AFOMS report ensures that all the parties start from the same point with the same information.

AFOMS reports are the departure point for decisionmaking on such key issues as:

- When and where tasks should be trained.
- Creating career plans for individuals.
- Rating of tasks to be included in training programs. Training emphasis for tasks is based on input from senior SMEs as to what tasks should be emphasized in entry-level training.
- Skills that are being trained but not used in the Air Force.
- Skills that are being performed but not trained.

Promotion tests are also based on the occupational analysis conducted by AFOMS, thus providing enlisted personnel with a strong incentive to learn the relevant skills. The tests are based on what tasks are done in the field and are written by operator SMEs who use AFOMS-provided data to write the tests.

AFOMS is an objective, stand-alone organization with no vested interest in the application of results or findings of the job analyses. The findings are a valid and reliable representation of the work that Air Force personnel perform, but AFOMS acknowledges there may be reasons other than performance to include or not include some tasks in the training program. AFOMS is not part of this decisionmaking process, which gives the office credibility with other stakeholders.

In summary, the Air Force views training and education of military personnel as an activity that promotes the overall mission of the Air Force, and systematically considers whether the training that is provided addresses the primary Air Force skill needs. AFOMS activities provide the data and venue for consideration of such issues.

Phase Two

It is the responsibility of the training centers (providers) to design and implement training content and actually evaluate the training activities. This level of assessment is done with input from the functional community. Phase Two assessment thus follows Model 3, in which providers assess their own performance with little input from or oversight by an intermediary. We did not examine the Phase Two activities of individual training providers in the Air Force as part of this research, but in-depth examples of Model 3 approaches are provided in Appendices K.1–K.4.

F.3. U.S. Navy Individual and Mission Training

Overview

In the Navy, the Chief of Naval Operations (CNO) oversees both individual training and mission training. Different types of individual training are offered, including accessions training, individual skills training, and professional development. All new recruits and officers begin their educational career with accessions training, during which time they are indoctrinated into the Navy and taught basic skills. Individual skills training includes either flight training or skill training. More than 100 bases offer close to 3,000 courses in skill training. Along with skill development, some recruits receive unit training, which consists of live training or simulation/war gaming. Depending on Navy and unit needs, as well as individual interest, Navy personnel may receive additional professional development, which typically lasts one to two years. Professional development includes professional military education, voluntary education, leadership training, internships or fellowships in acquisition or financial management, and graduate education. Navy personnel are required to constantly update or upgrade their skills in order to be promoted in the Navy.

The Navy distinguishes between education and training. One way to differentiate the two is to consider *education* as the broad-based skills required and acquired over the long term, and *training* as the particular skills required for seamen/officers to do their job.

Several entities are involved in both education and training of Navy personnel and in assessment. They include the Chief of Naval Education and Training (CNET), the Training and Education Assessment Division (N81) under the Deputy Chief of Naval Operations (Resources, Warfare Requirements and Assessments—N8), and naval academic institutions, which include the Naval Postgraduate School, the Naval War College, the United States Naval Academy, and the Joint Forces Staff College.

N81 is responsible for broad-based assessments on quality and cost across all areas within the Navy including training. N81 conducts high-level, independent analyses that are more capability-oriented.

CNO delegates most of training oversight to the Chief of Naval Education and Training, which is one of the largest shore commands in the Navy.

> The Chief of Naval Education and Training is responsible to the Chief of Naval Operations (CNO) for the education and training of Navy and Marine Corps personnel, both officer and enlisted. CNET oversees a network of training and education programs throughout the United States and on ships at sea.[1]

Specifically, CNET is responsible for recruit training, specialized skills training, officer accessions training, warfare skills training, and individual and team training. The assessment department within CNET conducts most of the program evaluation, while the Schoolhouse Operations department oversees the implementation of training at the different training sites.

The bulk of training assessment is done by CNET. However, the education assessment is much more fragmented, with all entities playing some role in the process. The purpose of the assessments is both improvement and accountability.

The academic institutions operate independently from CNET. In fact, most of them have or seek accreditation from national accreditation boards and follow the same assessment guidelines as civilian academic institutions. For instance, the Naval Postgraduate School has received both institutional accreditation from the Western Association of Schools and Colleges[2] and curricular accreditation from the National Association of Schools and Public Affairs and Administration for its Master of Science in Management degree, and from the Accreditation Board for Engineering and Technology for its degree programs in the engineering department.

CNET acts as an intermediary between the different resource sponsors that fund training and the providers (i.e., schoolhouses) that provide training and report directly to CNET. These schoolhouses offer different types of training at very different levels. CNET's collaboration, however, is mainly with resource sponsors who allocate funds for training.

Phase One

Multiple stakeholders are involved in the process of identifying Navy-wide education and training needs including system commands, resource sponsors,

---

[1]CNET mission: www.cnet.navy.mil/mission.html.

[2]For more information on WASC, refer to Appendix D.1 of this report.

and several departments from N8, including N81 and N82 (Fiscal Management Division).

The driving principles behind phase one efforts are to:

- Provide more training to more sailors at lower cost, and to make sure that each sailor succeeds. This is the philosophy of the time-to-train model.
- Provide sailors the skills that they need to do the job.

Cost reduction drives the assessment process, but these reductions should not compromise education quality. Currently, CNET expects to reduce system costs by 8 percent without lowering education standards. Costs are reduced through elimination and simulation of programs. Currently, $450 million is being spent on reengineering training systems. Reducing manpower and streamlining the process have the potential to save the government $1.2 billion in the future. The Navy also considers whether the funds are being spent in the right places.

Furthermore, the Navy is looking to outsourcing as a way of reducing education and training costs, partnering with civilian-sector institutions whenever there is a skill match. The Navy holds civilian-partner institutions to the highest standards; it requires these institutions to meet accrediting standards, and experts in the field must consider the education as one of the best in the country. Some of the training outsourced includes haircutting and cooking.

Stakeholders have access to the Baseline Assessment Memorandum (BAM), a publication used by CNET to disseminate information and study results. The publication is not disseminated widely and is not for public consumption. A handful of web sites—they include the fleet with publications on homeport training and the schoolhouses with publications on time to train—disseminate some information. These sites are also password protected. Efforts are under way to provide most of the information published in BAM electronically.

Phase Two

In this appendix, we consider the assessment activities of CNET, which uses the Model 2 approach. However, we point out that individual providers often conduct their own assessment, and thus Model 3 is also used in the Navy, although those activities are not considered here.

Identify Goals for Education and Training

CNET's assessment process is driven by education and training goals that are in line with the overall strategic plan of the Navy (*Forward from the Sea*) and of the Joint Chiefs of Staff (*Vision 2010*). To track progress toward goals, the Navy develops capability-based assessment to answer the question: What is the capability that the Navy is trying to achieve?

Develop Measures of Quality and Productivity

Typically, the Navy follows the education and training standards used in many academic institutions or in industry. For example, CNET tries to use indicators that measure learning. The measures must translate well into what the Navy is doing currently. Within industry, CNET looks at what different companies are doing. For instance, CNET looks at Cisco Academy because the company's target audience matches the Navy's. Specifically, CNET is interested in how Cisco evaluates employee knowledge of information technology skills after training.

CNET also follows current literature on the subject. In addition, the Navy follows closely current discussions on evaluation and technology. CNET sees evaluation via technology as an additional source for cutting the costs of evaluation and delivery.

CNET's measures are designed to measure progress while holding quality constant. The "time-to-train" concept adopted by the Navy focuses on how long it takes the Navy to train a single sailor for a job and on whether there are ways to improve total time needed to train. Several measures are considered:

- **Reduction in the individual's account:** The money in man-years set aside for training. If the Navy increased the number of sailors trained within one man-year, it could reduce costs by approximately 8 percent per year.
- **Reduction in permanent change in station costs:** Travel funds associated with training. Sailors often need to travel to other locations to receive training. In reducing travel and increasing homeport training, the Navy reduces the disruption in a sailor's life as measured by time away from home.
- **Reduction of attrition and setbacks:** Attrition measures the failure rate of sailors while setbacks measure average time required to get through the training. CNET looks at the reasons why setbacks in training occur.

- **Reduction in infrastructure costs:** CNET estimates that $5 million in homeport training results in $18 million worth of savings.

Measures are not selected necessarily on available data. CNET always tries to find new approaches in evaluation. The organization keeps abreast of the latest discussions and assessment processes used by academia and industry.

A CNET official explained that data and measures are obtained from all relevant sources. Some data are generated by schoolhouses, which measure quality of classroom instruction through student surveys and instructor feedback. CNET also pulls performance data on students who attended academic institutions.

In addition, CNET has two databases from which it draws most of its data. One database called NITRAS (Navy Integrated Training Resource Assessment System) tracks each sailor by Social Security number. The database profiles each sailor's education path. Tracking begins with the first day of training. Some of the information collected includes

- registration for specific courses
- specific courses completed
- courses still required to complete a particular training sequence
- systemic reasons for delay in training (e.g., inefficient system)
- individual reasons for interrupted training (e.g., injury, leave of absence).

A second database called SSTAS (Standard Schoolhouse Training Analysis System) was developed before computer-based instruction systems became available. The system tracks each student's performance on coursework from test scores to problem solving. The database even has information on what path a student took to solve a particular problem.

The cost of developing NITRAS was approximately $300,000, although CNET currently does not have any development costs. Total costs for assembling data are about $2.3 million per year—this includes direct labor costs of about $950,000 (i.e., staff, contracts).

Evaluate Quality and Productivity Using Measures

Evaluation of quality and productivity is based on the goals articulated for education and professional development. N81 conducts both quality and cost assessments, but admits having limited success evaluating quality, in part because tracking what happens in the fleet has proven to be quite difficult. Due in part to this limitation, N81 tasks other organizations to conduct quality and cost analyses of Navy divisions. For instance,

> N81 tasked the Center for Naval Analyses (CNA) to take a bottom-up look at each of the Navy's flagship schools. The main goals of the assessment were to evaluate the current quality and condition of the schools and to help determine the level of funding needed in the future to maintain Navy schools as top-tier institutions (Cavalluzzo and Cymrot, 1998, p. 1).

In the study, CNA examined the quality characteristics used by academic institutions and measured Navy schools against those characteristics. CNA compared cost data with peer academic institutions and analyzed whether these costs could be reduced without affecting quality. Within the quality framework, CNA reviewed outcome measures used by accrediting agencies, the Gourman report,[3] and the *U.S. News and World Report*. Quality indicators used by the National Research Council to review doctoral programs were also considered; indicators included institutional and departmental support, faculty involvement, student diversity, and program leadership. CNA summarized findings from these sources wherever available.

---

[3]The Gourman Report is an annual publication that ranks undergraduate and graduate programs in the United States and abroad. It considers such indicators as admission requirements, student qualities, faculty, school facilities, and resources.

G. Corporate Professional Development and Training

Overview

Our literature review on this topic includes material drawn from best-practice human resource departments and corporate learning organizations as well as corporate universities.[1] Throughout this appendix, we use the term "corporate learning organization" to reflect a high-level commitment to employee learning and a systems-based approach to providing for it, including a corporate university. Corporate learning organizations can be, but are not necessarily, associated with specific physical facilities.

The corporate learning organization represents an intermediary-aided approach to professional development and education, although many corporate learning organizations have some sort of provider role. Corporate learning organizations typically engage in Phase One system-level assessment activities; however, the structure of Phase Two functions often varies depending on the organization. Examples of each of Models 1, 2, and 3 can be found throughout different corporate settings. In corporate America, there is a growing interest in the role of the learning organization as an information gatherer and processor, knowledge broker and information clearinghouse, in addition to the role of developer and provider of content. The trend appears to be toward increased emphasis on the intermediary role and less emphasis on the provider role.

The intermediary organization, whether it is officially a corporate university or an in-house human resources unit, is increasingly likely to be headed by an

---

[1]In reviewing current literature on corporate professional development and education, our intent was twofold: to explore how corporate education and professional development may inform the development of a conceptual framework for thinking about DoD civilian education and professional development; and to identify lessons learned in that context that might be usefully transferred to the DoD civilian context.

For these purposes, we conducted a thorough search of online bibliographic reference materials related to corporate universities, professional education and training, and related evaluation practices. Relevant sources were retrieved from the Management Contents, ABI/Inform, PsycInfo, ERIC, and Business Periodicals Index databases. In our review, we gave highest priority to academic and professional society publications because of their attention to study methods and generalizability of results.

In addition, members of the project team attended the Corporate Universities 2000: Benchmarks for the New Millennium conference organized by Corporate University Xchange, Inc., in April 2000, where a range of corporate learning organizations presented their learning and development activities.

individual whose title is "chief learning officer" (CLO). Learning organizations are emphasizing their role as corporate-level partners and the importance of establishing learning as a strategic part of the future of the company, rather than a cost center. Formerly, training was controlled by individual lines of business and each had its own training activities to meet their specific needs. Now, the issue of training is being elevated to the corporate level, and activities are being consolidated and rationalized in the interest of both quality and efficiency. This is similar to the transition that information technology went through in the 1980s, when the term "chief information officer" was relatively new. Learning organizations have recognized the importance of getting buy-in from both the CEO and the lines of business in support of their efforts. Many are using "account management" to track the needs of the stakeholders, emphasizing communication and responsiveness. Learning goals must be tied clearly to business goals. Because human resource departments are often held in low esteem in large corporations, learning organizations are often advised to avoid "HR speak" and learn to communicate effectively with the business units.

Corporate learning organizations provide a range of services that are ultimately designed to promote workforce improvement. The intermediary role includes helping employees develop individual learning plans to meet their training needs as well as keeping track of their training needs and accomplishments. To this end, some learning organizations, such as the one at Sun Microsystems, have introduced information "portals" that organize information functionally allowing employees to easily find what they need about learning opportunities throughout the company. United Airlines provides another example. Its central unit that is responsible for leadership training is developing an interactive web site that includes online assessments that help an employee determine the skills (math, verbal, and leadership) he or she is lacking. The web site is a huge information clearinghouse, organized on the basis of the assessments and other information for the benefit of the user. For example, the learner can pull up a list of learning opportunities, both internal and external, that are available through United. Using well-developed web tools, learning organizations can connect and coordinate learning experiences for employees.

In the corporate learning environment, customers are broadly construed to include both learners (employees at all levels of the organization) and managers of the line units whose employees receive education or training. Often intact teams or entire units are engaged in the learning experience. Further, there is increasing interest in including other members or components of the value chain as learners (e.g., suppliers or customers of the line unit, and occasionally collateral units). Such efforts evidence a systems-based approach to learning.

Providers of training, education, and professional development in the corporate setting are a diverse collection of individuals and organizations whose activities are carried out in close collaboration with the intermediary unit. Providers include nonprofit educational institutions (especially if they are flexible about customizing or tailoring coursework and schedules) and for-profit training firms. Frequently, line managers and even senior managers in the organization are also being asked to serve as educators, with assistance from the intermediary unit. In addition, companies develop and deliver their own course materials as well. As a first step, the intermediary must identify the appropriate delivery mechanism and provider. Partnering with existing educational institutions is highly desirable because courses and programs are likely to be accredited or certified; on the other hand, they may have less flexibility and less motivation to adapt their procedures to the needs of corporations than private, for-profit training firms. Learning organizations may elect to develop their own courses. In any case, the intermediary must constantly broker, monitor, and manage relationships between providers and customers of professional development and education. The intermediary must also work with customers and providers to develop learning evaluations.

In spite of all the interest in new technologies for education delivery, many providers still rely on classroom-based instruction. Based on the learning pyramid from National Training Laboratories, popular opinion about the relationship between information retention and education delivery methods posits that students retain 5 percent from lecture, 10 percent from reading, 20 percent from audio-visual aids, 30 percent from demonstration, 50 percent from discussion, 75 percent from practice by doing, and 90 percent from teaching others. Interestingly, while this belief is widely held, there are no data supporting the numbers.

In terms of assessment, the human resource office, corporate university, or corporate learning officer is responsible for designing or guiding the assessment, and potentially for implementing or helping to implement it. The intermediary will also take the lead in using assessment results to revise course offerings and give improvement-oriented feedback to providers.

Ultimately, attention to the quality and productivity of professional development and educational activities is motivated by interest in promoting the long-run health and competitiveness of the corporation. However, while the benefits to the corporation are the clear driver, assessment often benefits the employee learners as well. For example, academic accreditation and professional certification are taken by corporations as marks of the quality of courses offered, but corporations also believe it is beneficial to employees to have such accomplishments on their records. Achievement in externally validated courses, they believe, helps assure lifetime employability in a period when corporations can no longer promise lifetime employment.

Although the reviewed literature reflected a highly diverse collection of businesses and industries, a number of common assumptions underlie and drive their concern for quality and productivity in professional development and education. One dominant theme, for example, is knowledge work as an ever-increasing proportion of the total work of organizations. In the United States, as in most developed economies, firms' core competencies are being defined in the context of information-intensive activities. Key corollaries of this theme are systematically increasing skill requirements for most jobs (to produce value-added, knowledge-based goods and services) and continuous learning needs related to technological advance (since information-intensive tasks are highly technology dependent).

A second major theme in the literature has to do with corporate restructuring. Downsizing and other business process redesign efforts have reshaped organizations, making them flatter, leaner, and more competitive. As a consequence, today's employees are expected to work "smarter"—to become effective self-managers and problem solvers. Emerging interest in knowledge management and intellectual capital suggests that firms are giving more attention to the value of their human resources.

Emphasis on high-performance work systems throughout the value chain is a third noteworthy theme. Line business units in organizations are being asked to reexamine their roles, to align their processes with mission-critical enterprise goals, and to demonstrate measurable results from their performance improvement strategies. Corporate professional development functions are experiencing these same pressures.

Taken together, these cross-cutting trends appear to have greatly increased the importance of workplace learning in the corporate literature we reviewed. The growth of corporate universities—from about 400 in 1990 to an estimated 1,000 or more today—signals the renewed interest in professional development and education.

As learning and knowledge management become increasingly important to organizations, the value of the learning organization as a strategic partner in the continuous improvement of business processes is emerging as an important trend. Quality assessment results are expected to be useful both for improving learning processes and for providing insights on factors that affect organizational performance.

At the employee level, student assessment results are sometimes fed into performance reviews and future career path plans. The literature recommends employee incentives for learning as a way of linking employees' individual goals to organizational performance improvement goals.

Finally, corporate universities and corporate learning units are increasingly being expected to operate on a fee-for-service basis, recovering their operating costs from business units that supply them with customers (learners). Thus they have a strong incentive to monitor their productivity; and it is in their best interests as well to gather and disseminate quality evaluations to potential customer units.

Phase One

Details of corporate university approaches to identifying goals for professional development and education vary in a number of firm-specific ways. However, they evidence some common systems-level features. Typically, the learning goals are based on the corporation's strategic plan, plus core and other competencies taken as critical to the mission success of the enterprise's several lines of business.

The intermediary organization is often responsible for setting out the top-level goals for professional development and education activities but has to act entrepreneurially to sell the learning agenda within the corporation. It is crucial to enlist strong and visible commitment and support from the corporation's CEO—if the CEO was not a prime mover in creating the corporate university or CLO position. Often, but not always, these learning initiatives are driven from the top. Additionally, it is critical to convince key managers in all lines of business that intellectual capital investment is a necessity for survival and success in the current economic environment.

The intermediary's role in goal identification and needs analysis differs among learning organizations. In some cases, learning organizations are responsible for both goal identification and needs analysis to determine in what key areas education and professional development efforts should be directed. At Sun Microsystems, for example, a framework was developed that can be applied to individual lines of business for identifying goals and establishing where needs exist. For each line of business, the Sun Microsystems corporate university focuses on knowledge management to establish what learners know, competency management to determine what learners need to know, and performance management to help learners use what they know. The Grainger, Inc., learning center has adopted a more bottom-up approach to goal identification. By taking an inventory of the training and education activities going on in the company, they have identified 108 "learning solutions" or training modules and have developed a core curriculum that encompasses 27 of those learning solutions. The core consists of four areas: leadership and management, quality, sales and customer contact, and "digital Grainger." Other learning organizations, such as the United Airlines leadership training unit, have their goals established by corporate headquarters and focus on needs analysis. The training unit has built the curriculum for leadership development around the corporate goals and corporate definition of good leadership and considers its core competency to be needs analysis based on that definition.

A common strategy for selling the learning agenda within the company is to create a governance structure for the corporate university that puts representative managers for primary lines of business on a board of trustees or board of advisors. This structure creates direct formal links between the business units and the intermediary organization and allows business units to help determine the learning goals.

Productivity improvements in professional development and education, in contrast, are often sought to make two main types of changes to the corporate university or corporate learning effort: reorganizations that decrease the administrative costs associated with providing these programs, and innovative uses of information and communication technologies to create more efficient ways of delivering them.

Phase Two

Many corporate learning organizations are moving toward a lesser role in the actual provision of education and training, and increasingly exemplify a Phase Two, Model 2 structure where the intermediary assesses the quality and productivity of outside providers. It is still common, however, for corporations to assume Model 3 in their Phase Two activities where the corporate learning organization acts as provider of professional development and training and assesses its own quality and productivity (e.g., Lucent; see Appendix G.1). Finally, some corporate learning organizations serve as advisors to corporate business units that are providing their own training. In this capacity, they assume a modified version of Model 1 where they make recommendations and guide provider assessment.

Identify Goals for Education and Training

The intermediary works with major stakeholder groups to jointly articulate more-specific goals and objectives for the varied business lines or directions that professional development and education will take. Subsequently, the intermediary designs curricula in collaboration with customers and providers. Customization aims at developing curricula that will boost the customer unit's successful performance (as determined by the unit's role in the corporate business strategy). Tailoring curricula is regarded as important for assuring that courses directly address firm-specific and unit-specific performance goals and also to help reconcile provider schedules (e.g., academic terms) with customer schedules (e.g., fiscal cycles). In other words, the goals relate mainly to business outcomes.

Develop Measures of Quality and Productivity

Corporate mission goals and objectives typically form the basis for assessment procedures, which must be designed to reflect performance outcomes that are desirable in light of the corporation's strategic plans and the role that employee professional development and education plays in them.

Our review of corporate literature revealed a variety of measures in use for assessment purposes. In general, in the reviewed literature, productivity assessment received far less attention than quality assessment. The productivity assessments we found are generally based on inputs, assuming that outcome quality remains constant. Common examples of productivity measures in use include

- the number of instructional days provided per unit of cost
- the total cost to deliver a course, per student
- the total time required to complete a course, per student.

As noted, these tend to be input measures. The unit of analysis for productivity measures is generally the learning organization or provider of the education.

In contrast, most of the specific measures of quality we found reflect processes or outcomes; and their relationship to business performance goals and objectives is generally highly inferential. Because this project emphasizes academic quality over productivity, we identified a number of examples in the corporate literature for several categories of quality measures. The unit of analysis for quality measures can be the business units, the educational providers, or the students.

Input measures are sometimes used as quality metrics in the corporate training environment. From a quality perspective, the underlying assumption is that more inputs generate better or more outcomes. Common input measures include

- education/training expenditures as a percentage of payroll
- hours of training per employee per year
- percentage of employees trained per year
- education/training expenditures per employee
- ratio of employees to trainers.

Such external certification as the accreditation or certification of courses is sometimes used as a measure of quality. Organizations may also choose to participate in outside certification of unit processes or recognition of performance (e.g., ISO or Baldrige Award) as a way of determining quality.

Measurement of the quality of professional development and education in the corporate sector continues to rely heavily on the Kirkpatrick framework, which consists of four levels of assessment. The first level is reaction, or trainee satisfaction with the course. The second level is learning and measures how well participants have mastered the course material. Level three is transfer to the job, or how the learning and development is being used on the job. The fourth level is organizational effects and measures changes in the business process itself.

Table G.1 summarizes the four Kirkpatrick levels and provides examples of measures used at each level.

There is currently a strong emphasis on levels 3 and 4 in corporate professional development and education. However, in practice, most assessment is still being done at level 1, with some assessment at level 2. While many learning organizations consider assessment at levels 3 and 4 to be desirable, they are not able to carry it out in most cases. The value chain has been incorporated into how Kirkpatrick levels 3–4 are understood and operationalized. It is regarded, however, as quite difficult and costly to obtain quantifiable measures of performance improvements at levels 3–4 and to associate such changes with bottom-line improvements.[2] For instance, Motorola's rigorous effort to estimate the return on its investment in education and training is rumored to have cost over $1 million.

---

[2]These findings from our site visits and literature review parallel those reported in an earlier *Annual Review of Psychology* article by Tannenbaum and Yukl (1992).

Table G.1

Kirkpatrick Model

Kirkpatrick Level	What It Measures	Examples of Measures
One—reaction	Learner satisfaction with course, other aspects of the learner's experience	Course/instructor evaluation Employee job satisfaction survey Employee (pre/post) self-assessment
Two—learning	How well participants have mastered the course material	Technical skill test (pre/post) Observation of standardized task performance (post only) Retention tests
Three—transfer to the job	How learning and development is being used on the job	Qualitative interviews with the learner Focus groups with managers of learners Improvement ratings collected from managers Direct measurement of employee performance (e.g., reduced time-to-completion of tasks)
Four—organizational effects	Effects on the business process itself	Number of defective parts Satisfied-customer index Customer retention Return on investment Return on expectations, where expectations are indicators of valued performance derived and operationalized collaboratively from missions and goals Demand for education/training as a measure of its quality and relevance Desired effects on organizational culture (ethnographic studies pre/post)

Despite its widespread use, there are several limitations of the framework. First, it focuses on student learning, which is an important goal of education and professional development, but may not be the only goal of interest to an assessor. Second, what little empirical research there is on Kirkpatrick's typology of measures provides weak evidence of correlation among levels 2–4 and no evidence that level 1 outcomes are related to the others (see Tannenbaum and Yukl, 1992). As noted, levels 1 and 2 are the most commonly used measurements because of their low cost and ease of administration. However, business organizations are generally less interested in individual-level measures of course satisfaction and learning than in the effects of the education and development activities on job performance and business processes. Using level 1 or level 2 measures as proxies for higher-level outcomes, such as task or process improvements, is not appropriate and may lead to flawed conclusions.

Some learning organizations have undertaken return-on-investment (ROI) evaluation to underscore the effects that investments in learning and development have on a company's productivity. By measuring increases in productivity as a result of education and professional development, the activities of the learning organization are elevated to the level of importance comparable to other strategic investments. The process of ROI evaluation facilitates better management of these activities and promotes their continuous improvement. It is not, however, a viable method of self- or budgetary justification (Bassi, 2000). ROI measurement involves determining the intended business result, establishing the causal relationship between learning and development activities and the result, quantifying the value of that result, identification of metrics, and evaluation. Measurement of the three categories of provision costs is critical for a credible ROI evaluation: direct costs, including payments to vendors and materials; indirect costs, including overhead; and opportunity costs, such as lost productivity (Bassi, 2000). Establishing causal links between learning and development efforts and ROI effects (or other organizational performance effects) is likely to be another difficult step toward the credibility of level 4 evaluation efforts.

While some learning organizations emphasize the importance of ROI assessment (e.g., United Airlines) or an ability to demonstrate the value to the firm, others are moving away from this type of measurement. For example, Cisco focuses instead on the effect of training on the revenue stream. They claim that this is a more "strategic" focus (as opposed to a cost center perspective).

Evaluate Quality and Productivity Using Measures

As explained earlier, productivity assessments typically turn on input measures, assuming quality of output is held constant. Using these measures, productivity is then evaluated by comparing an organization's current resource-to-output ratio with a prior baseline rate; such methods have been used, for instance, to evaluate whether the introduction of network-based distance learning techniques for a particular course of instruction yields productivity improvements. Alternatively, productivity can be evaluated by comparing the productivity of an organization's education or training activities with those of a benchmark organization. Use of benchmarks for productivity evaluation is dependent on finding appropriate organizations and courses for comparison; this approach is most successful when organizations use similar techniques for determining costs and where equivalence of outputs can readily be established (e.g., for certain kinds of technical training).

Additionally, corporate universities also rely on benchmarking (comparison to leading-edge peers) and standards (e.g., accreditation or certification) in quality evaluations. At least two objectives are served by accreditation or certification of courses. On the one hand, such processes provide the corporate university with an independent and objective evaluation of the quality of specific courses or programs. On the other hand, having taken accredited or certified courses gives employees a portable credential; given that companies cannot promise lifetime employment, they are attempting instead to provide lifetime employability. In return, companies say, they are able to attract and retain better workers.

Benchmarking as a tool for quality evaluation is a widely accepted and familiar practice in the corporate world and was readily extended to serve needs for evaluating the quality of professional development and education. But it is recommended with some caveats: Processes closely linked to performance improvements in one company might not have the same relationship to performance in another; and in any case, benchmarked processes probably have to be tailored to particular contexts rather than adopted as is.

Typically, performance measures of the effects of professional development and education on the performance of units, lines of business, and/or the entire enterprise are evaluated in one of two ways. One involves examining face-valid indicators of performance improvements (indices based, for instance, on defined mission objectives); corporations rarely make the investment of time and funds necessary to establish the predictive validity of these measures or to link them directly with ROI. An alternative is to rely for evaluative purposes on measures of processes that have been independently benchmarked to performance improvements (e.g., the American Society for Training and Development has defined a set of input and process measures associated with performance improvements in a set of best-practice organizations).

Apart from consortia that establish procedures for collecting and sharing data for benchmarking purposes, evaluation information is not widely shared; and typically consortium members hold the information as confidential or proprietary to the association.

Although assessments need to be specific to courses and to business processes, the intermediary organization is expected to establish general evaluation standards and procedures and to assure their implementation.

G.1. Lucent Technologies Learning and Performance Center[1]

Overview

Lucent Technologies is a spin-off from AT&T, specializing in telecommunications equipment. This description was written in the spring of 2000. At this time, the company is moving away from routine manufacturing and concentrating more on high-end manufacturing and telecommunications technologies. It has about 150,000 employees, 45,000 of whom work outside the United States in 67 different countries. Lucent's annual revenue is about $38 billion.

Education, development, and training activities occur throughout the entire corporation at Lucent and are budgeted at about $225 million per year. Much of this activity occurs under or is guided by the Learning and Performance Center (LPC). While the LPC performs the functions of a corporate university, namely, designing and delivering learning opportunities, it also serves a broader function as the leader of the Lucent learning network. The LPC was established in 1996 and currently provides 250,000 learning days per year with a budget of $70 million. Twenty-five percent of the budget comes directly from a corporate allocation, and the remainder comes from tuition charged to the business units that use the training. About 25 percent of the learning days are delivered using technology. The primary purposes of establishing the LPC were to improve content and delivery, reduce costs, and eliminate redundancies.[2]

The LPC has many roles. It monitors both stakeholder and system needs for education and professional development and assesses whether the provision is meeting quality and productivity standards for the organization.

Phase One

LPC's vision is "to be recognized as a critical business partner in achieving Lucent's success"; its mission is "to provide innovative learning solutions,

---

[1]This appendix is based primarily on a conversation with and briefing given by Learning and Performance Center Vice President Bill Harrod. Unless otherwise noted, quotes are from that briefing.

[2]*Lucent Magazine*, March/April 2000, pp. 14–17.

readily available and highly valued worldwide, that measurably improve Lucent's organizational and individual performance."

Bill Harrod, LPC vice president, noted that many large organizations have an education committee, but that generally such committees do not include people who are well informed about business needs. At Lucent, the education and training activities are divided into 15 curriculum areas. Examples of curriculum areas include software, wireless, diversity, and program management. Each curriculum area has a business performance council, composed of powerful people in the company. For example, the software committee is headed by the vice president for software. There are over 160 people on these councils. There is a dean for each curriculum, and about 20 subject matter experts help with curriculum design.

The business performance councils are responsible for much more than education and training. They consider all strategic issues related to the particular area. The point is that they specifically consider education and training as part of key strategic business issues. The success of the business performance councils and of the learning and development activities in general is driven by several factors including strong executive-level leadership and support and broad involvement with the business units.

The goal of the LPC unit is to be a valuable member of a team whose focus is much larger than learning. However, the learning staff have to earn their way to the top management table by demonstrating how learning affects key business performance. The key to doing this is to understand the proficiency gaps in given business domains, determine which can be addressed by learning solutions, and develop learning solutions to help close those gaps.

The different business performance councils are at different stages in the development of tools for identifying competency gaps. A state-of-the-art tool, the Kiviat, is used by the software council. This tool helps assess proficiencies and identify gaps in eight software project areas: customer focus, project management, project team variables, tools, quality focus, methodologies, physical environment, and metrics. The tool includes a detailed instrument for measuring Lucent's performance (there are about 20 metrics in each area) on a five-point scale ranging from 1 (leading edge) to 5 (high risk). The performance measures are evaluated on the basis of ten years of industrywide data. The tool points out areas where Lucent's performance is not leading-edge; these are areas where learning might be able to improve business performance.

Harrod emphasized that just dumping courses out there will not solve the company's problems. There is a tendency to view all performance problems as "training problems"; however, not all proficiency gaps are due to a lack of skill or training. Individual jobs must be structured in such a way that employees can use the training they receive. A new initiative of the LPC is a consulting effort that works with the business units to identify the problems that are learning related and design learning solutions for them. Rather than being an advocate for any and all education and training activities, the role of LPC is to help the company determine the most effective way to deploy limited education and training resources in such a way as to promote overall corporate goals. Part of that role is identifying where training is *not* appropriate. LPC recently established a consulting service that is specifically designed to work with the individual business units to help them find learning solutions when they are appropriate.

Another element of the LPC role is helping the company identify which stakeholder needs deserve attention from the learning and development unit. The purpose of learning activities at Lucent is to help the company achieve growth in key markets. If an activity is not important to Lucent from a business perspective, Lucent will not train it. LPC focuses on what people need to succeed on the job. Its activities focus on business needs, as distinct from student demands. Harrod noted that if Lucent were to offer a course on taxes on April 14, a lot of employees would take the course. Employees would like it, but it is not relevant to business goals. In other words, there are "nice to have" courses and "need to have" courses. Lucent wants to focus on the "need to have."

As mentioned above, an important part of LPC's early efforts were focused on eliminating redundancy and reducing cost. Much of this was achieved by consolidating approximately 70,000 courses taught throughout Lucent into about 2,000. For example, there were originally about 700 courses on fire extinguisher operation. It has also decreased the number of vendors from which it purchases course content and eliminated certain high-cost programs whose value did not justify their continuation (such as the Wharton executive MBA). LPC has also improved its focus in terms of the courses it develops internally, having reduced that number from 800 to 390. Additionally, technology-enabled courses have reduced some travel costs. The total number of learner days has increased by over 60 percent.

The consolidation of courses has made it easier for Lucent to integrate training records with personnel records. Formerly, Lucent kept training records on employees, but the records were not centralized. This made it difficult to construct a training history on an individual. Now, if a learner successfully completes a course, then course completion is recorded in the person's record. Lucent was using PeopleSoft for that purpose but has recently moved to a training server to track all training. In addition, the system allows students to search for and enroll in courses online.

Phase Two

The LPC provides some, but not all, of the education and professional development opportunities. The term "provider" is used loosely in this context and often refers to a situation where the LPC makes available to the business units a learning opportunity that was developed by an external provider. As a result, the LPC tends to operate as more of an intermediary (between the business units and the array of providers) than a provider, and Phase Two assessment is most similar to Model One.

Identify Goals for Education and Training

The Lucent LPC has four layers of internal clients, ascribing different goals to learning activities. The executive leadership of Lucent wants LPC to promote cultural change (make Lucent look less like AT&T and more like a dot-com). Leaders at the vice president level want learning to promote strategic knowledge in the corporation. Mid-level managers are looking for tactical knowledge, and employees in general want the knowledge necessary to strengthen their role in the company.

The goals of the learning activities are driven by input from business line leaders through the business performance councils. These councils have staff associated with the chief technical officer as well as the chief education officer. Because the same group of people is considering the technical and the training issues, the learning goals are driven by business needs.

Ultimately, the purpose of learning is to change an employee's behavior. Whereas education used to be just learner focused, now it is business focused.

Develop Measures of Quality and Productivity

The main productivity measure used in LPC is cost per learner day (measured as eight hours spent in a learning activity). The LPC finds it is better to use the learner day as the unit of analysis, rather than a course, because "courses" vary tremendously in their duration. The LPC would like to break the learning unit down further. Another metric it tracks is the percentage of programs that are technology enabled.

In terms of quality measurement, Lucent has made the most progress in two domains: software and program management. These are areas where there are externally based standards of knowledge and performance. In the area of program management, the Program Management Institute certifies program management skills and accredits courses designed to prepare learners for the tests.

Lucent uses the Kirkpatrick framework to develop measures of quality for education and development. It measures performance at levels 1, 2, and 3 and views level 1 as extremely important. Level 1 performance measures go beyond making training fun (or serving good food) so that the student provides positive course evaluations. The ultimate goal of a learning activity is to change the behavior of workers. If learners are not getting something they think they need, then they will not learn.

Level 2 is conducted for all learning experiences. Students must pass a test of some sort, and then successful completion of a learning module is recorded in their records (nothing is recorded if they fail). Level 3 assessment is being used in 30–40 percent of the learning activities; these assessments rely primarily on judgments made by managers of learners. LPC has not been asked to do level 4 assessment. Harrod believes that it is not possible to measure only the effects of learning activities because job performance is influenced by so many variables. In the future, LPC expects to adopt a balanced scorecard approach to identify goals and develop measures.

Evaluate Quality and Productivity Using Measures

LPC wants to see high learner satisfaction (level 1) results because it believes that this is a good measure of whether students found the coursework relevant to their jobs.

To the extent possible, LPC benchmarks itself against other learning organizations and strives to be at the leading edge of such organizations. It also compares current performance to previous performance. LPC has reduced the average cost per learner day from $520 to $284. The primary source of savings comes from the use of technology and the use of courses that are developed in the marketplace. Currently, 20 percent of the learning is technology enabled. The goal is to reach 50 percent.

The learning network model suggests a continuous process of assessing competency gaps, feeding results to the business councils, changing training to address the identified gaps and other needs. The whole point is that the results of learning activities and the assessment of those activities will influence the day-to-day operation of Lucent. Harrod emphasized the power of measurement to drive performance.

H.1. *U.S. News and World Report*

Overview

Since 1983, *U.S. News and World Report* has published an annual ranking of U.S. colleges and universities based on various dimensions of quality. The special issues have attracted millions of readers and have become a huge market with other publishing companies joining *U.S. News* in putting out their own annual rankings (e.g., *Time, Barron's,* and others).

U.S. News is neither a customer nor a provider. Aware of this role, most institutions voluntarily provide the company with the data needed to rank top programs in defined disciplines. The company plays the role of an intermediary and sees itself as one potential source of information to customers of higher education. In this capacity as an intermediary assessing the quality of institutions, the *U.S. News* rankings exemplify a Model 2 approach to Phase Two provider assessment.

U.S. News assessment ranks institution programs according to a score that is a composite of several quality measures. The system defines quality along dimensions including reputation of a school, selectivity, faculty resources, financial resources, and many others. The organization publishes three different rankings: (1) best colleges, (2) best value (based on quality and cost), and (3) best graduate programs. The assessment is intended to benefit customers by helping students and their families determine the right school for them based on the specific dimensions of quality considered in the rankings.

The implicit assumption of this assessment system is that the same yardstick can be used to evaluate the quality of education in a variety of institutions serving a wide range of students. *U.S. News* assumes that the rankings will help students make an informed decision about appropriate colleges and universities to which they will apply. The company explicitly states that the rankings should serve as only one source in the decisionmaking process.

U.S. News does not hold universities and programs accountable based on these measures. However, the rankings generate strong readership, and some customers may hold schools indirectly accountable based on these measures because of market pressure. Although the assessment was not designed to help improve school quality, there is evidence that schools do modify their behavior in pursuit of higher scores on the dimensions of quality considered by *U.S. News*. Although some providers would argue that rankings are a detriment to the education system, they readily accept and publicize high rankings in their marketing literatures. Some institutions have even incorporated the *U.S. News* ranking as a quality measure in their internal assessment process.[1]

The process does not encourage any formal collaboration among key stakeholders at any step of the assessment process. *U.S. News* determines the assessment criteria, conducts the analysis, and provides the results to the consumer. The company is dependent, however, on stakeholders (i.e., colleges and universities) to provide accurate data. Indirectly, external criticisms are reviewed and may lead to changes in the assessment protocols. The rankings have drawn criticism for the way that measures are weighted in an approach that "lacks any defensible empirical or theoretical basis," according to a report by the National Opinion Research Center (Reisberg, 2000, p. 1). *U.S. News* has also been criticized for changing the weighting method periodically, preventing accurate comparisons from year to year. Critics find weakness in the way that some measures are used more than once for certain indicators and others that are considered by the higher education community to be important measures of quality, such as student experiences and curriculum, are not used at all. For example, the absence of both a good student satisfaction measure as well as a measure of the difficulty of the curriculum is seen as a flaw in the rankings (Reisberg, 2000).

The information is published and sold at all major newsstands, and some of the information is also available on the Internet for free. The publications have been very popular among students and their families as a source of information on the quality of institutions of higher education and a comparison of best values for their education dollars. With the growing popularity of the publication, universities fear that they may lose their customers if they are poorly ranked. Reputation of institutions are enhanced or tarnished to some extent based on the position in the rankings.

Phase One

U.S. News rankings consider individual institutions, rather than the higher education system as a whole. Therefore, Phase One assessment is not part of this effort.

---

[1]See Appendix K.3 for a description of the USC School of Education, which uses *U.S. News* rankings as a measure of quality.

Phase Two

In ranking colleges and universities along specified dimensions of quality, the *U.S. News* acts as an intermediary assessing the quality of provider institutions and thus illustrates a Model 2 assessment approach to Phase Two.

Identify Goals for Education and Training

The *U.S. News* rankings system implicitly attributes goals to institutions. The ranking system is based on indicators that are thought to measure academic quality, such as reputation and faculty, and on a ranking formula that weights the indicators by level of importance. The criteria used to calculate a school's score and ranking are based on an understood model of what a "good college" or "good graduate program" is. The goals are attributed to institutions of higher education in general. They are not linked to the mission of a specific institution or tailored to individual institutions.

The assessment is completely intermediary driven. *U.S. News* determines the variables used in the ranking, and the only role that universities play is to provide data to the company. Input from schools on the actual assessment process is virtually nonexistent; only when universities went public with their criticisms did the *U.S. News* take action in adjusting its variables. The goals are mainly input- and outcome-focused. Typical categories of goals include the following:

- *Academic Reputation* captures the quality of programs offered by the academic institutions.
- *Selectivity* captures the academic strength and overall ambition of the student population.
- *Faculty Resources* captures the strength, quality, and accessibility of each institution's professors.
- *Financial Resources* is used to capture the variety of things (e.g., student services, physical plants, research opportunities) available to students.
- *Retention* is used to indicate student satisfaction and success.
- *Alumni Giving* is used to indicate alumni satisfaction with their undergraduate experience at the institution.

Develop Measures of Quality and Productivity

According to *U.S. News*, "the ranking system relies on quantitative measures that education experts have proposed as reliable indicators of academic quality." Published reports by the company reveal little about who these experts are and how the particular measures are selected.

The "best colleges" ranking system is based on groupings developed by the Carnegie Foundation for the Advancement of Teaching, "the generally accepted classification system of colleges and universities that defines schools by their mission." Almost 1,400 accredited four-year institutions are considered for the rankings: 228 "national universities," 162 "national liberal arts colleges," 504 "regional universities," and 429 "regional liberal arts colleges."

While *U.S. News* may define its rankings differently for colleges and graduate programs, some of the same quality dimensions (i.e., academic reputation, selectivity, and faculty resources) are used across rankings; the measures may have been adapted slightly or weighted differently to fit the needs of the ranking. For instance, in evaluating selectivity scale, the "best colleges" ranking includes SAT scores while the graduate programs ranking includes the GRE, GMAT, and others. Tables H.1.1 and H.1.2 summarize the measures used for the best colleges and best graduate programs rankings.

The "best-value" ranking considers the following:

- The ratio of quality to price. A school's quality ranking—its overall score in America's best colleges survey—was divided by the cost to an average student there receiving a grant meeting his or her financial need. The higher the ratio of quality rank to the discounted cost, the better the value.
- Percentage of all undergraduates receiving grants that meet financial needs during the 1997–98 academic year.
- The percentage of a school's total costs covered by the average need-based grant to undergraduates.

Table H.1.1

Measures Used in Best Colleges Ranking

Quality Dimension	Measures
Academic reputation	Survey rating in academic programs of peer institutions on a 5-point scale (1 = marginal to 5 = distinguished). A "don't know" option is also available.
Selectivity	Acceptance rate. Percentage of admitted students who enrolled. Average SAT1 scores of enrolled students. High school class standing of entering freshmen.
Faculty resources	Ratio of full-time faculty to full-time students. Percentage of full-time faculty with doctorates. Percentage of faculty with full-time status. Average salary for all full-time faculty, adjusted for cost of living using the Runzheimer International indexes. Class size: both the percentage with less than 20 students and the percentage with more that 50 students.
Financial resources	Total expenditure for education programs per full-time equivalent enrollment. Expenditure for research, financial aid, public service, operation, and maintenance per full-time equivalent enrollment.
Retention	Average percentage of students graduating within six years. Average percentage of entering students who returned for the sophomore year. The graduation rate performance: difference between the school's predicted graduation rate and its actual graduation rate.
Alumni Giving	Average percentage of undergraduate alumni who donate to the university.

Table H.1.2

Measures Used in Professional and Academic Graduate Program Rankings

Quality Dimension	Measures
Reputation	Two survey ratings: quality of programs on a 5-point scale (1 = marginal to 5 = distinguished), and the top 25 graduate programs.
Selectivity	Standardized test scores (GMAT, MCAT, LSAT, GRE). Undergraduate grade point average. Acceptance rates.
Placement success	Employment rates after graduation and several months after. Total compensation (business programs). Bar passage rates (law schools).
Faculty resources	This measure differs to some degree for each area of study. Only the scale for business programs did not take into account this measure.
Financial resources	Expenditures per student for instruction, library, and supporting student services; student-to-teacher ratio. Expenditures per student for financial aid and other expenditures. Total number of volumes and titles in the law library (law schools).

NOTE: Ph.D. programs were considered on the reputation scale only.

Surveys and university data from enrollment rates to expenditures are the data used in the assessment process. *U.S. News* is dependent on the academic institutions to provide data and to complete the surveys. Missing data are retrieved from other sources such as the Wintergreen Orchard House and the National Collegiate Athletic Association. Data are also cross-referenced with other associations for accuracy.

For the academic reputation scale, surveys are sent to 4,200 college presidents, deans, and admissions directors. Each of the surveys accounts for a share of this scale. For the remaining scales, *U.S. News* requests data from institutions that are used to conduct the analyses.

Evaluate Quality and Productivity Using Measures

The ranking system is inherently a peer benchmarking activity. Overall rank is determined by tabulating and weighting the data along the variables listed in each of the categories above. The scales (e.g., reputation, selectivity) are also weighted. Institutions are ranked according to the overall weighted score. Weight given to the different categories are listed in Table H.1.3 by type of school.

Table H.1.3

Weight Given to Different Categories of Measures by Type of School (in percentage)

Category	National Schools Weight	Regional Schools Weight
Academic reputation	25	25
Selectivity	15	15
Faculty resources	20	20
Financial resources	10	10
Retention	20	25
Alumni giving	5	5
Graduation rate performance	5	0

A similar approach is used for graduate professional programs. Weighted average of several scales are used to determine the overall ranking of schools. The scales differ slightly from one professional area to the next.

To determine best value, overall rank was determined by converting the scores achieved by every school in each of the three variables discussed above into percentiles. The highest score on each of the variables was valued at 100 percent. The scores for the other schools were then taken as a percentage of this top score.

The first variable—the ratio of quality to price—accounted for 60 percent of the overall score, the percentage of all undergraduates receiving grants accounted for 25 percent of the score, and the average discount accounted for 15 percent of cost. The weighted percentage scores for each school were totaled. The school with the highest total weighted points became number one in its category. Next, its score was converted into a percentile of 100. The scores for the other schools were then converted into a percentage of that achieved by the number one school and ranked in descending order.

School administrators provide their input in the evaluation process when they complete the surveys on the reputation scale. However, *U.S. News* conducts the overall assessment from scale analysis to ranking of institutions.

I.1. Baldrige Award

Overview

The Malcolm Baldrige National Quality Award program seeks to assess the overall performance management system of participating organizations and to recognize those that excel. The objective of the award is to help U.S. organizations meet the highest standards by improving current practices in performance and quality.

The Baldrige Award program was established in the late 1980s as many industry and government leaders recognized the need to establish a standard of excellence for organizations striving for quality and efficiency. These efforts resulted in the passage of the Malcolm Baldrige National Quality Act of 1987 (Public Law 100-107). Over the years, the award has gained significant prestige within industry and government. Because of high demand for the program, last year it was expanded to include organizations from education and health care sectors as well.

The Department of Commerce is responsible for the award, and the National Institute of Standards and Technology[1] (NIST) manages the program with assistance from the American Society for Quality. A board of overseers, made up of members from industry handpicked by the Secretary of Commerce, directs the award program and determines whether the evaluation process and requirements are adequate.

The annual award is presented to three organizations from five different sectors. The board of examiners[2] conducts evaluations of all participating organizations and recommends approval of award winners to NIST. Regardless of award status, each organization is given detailed feedback of strengths and areas for improvement. Award recipients are required to share their performance and quality strategies with other institutions that may be interested in improving their own standards.

[1]NIST is a U.S. Department of Commerce agency.

[2]The board of examiners consists of expert volunteers from the business, health care, government, and education sectors.

The purpose of the award is to help organizations improve and gain a competitive edge by delivering better value to customers and by improving their performance. The award has three main objectives (NIST, 1995):

- to promote awareness of the importance of quality improvement to the national economy
- to recognize organizations that have made substantial improvements in products, services, and overall competitive performance
- to foster sharing of best practices information among U.S. organizations.

This purpose is linked to the Department of Commerce's mission of improving the competitiveness of each participating organization in the global marketplace.

The award criteria set standards for the level of assessment that institutions must undertake and evaluate them along specified dimensions related to quality. Organizations volunteer to participate in the program's assessment process because they view it as a means of self-improvement. Many organizations report having better employee relations, higher productivity and profitability as a result of their participation. Companies also report improved customer satisfaction after implementing Baldrige recommendations.

Organizations from several sectors including manufacturing, service, and small business participate in this program. The Baldrige model assumes that different business sectors share common core requirements for excellence in quality and productivity. It is the manner in which these requirements are addressed that may vary between organizations. Because the measures are not specific, the approach is adaptable; the assessment focus is on outcome and on common requirements rather than on detailed procedures.

Among the business community, the award is held in high esteem. Winning companies become quality advocates for other institutions and inform them on the benefits of using the Baldrige framework. In fact, companies are also asked to provide information on their performance strategies and methods so that others may learn from them.

Phase One

The Baldrige program is concerned with the quality and productivity of organizations, not systems. Therefore, Phase One does not apply.

Phase Two

In administering the Baldrige program, NIST acts as an intermediary in assessing the quality and productivity of institutions and thus exemplifies Phase Two, Model 2.

The Baldrige Award criteria are designed to evaluate institutions based on seven specified dimensions that have been identified as leading indicators of quality.

Identify Goals for Education and Training

The underlying assumption is that organizations can improve quality if they have a process in place that can measure quality. The Baldrige Award focuses mainly on outcome goals that are structured around seven categories:

- leadership
- strategic planning
- customer and market focus (students and other stakeholders)
- information and analysis
- human resource focus (faculty and staff)
- process management
- business results (school performance).

Each category is reviewed and adapted to fit the needs of a given sector. To this end, appropriateness of core concepts and criteria elements are considered.

Several stakeholders provide input into the goal determination process. Stakeholders include the following:

- U.S. Congress, which passed the bill creating the award. It also has the authority to add additional sectors as it sees fit.
- Trustees of the Foundation for the Malcolm Baldrige Award; they include prominent leaders from U.S. organizations who raise funds for the program.
- The Secretary of Commerce.
- The National Institute of Standards and Technology, which manages the program.
- The board of overseers, which is an advisory committee of distinguished leaders to the Department of Commerce.

It is unclear how the original seven criteria in the assessment process were selected. With regard to the education criteria, however, we do know that the measures were adapted from the original protocol developed for the business community. In 1995, NIST launched a pilot study to determine the appropriateness of the protocol for the education industry. First, the Baldrige criteria were distributed to educational leaders who reviewed the core methodology and provided feedback. Second, an education protocol was adapted to include industry-specific issues and language. The protocol was then distributed to a team of evaluators for training and implementation.

Develop Measures of Quality and Productivity

The model for education uses mainly outcome measures and some input measures which include the following:

- The leadership indicator measures system level decisionmaking and public responsibility. It focuses on the leadership's ability to integrate key objectives (e.g., clear goals, high expectations) in the institution's management system.
- The strategic planning indicator measures the institution's overall strategy development and deployment. It focuses on the institution's ability to set appropriate directions and to implement action plans effectively.
- The student and stakeholder indicator examines whether the institution understands the needs and expectations of students and other relevant stakeholders, such as parents or employers. The indicator also captures an institution's relationship with key stakeholders.
- The information and analysis indicator measures the selection and use of information and data and of comparative information, and it reviews school performance.
- The faculty and staff focus indicator examines

  > how the school enables faculty and staff to develop and utilize their full potential, aligned with the school's objectives. Also examined are the school's efforts to build and maintain an environment and climate conducive to performance excellence, full participation, and personal and organizational growth (NIST, 1999).

- Educational and support process management is an indicator that focuses on how educational programs and support functions are designed, implemented, and improved.
- The school performance results indicator focuses on measures that capture the success of an institution's overall mission.

Table I.1.1 indicates some of the specific measures used in the assessment process for each of the seven criteria.

Evaluate Quality and Productivity Using Measures

Evaluation of each organization is conducted in four stages. In the first stage, each institution submits a written application, which is reviewed by five evaluators who score and provide comments along the seven different dimensions. In this application, an institution must submit information on key processes along with information on the seven award criteria. Since participation is voluntary, institutions are motivated to provide all the required information. The information is provided completely by stakeholders within a given institution including students, staff, and faculty. Comments on strengths and areas for improvement are written in the application scorebook, which determines whether an applicant moves to the next stage. If an applicant is not selected, the applicant receives a detailed feedback report. In the second stage, a team of evaluators determines through a consensus review which higher scoring applicants will be visited. Applicants not selected for the site visit will receive feedback reports based on written comments from this review. The evaluation process is based on a point system. Each organization is scored on the seven criteria weighted by level of importance and may receive a maximum score of 1,000. Table I.1.2 indicates the point distribution for each criterion.

In the third stage, a team of evaluators conducts site visits to promising institutions. The evaluators up to this point in the evaluation accept the information provided by the institutions at face value. The purpose of these visits is to see firsthand the organization's performance, to investigate information and claims made by the institution, and to clarify key questions or issues discussed in earlier reviews. After the visit, a feedback report is prepared for the applicant.

In stage four, all written documentation is reviewed, and the evaluators' recommendations are passed on to NIST. More than 300 people, largely from the private sector, volunteer to join the board of examiners to evaluate the organizations that have been selected as semifinalists. The evaluators are leading experts from the five different sectors and are selected through a competitive application process. The Secretary of Commerce selects several judges among the list of examiners who will determine which organizations will be finalists for the award. Finally, NIST reviews the nominations and determines the winners. Award certifications are marked with the presidential seal.

Table I.1.1

Examples of Measures Used in the Baldrige Award

Core Concept		Some Examples
I.	Leadership	
	Leadership system	Description of school leadership system and operations. Description of the role of senior leaders.
	Public responsibility	Current and potential impacts on society due to operations.
II.	Strategic Planning	
	Strategy development process	Needs of stakeholders, internal and external factors, and opportunities.
	School strategy	Summary of strategy and action plans (e.g., differences in short- and long-term plans, tracking of performance relative to plans).
III.	Student and Stakeholder Focus	
	Knowledge of student needs and expectations	How are needs determined and analyzed? How does the school determine and anticipate changing needs and expectations of future students?
	Student and stakeholder satisfaction	Strategies used to provide effective relationships to key stakeholders. Processes in place to determine stakeholder satisfaction.
IV.	Information and Analysis	
	Selection and use of data	Overall information management in support of institution goals.
	Selection and use of comparative information and data	Which needs and priorities drive the data collection effort? For what purpose? What sources are used? How is the information used to drive improvement?
	Analysis and review of school performance	How are the different data gathered integrated to evaluate school performance? What analyses are conducted? How are the analyses used to review and improve performance?
V.	Faculty and Staff Focus	
	Work systems	How do work and job design and faculty and staff compensation and recognition affect student and institution performance?
	Faculty/staff education and training	How does the institution meet these needs? How do these needs, once fulfilled, affect both personnel and institution performance?
	Faculty and staff well-being and satisfaction	What assessment strategies are used to measure the maintenance of a healthy work environment and climate?

Table I.1.1—continued

Core Concept	Some Examples
VI. Educational/ Support Process Management	
Education design and delivery	Information on design and delivery of programs, on types of programs offered, and on processes in place to achieve better performance.
Education support processes	How does the institution design, maintain, and improve its support processes?
VII. School Performance Results	
Student performance	Trends comparison within and across institutions to detect longitudinal improvements and sensitivity of the institution to improve education for all students.
Student and stakeholder satisfaction results	Trends in satisfaction that are also compared with peer institutions.
Faculty and staff results	Generic and/or institution-specific human resource factors.
School-specific results	Other specific information that helps the institution achieve it goals (e.g., cost containment, school innovations, community contributions).

SOURCE: NIST, *Education Criteria for Performance Excellence* (1999). Malcolm Baldrige National Quality Award.

Table I.1.2

Baldrige Scoring System: Points Awarded by Area

Criteria	Total Points
Leadership	110
Strategic planning	80
Student and stakeholder focus	80
Information and analysis	80
Faculty and staff focus	100
Education and support process management	100
School performance results	450

With more than 400 evaluators and staff involved in the award process, the cost is fairly high. The federal government contributes about $4.9 million to NIST for the program. This investment is leveraged by millions of dollars in contributions from the private sector as well as from state and local organizations. The program also generates funds by charging participating institutions application fees. Companies with more than 500 employees are charged close to $4,500, while those with fewer employees are charged $1,500. Nonprofit institutions are charged only $300. Of course, the internal costs beyond fees are unknown, although they are probably high.

Most often, the evaluation process is used by the participating organizations for self-improvement and for comparison with peer institutions. The goal is to self-evaluate, compare, reflect, and develop processes for improvement. Excellence in quality and productivity is perceived as an outcome of a continuous evaluation process.

J. Certifiers of Student Competencies

Overview

Certifiers of student competencies are intermediaries in the education and professional development process, even if they happen to provide education as well. Their purpose is to certify that students have achieved a clearly defined level of knowledge, skill, ability, expertise, or aptitude. The focus of assessment is on the learner rather than on the provider.

In competency-based education and training, where the certifier also provides education, assessment (including the design of assessment instruments) is often integrated into the education and training activities. Curriculum development is closely linked to and even driven by the definition of competencies and the operationalization of those competencies in the assessment instruments.

In recent years, there has been increased attention focused on the concept of student competencies by government, business leaders, and educators as an innovative approach to education and training, as well as assessment. Competency-based assessment focuses on individual student outcomes and operationalizes the specified competencies and helps determine where instruction is needed (Pottinger and Goldsmith, 1979). This allows educators to organize courses and instruction around the gap between what students already know and what they should know to demonstrate a level of proficiency in a particular area.

Competency-based education benefits students because it gives them recognition of past achievements, portability of course credits, and a system for lifelong learning (Paulson and Ewell, 1999). Institutions value competency-based education and training because they encourage stakeholders to closely examine what is important for students to know and instructors to teach as well as target scarce resources where they will be most effective (Mager, 1997).

Phase One

When the certification of student competencies is conducted by a system-level intermediary, there is substantial overlap between Phase One assessment and the process of identifying goals in Phase Two. However, if the certification of student competencies is conducted by a provider serving many customers, then

Phase One will normally be conducted by the customer or stakeholder (if at all), while Phase Two is conducted by the provider. Because the latter example is more common in the education and professional development arena, we discuss the approaches used to define goals in terms of Phase Two assessment here. Many of the techniques described here could also be used in Phase One by a system-level certifier interested in a Model 4 approach.

Phase Two

Competency-based education and professional development provides examples of Model 4 assessment approach.

Identify Goals for Education and Training

The competencies identified as critical to a customer or other stakeholder embody the goals of education and professional development.

There are different ideas about how to define competencies. The most common method is to identify tasks and a definition of their successful accomplishment that define competency in a certain domain. Critics argue that this oversimplifies performance in the real world by ignoring the relationship between tasks and other factors that influence performance. Another approach to competency definition looks only at general characteristics needed for effective job performance, for example, critical thinking skills or communication skills. This method of competency definition ignores the need for different skills in different domains and that

> individuals demonstrate little capacity to transfer expertise from one area to another . . . and [this] provides limited help for those involved in the practical work of designing education and training programs for specific professions (Gonczi, 1994, p. 29).

A more integrated approach combines defined tasks as well as cross-cutting skills to define the knowledge, skills, and abilities needed to perform effectively in particular domain areas. In this approach, "competence is conceived of as complex structuring of attributes needed for intelligent performance in specific situations" (ibid.).

The steps involved in defining competencies are a "reverse engineering" process where jobs are broken down, organized into domains, and an assessment system developed around them. Most approaches begin with a job analysis and the decomposition of roles by defining what an individual should be able to do under particular circumstances. These performance descriptions should be developed by all the stakeholders who have an interest in the degree or certification being awarded. Performance descriptions should be specific to the institution and degree and specified as valid for a determined time period (Paulson and Ewell, 1999).

The next step involves "chunking" or grouping the competencies into domains and subdomains, rather than just producing a laundry list of tasks that individuals should be able to perform. This step allows flexibility in awarding degrees and credentials because students can focus on subareas and earn lower-level certifications without having to complete an entire sequence of courses that may not be useful to them. This allows institutions to serve the wide-ranging needs of a diverse student body.

The federal government has recognized the benefits of conducting job analysis to identify the necessary competencies for certain jobs. The Department of Labor Secretary's Commission on Achieving Necessary Skills (SCANS) initiative was undertaken with the intent of linking competencies and skills needed by the business community and government to what is taught in schools.

SCANS aims to "define the skills needed for employment, propose acceptable levels of proficiency, suggest effective ways to assess proficiency and develop a dissemination strategy" (SCANS, 1991, p. xv). The SCANS team had meetings and discussions with business and government leaders, created six special panels, and commissioned researchers to conduct interviews throughout the business sector. The competencies and foundation skills that they identified are based on an analysis of 15 jobs,

> through detailed, in-depth interviews, lasting up to four hours each, with job holders or their supervisors. The interviews explored the general job description, confirmed ratings of the importance of skills, and inquired about "critical incidents" and illustrative tasks and tools used on the job (SCANS, 1991, D-1).

While SCANS acknowledges that technical expertise varies between industries, it posits that the basic competencies or "workplace know-how" is the same for all types of jobs. SCANS identified five major categories of skills that are needed across the spectrum in all industries: resources, interpersonal, information, systems, and technology. In addition, according to SCANS, students need a three-part foundation consisting of basic skills, thinking skills, and personal qualities.

Private industry has also acknowledged the benefits of identifying competencies. American College Testing (ACT) has developed a program called Work Keys, which is a system for employers to use in hiring to determine how candidates match job requirements and where they need training.

Using SkillPro (ACT proprietary software), an analyst develops a list of tasks most relevant to the job under review using company information, job descriptions, and the Dictionary of Occupational Titles. It is then revised and amended by experienced employees who decide which tasks are most critical to the job. This is followed by an assessment of which Work Keys skills are relevant and at what level they are needed for the job. The desired skill level is determined "on both importance (significance of task to overall job performance) and relative time spent (compared to other tasks)" (ACT, 1999). ACT also conducts assessments of current skill levels in up to eight critical areas: reading for information, applied mathematics, applied technology, teamwork, listening, locating information, observation, and writing. In addition, Work Keys includes an instructional support component to help educators assist students/learners improve their workplace skills. ACT also developed a series of guides called *Targets for Instruction,* which give

> detailed descriptions of particular skill areas and of characteristics that distinguish each skill level. The targets are designed as springboards for building curricula and training materials tailored to the specific needs of the client (ACT, 1997, p. 8).

Work Keys is used in a wide variety of industries including technology, manufacturing, service, and retail. ACT has profiled over 5,000 jobs in both white- and blue-collar occupations (ACT, 1997).

Develop Measures of Quality and Productivity

Competency-based education uses student tests as a measure of performance. These tests may be traditional standardized, paper-and-pencil or computer-based tests (such as state licensing examinations or tests sponsored by ACT) or tests that require a learner to demonstrate a skill in a practical setting.

The organization of competencies into domains and subdomains also aids in the process of developing measures by distinguishing between job-specific competencies and more-generic skills. The skills can be categorized separately, allowing assessments to be customized for a wide range of degree and certification types using the cross-cutting skill assessments to augment the profession-specific measurement tools (Paulson and Ewell, 1999).

Evaluate Quality and Productivity Using Measures

As described above, the development of measures and evaluation of performance follows directly from the process of identifying goals (i.e., identifying competencies). The defined competencies reflect the desired endpoint—what is required of students to know or do. Performance measures are designed to reflect how much they know or how much they can do. Normally, performance is compared to some objective standard or desired end state that is specified in the process of identifying the goals of education and professional development.

The competency-based evaluation method is appealing because it

> enables us to come closer than we have in the past to assessing what we want to assess—the capacity of the professional to integrate knowledge, values, attitudes and skills in the world of practice (Gonczi, 1994, p. 28).

It requires an integrated approach because knowledge, skills, and attitudes are closely connected in their influence on job performance. Such evaluations not only "directly test performance but also suggest how individual knowledge and skill elements should be combined" (Paulson and Ewell, 1999, p. 10). To the extent that competency-based assessment is a tool for measuring the need for instruction, it is also a tool for determining when education or training is not necessary. A variety of methods should be employed in competency-based assessment and efforts made to evaluate performance directly in real world situations when feasible (Gonczi, 1994). It is, however, time consuming and expensive to go through this process, and to update the competencies and the assessment mechanisms. In addition, many observers are skeptical that a competency-based education approach will be embraced by the academic community (Carnevale, 2000).

Example: The Western Governors University

The Western Governors University (WGU), established in 1997, has been a leader in higher education's competency-based approach to education. The university was created to address several challenges, including

> a wide geographic dispersion of students; non-traditional students, such as adults employed full time, seeking part-time enrollment; scarcity of workers in certain highly trained occupations; rising student costs of attaining higher education; existing and potential duplication of effort among states in developing courses and programs; failure of existing higher educational institutions to recognize and acknowledge skills and

> abilities which students already possess; and inadequate information to students about educational opportunities and choices (Testa, 1999, p. 3).

WGU differs from traditional institutions of higher education in that the degree and certificate programs[1] are defined by a set of competencies that students must demonstrate rather than a set of courses they must take. Thus, WGU's primary effort is directed toward defining an appropriate set of competencies, developing valid and reliable methods for measuring those competencies, and helping students identify learning opportunities that can help them acquire competencies they are lacking. The attainment of a degree or certificate is not based on credit hours, but the successful completion of a set of competency tests. In fact, students may earn a degree or certification without taking courses if they can demonstrate competency in a domain area (ibid.).

WGU faculty plays a key role in the design and development of programs and tests designed to assess performance. Actual courses are delivered by distance learning providers, which are approved by WGU for providing education that fosters the development of specific competencies. Programs are developed through analysis, research, competency and assessment development, content identification, implementation, and a review and evaluation process. The research and analysis portion of program development ensures that there is a demand in the proposed subject area, both by students and the job market, and information is collected on content, providers, and assessment.

The competencies are developed by special program councils that are composed of experts in the field. The council members come together to identify the required "knowledge, skills and abilities (ksa's) that students would be required to demonstrate within a discrete area of competence" (ibid., p. 5). These "ksa's" are organized into domains and more-detailed subdomains of competencies required for a degree or certificate. In developing competency statements, council members consider the target audience, including their educational and skill level; characteristics of the students enrolled in the program (adult, full or part-time); the types of jobs that the degree or certification may lead to; and finally, the types of skills and abilities that should be demonstrated by successful graduates.

The WGU appoints an assessment council for "overall oversight for the development, approval and delivery of WGU assessments" (ibid., p. 8). The

[1]WGU is currently a candidate for accreditation. Current degree programs offered include a general AA, an AAS in electronics manufacturing engineering, an AAS in information technology, and an MA in learning and technology. WGU is building a bachelor's degree in business.

assessment council works with the program council to ensure that assessments are appropriate for the competencies being measured.

K.1. University of Phoenix

Overview

The University of Phoenix, formed in 1976, is a for-profit higher education institution. Offering mainly night classes, it serves working adults, generally 35 to 39 years old. Students take five- or six-week-long courses, one at a time. Many of the faculty are part-time instructors who have full-time jobs elsewhere. The school serves approximately 49,000 students at 65 campuses in 15 states, Puerto Rico, Vancouver, British Columbia, and via distance education. About 9,500 students are served via the distance education program.

The University of Phoenix has a centrally developed curriculum for every program, which facilitates centralized assessment. No matter who is teaching a course, certain baseline content is observed, and specific outcomes are expected (so students know what is expected of them). All of the courses are developed by content experts. The general education curriculum consists of courses that focus on written communication skills, oral presentation skills, critical thinking skills, problem-solving skills, self-reflection, and an appreciation of diversity. In addition, the university offers certificate and degree programs in a number of fields, such as business, health care, education, counseling and human services, technology, and management. Campuses cannot develop new credit-bearing courses.

Assessment practices were not developed until the mid-1980s. The University of Phoenix has a number of different mechanisms in place for measuring quality, most of which were originally implemented to demonstrate the school's quality to the external world, but are now used for internal improvement purposes as well. For example, faculty can be recruited and trained.

The purpose of the assessment process is to measure value added, customer satisfaction, and to ensure that certain inputs and processes are in place across the campuses. The portfolio of assessment practices enables the University of Phoenix to measure the quality of the curriculum as well as the quality of administrative practices.

The university has regional accreditation from the Commission on Institutions of Higher Education of the North Central Association of Colleges and Schools. It also has programmatic accreditation in nursing and counseling. The North

Central regional accrediting agency is moving toward outcomes assessment, which suits University of Phoenix purposes well.

Phase One

Since the customers served by the University of Phoenix do not compose a system as we are using the term, Phase One assessment is not relevant.

Phase Two

The University of Phoenix provides a clear example of a Model 3 approach—the university is the provider and it conducts its own self-assessment. Below we provide detailed descriptions of the various assessment processes carried out by the university. The university's assessment practices are consistent with the centralized structure of the university's operations, curriculum development, etc. Since it is accredited, it also makes use of Model 2, but we are focusing on its internal assessment.

Identify Goals for Education and Training

The University of Phoenix is both the provider and assessor. As a for-profit provider of education, the institution focuses on what customers (both actual students and their employers) want. Market forces imply that the University of Phoenix's goals are linked to the needs and desires of the student body and the career orientation. To provide customers with an opportunity to express their opinions, the university makes extensive use of student and employer surveys and conducts extensive market research. A variety of stakeholders, including students, alumni, faculty, and employers, are surveyed to gather information about how well courses are meeting each group's needs.

The University of Phoenix assessment practices are focused on the following goals:

1. Ensure students are learning.
2. Ensure students are learning the right things.
3. Ensure students are successfully employed.
4. Ensure students and employers are satisfied.
5. Ensure the university is making a profit.

Develop Measures of Quality and Productivity

To measure progress toward the myriad goals listed above the university has developed a number of assessment tools. Given its unique position in higher education, the university had to create its own assessment tools—none of the existing approaches fit its specific needs.

The primary assessment efforts are the Cognitive Outcomes Comprehensive Assessment (COCA), Adult Learning Outcomes Assessment (ALOA), Academic Quality Management System (AQMS), and Services Operating Report (SOR). The university's Institutional Research Department (IR) has primary responsibility for selecting the measures (and procedures) used by the entire system of campuses. The measures in use by the university focus on outcomes (student, instructor, and faculty satisfaction; student test scores), and inputs (resources are measured as part of the SOR, and faculty are queried regarding their satisfaction with resources provided to them). The unit of analysis may be the student, course, or campus. Both the student and teacher end-of-year surveys ask about the quality of the curriculum, the books, and supplemental materials. Students are also asked about the quality of the teaching and how well the class fits into their sequence of courses. Teachers evaluate the students (how well prepared they were), the classroom (physical space), and support from the central office. And, as noted, graduates, alumni, and employers are regularly surveyed.

COCA and ALOA Address Goal One: Ensure Students Are Learning. Students are tested at the beginning and end of each course to measure what they have learned. COCA is a cognitive assessment tool, while ALOA is an affective/behavioral assessment. The tools are developed by Phoenix faculty and IR. Faculty focus on content, while IR is responsible for ensuring the validity and reliability of the instruments. These tests are curriculum specific.

All students take the COCA and ALOA as a matriculation and graduation requirement. The instruments are revised whenever the curriculum is substantially changed. The results are given to the students, but not to faculty. Originally there was a problem with students not taking the tests seriously since they were not graded, but now students' scores count somewhat toward their capstone course grade, so they take the tests more seriously.

The cost of developing and administering these tests varies depending on the program, but it is not insubstantial (because the tests are developed internally). The university would like to utilize externally developed tests so it could do national norming and such, but there are no good tests available in most of the subject areas needed.

AQMS Addresses a Combination of Goals Two, Three, and Four: Ensure Students Are Learning the Right Things, Ensure Students Are Successfully Employed, and Ensure Students and Employers Are Satisfied. The university conducts several surveys to measure customer satisfaction. It surveys students and faculty at the end of each course, and these end-of-course surveys are similar. Both ask about the quality of the curriculum, the books, and supplemental materials. Students are also asked about the quality of the teaching and how well the class fits in their sequence of courses. Teachers evaluate the students (how well prepared they were), the classroom (physical space), and support from the central office. It typically gets a very high response rate from students (close to 100 percent). The faculty members' response rate is lower, probably about 60–70 percent (there is no penalty for them if they do not respond).

The university also regularly surveys alumni and employers. It asks alumni questions about whether they are getting promoted and how well their training met their employment needs. Employers are asked whether University of Phoenix graduates have the right skills. Alumni are typically surveyed at one, three, and five years out. The university sends surveys to all alumni but does not get a very high response rate.

Employers are surveyed periodically. The university considers employers to be its "shadow" consumers. It needs them to be happy since many firms provide tuition reimbursement to their employees. The response rate for employers is low.

AQMS includes more than the surveys; students also participate in exit interviews. Students are asked questions about such issues as financial aid, graduation requirements, and their satisfaction level. This is an ongoing process, since they continually conduct interviews. In addition, AQMS also includes a series of quarterly and monthly reports that address such issues as average class size.

IR develops the surveys and revises or updates them on an as-needed basis, but only when it is truly necessary. IR does not want to tinker with the instruments unnecessarily because it wants to be able to look at long-term trends. It will change surveys to reflect a change in direction at the university. When computer access became a major goal, for example, the surveys were changed to reflect that. The overall goal of the surveying is to gauge continued customer satisfaction.

IR ensures survey validity and reliability. The surveys are not expensive once they have been piloted or on a per-unit basis. Quarterly reports are sent to stakeholders; results are provided to campuses as an improvement device.

SOR Addresses Goal Five: Ensure the University Is Making a Profit. SOR focuses mostly on services and business operations. The vice president of the university generates the report that compares the campuses to create "healthy competition" between them. The report is used for "assessment of compliance with policies and procedures, work-flow enhancements, computer system development and prioritization needs, and training" (APQC Institute for Education Best Practices, 1987, p. 40). It looks at such things as student numbers, whether learning centers are turning their paperwork in on time, whether they are recording student numbers, and if group size is appropriate.

Other Efforts. Another element of the university's assessment is rigorous training of faculty. New faculty are assessed up front and enroll in a six-week-long training course. The training covers content-specific material as well as more general topics such as adult-learning theory. In addition, faculty are peer reviewed once every year and reviewed by the administration every other year.

Evaluate Quality and Productivity Using Measures

Evaluation of quality occurs on an ongoing basis, very much in a continuous process improvement model. Institutions are not graded, but they are compared with one another. The evaluation results are used to help institutions improve their performance. Campuses are not penalized per se for poor performance, but there is a quarterly incentive plan to link rewards with outcomes. Senior managers are the beneficiaries of the plan, but many of the judged areas depend on people working together.

All the data are analyzed at both the program and campus level, enabling comparisons across institutions at two levels. Benchmarking consists of comparing peer institutions (all of which are part of the university) and individual campus performance over time.

The data are also being used for improvement purposes. Specifically, the administration uses the results of the COCA and ALOA for institutional improvement. If students did poorly on a section of the test at one campus, the administration would work with the campus to improve. Or if students everywhere did poorly on a particular section, the administration would revise the course curriculum or determine if there is a problem with the teaching of the material. It does not try to link individual faculty to "poor" student cognitive outcomes.

The philosophy is "managing by exception"; the administration looks at outliers and then works with them to improve. It has also set up a buddy/mentorship program so schools that are not performing well in a particular area are matched with a campus that is doing well in that area. The university is committed to continuing with its assessment practices—"if it moves we measure it."[1]

The administration also conducts "campus reviews," which are very much like an accreditation visit. During campus reviews, the review team will look at financial, academic, and student information. It will conduct a debriefing at the end of the visit to discuss strengths and weaknesses, but a formal report is not issued.

The administration finds all of the assessment practices to be useful. And while campuses originally considered all of the assessment efforts to be a burden, assessment is now a valued part of the University of Phoenix culture. Campuses now want the information and complain when reports are delayed or cut back in any way. The data are available on a web site for speedy dissemination.

---

[1]Personal conversation with L. P. Noone, Provost/Senior Vice President, Academic Affairs, May 9, 2000.

K.2. U.S. Air Force Academy, Department of Management[1]

Overview

The U.S. Air Force Academy (USAFA) is an accredited[2] institution that provides undergraduate education to over 4,000 students. It is also an operational Air Force organization. Between 80 and 100 students per year have majored in management in recent years, and the department's "Introduction to Management" class is a required part of the core curriculum for all cadets.

The Department of Management (DFM) at the USAFA has a number of internal mechanisms in place for assessing quality and is also currently a candidate for accreditation by the International Association of Management Education/ American Assembly of Collegiate Schools of Business (IAME/AACSB).[3] Thus, DFM is using a combination of provider-based assessment and intermediary-based approaches to assessment. Because it is part of a U.S. military service academy, DFM has some unique characteristics relative to management schools at traditional universities. IAME/AACSB has been working to make the accreditation process more flexible and relevant for schools with specialized missions. This increased flexibility made accreditation a real possibility for DFM. DFM has chosen to pursue accreditation but is not required to do so.

Representatives from DFM feel that pursuing accreditation is not unreasonably expensive. They noted that they were already doing or planning to do many of the assessments, so that the cost of accreditation was really just the fee of $3,000 per year (which includes national testing materials) charged by AACSB, and they welcomed the opportunity to document what they are doing. In addition, they consider that the costs are amortized over a multiple-year period.

The department is in the process of strategic planning, which has involved several stages (U.S. Air Force Academy, 1997b, p. 3):

[1]The information contained in this appendix is based on a site visit with department of management faculty and a review of documents.

[2]USAFA is accredited by the North Central Association of Colleges and Schools.

[3]IAME/AACSB accredits business and management schools; formerly just the AACSB, it recently added IAME to its title, emphasizing its global perspective and management focus.

- Develop "adaptive" pedagogies (such as team teaching, seminar methods, and collaborative learning).
- Integrate the adaptive capacity into management courses.
- Develop a department mission statement and educational outcomes.
- Assess the accomplishment of mission and learning outcomes.
- Pursue program accreditation by IAME/AACSB.

DFM considers its current efforts to be for the benefit of the students, the Air Force, and DoD. With the increased emphasis on applying private-sector management practices in DoD, DFM teaching, research, and consulting activities can have important effects on the Air Force and DoD. The external recognition associated with IAME/AACSB accreditation can help amplify those effects. Accreditation would also help graduates of the program because many schools reduce the number of graduate credit hours required for an MBA for students who hold bachelor's degrees from accredited business programs. Accreditation may also help DFM attract high-quality faculty.

Phase One

The Department of Management does not engage in Phase One assessment per se. While it does consider the needs of its students as a whole, it does not conduct needs assessment of the entire Air Force as a system. The department staff clearly want the curriculum to meet the needs of the total Air Force but focus their efforts more on the cadets at the academy enrolled in the department's courses.

The department's vision is "to become the Air Force's renowned center of Management education and expertise." Its related mission statement describes how this vision will be operationalized:

> In our teaching, we faithfully develop cadets to become life-long learners who can creatively solve complex organizational problems through the adaptive use of information and communication. In our pursuit of knowledge, we continually advance and apply innovative, successful business practices. In our dedication to service, we actively value involvement with the academy, community, and other stakeholders. (Both the vision and mission appear in U.S. Air Force Academy, 1999b, p. 1.)

Phase Two

DFM provides an example of Model 3; it is a provider that conducts its own self-assessment. To do this, it has adopted the approach of requesting feedback both from internal and external stakeholders. By pursuing accreditation, DFM will be introducing elements of Model 2, since accrediting agencies are an intermediary form of assessment.

Identify Goals for Education and Training

Its assessment practices follow from and are linked to the vision, mission, and goals and are based on a balanced scorecard approach reflecting the perspectives of all stakeholders. The "suite" of assessment tools is designed to "provide critical information for key organizational decisions to DFM" (ibid.). Each of the tools is linked to one of the department's goals (teaching/curriculum, intellectual contribution/service, faculty).

At the institution level, interest in total quality management eventually evolved into the Educational Outcomes Assessment Working Group. The group identified the primary outcomes of interest for assessment: written communication, the ability to frame and resolve ill-defined problems, and intellectual curiosity.

During the process of seeking accreditation, the department has solicited input from numerous stakeholder groups including students in the capstone course, department faculty members, senior academy and Air Force leadership, targeted Air Force members, and recent graduates. DFM broadened its definition of stakeholders, realizing the potential importance of the local community. Therefore, it now considers owners and managers of businesses and not-for-profits in Colorado Springs to be its stakeholders and plan to solicit their input regarding course content and research and consulting activities.

Develop Measures of Quality and Productivity

The categories of measures relate to mission, faculty composition and development, curriculum content and evaluation, instructional resources and responsibilities, students, and intellectual contributions by faculty. The Director of Assessment is responsible for many of the procedures, others involved are the Director of Accreditation, AIC (Advisor in Charge), Director of Research, Director of Personnel, Director of Faculty Development, Department Head, and Appointees of the Dean of Faculty.

DFM has a number of measurement procedures in place including the following (U.S. Air Force Academy, 1999b):

- **Teaching/Curriculum**
  - EBI (Educational Benchmarking Institute) Student Satisfaction Survey: This is annually administered to gauge student satisfaction with teaching, advising, curriculum, facilities, career services, and student services. The results are benchmarked with a select group of comparison schools. EBI designs and administers the survey and performs the benchmarking.
  - ETS (Educational Testing Service) Content Exam (Major Field Test): Each year graduating students are given this exam, which addresses accounting, economics, management, quantitative business analysis, finance, marketing, legal and social environment, and international issues. The examination is developed, administered, and scored by ETS.
  - Course critiques: This instrument is used throughout the academy to solicit student feedback on the course and instructor. It is administered at the end of the course.
  - Focus groups (management major): Each spring semester, focus groups are held with 12–15 majors to gain insight on strengths and weaknesses of the major and learn more about students' experiences.
  - Focus groups (management core course): Each semester focus groups with 12–15 students from the core management course are held to solicit input from students about their experiences in the course.
  - Graduate survey: This survey, pilot tested in spring 1999, will be mailed to graduates one, two, and five years after graduation. The survey addresses students' perceptions of the major and degree, specifically the skills they learned and how useful those skills are after graduation.
  - Stakeholder interviews: These semi-structured interviews will be done periodically with different stakeholders to learn more about their perceptions of the major.
  - Number of management majors: An actual count of management majors to determine course offerings and manpower requirements.
- **Intellectual Contribution/Service**
  - Faculty presentations, publications, consultations, and faculty involvement: DFM tracks the number of presentations, publications, and consultations to gauge faculty research contributions.
  - Climate survey: Faculty are surveyed annually to assess their perceptions about such "climate" issues as leadership, communication, job design, etc.

- Promotion rate: DFM tracks the military and academic promotion rates of the faculty.
- Mid-year feedback: Midway through the academic year, the department solicits anonymous feedback from faculty on "things we do well" and "things we could do better."
- Faculty development: Attendance at faculty development courses provided by the USAFA Center for Educational Excellence is tracked.
- USAF and civilian appraisal systems: Each year faculty are evaluated (via forms and face-to-face meetings) on criteria such as number of presentations, publications, and consultations.

• **Faculty**

In addition to the department-level assessment efforts, DFM participates in a number of USAFA-wide assessment efforts.

- Unit self-assessment: Every three years (with annual updates), units report to the dean on such issues as leadership, information management, strategy, operational planning, etc.
- Educational outcomes assessment working group assessment phase one: A team representing multiple functions at the academy met for 18 months to study educational outcomes including senior cadet's ability to frame and resolve ill-defined problems, development of intellectual curiosity, faculty practices, and correlates of course and faculty-perceived effectiveness.
- Educational outcomes assessment working group assessment phase two: This team

  > met for 24 months to examine the core course contribution to three educational outcomes: breadth of fundamental knowledge, ability to frame and resolve ill-defined problems and intellectual curiosity (U.S. Air Force Academy, 1999b, p. 10).

- The academy surveys graduates and supervisors of USAFA graduates. They conduct time studies of how cadets spend their time, social climate surveys, and various tests to assess moral reasoning.

These assessments appear to emphasize improvement. DFM conducted a self-assessment based on the accreditation standards (which is part of the accreditation process). In addition, as a publicly funded institution, the staff feel a need to demonstrate accountability.

Evaluate Quality and Productivity Using Measures

A few of the measures in the above-mentioned categories include specific objective criteria against which performance can be evaluated. For example,

DFM wants to "recruit and attract qualified civilian instructors to maintain a 75/25 mix between Air Force and civilian faculty" so they can easily keep data on the mix of faculty. Many of their measures are not quantifiable (e.g., "continue overall faculty planning process in the 'big picture' format") so data will be harder to collect for such measures (U.S. Air Force Academy, 1999a, p. 9).

DFM is also making use of external benchmarks: other USAFA departments and management programs at other schools. DFM would like to be in the top 15 percent on 80 percent of the EBI Student Satisfaction Survey factors that apply to USAFA. With the ETS Content Exam, DFM would like the student score to be above 95 percent overall. DFM would like to be above the USAFA average for the course critiques (greater than 5.0 on instructor items). DFM would like to have a minimum of 100 majors per class to maintain their functional expertise level. Presentations, publications, and consultations should total at least 50 intellectual contributions for the department annually, with 100 percent of the faculty involved in outreach and dissemination activities. DFM strives to be above the USAFA average on three of the climate survey outcome measures (overall satisfaction, morale, and department effectiveness). DFM would like to achieve a promotion rate of 90 percent for academic positions and rates above the USAF average for military promotions.

IAME/AACSB sponsors tests and surveys that allow the institution to compare itself with other institutions. For example, there is a standardized content exam run by ETS. These tests allow the institution to compare how the students at the USAFA are doing overall. USAFA students have been scoring extremely well on these tests. They also allow the school to evaluate the effects of changes in the curriculum. For example, the school recently added a course on international business to the core, and the scores on the international business test went up.

K.3. Balanced Scorecard

Overview

The balanced scorecard is a framework designed to help organizations translate their vision and mission statements into measurable performance goals and objectives while taking into account multiple perspectives, including customers, internal business processes, learning, and growth. As an assessment tool, the balanced scorecard is used primarily by provider organizations to identify goals and translate those goals into operational measures of performance. The balanced scorecard is primarily associated with Phase Two, Model 3.

Recognizing its value as a means to link short-term goals and objectives to long-term strategy, a wide range of organizations (including corporations, universities, nonprofit organizations, and government agencies) has adopted the balanced scorecard framework as a strategic management system. It is valued for its flexibility in implementation and reasonable requirement of time and resources and because it can be easily adapted to incorporate new initiatives in the organization.

The balanced scorecard approach is based on four main processes: translating the vision, communication and alignment, business planning, and feedback and learning. All four processes aim to create consistency and integration of priorities across the organization and to determine the right performance measurements. The translation of the vision is meant to create an understanding of the organization's vision through an "integrated set of objectives and measures that describe the long-term drivers of success" (Kaplan and Norton, 1996). The vision and strategy should then be communicated throughout the organization to ensure that departmental and individual employee goals and objectives are properly aligned with the long-term strategic vision. The business planning aspect links the budget to strategic planning and performance measurement, allowing decisionmakers to direct resources appropriately. Finally, the feedback and learning mechanism provides an opportunity for decisionmakers to review performance results and assess the validity of the organization's strategy and performance measures. The balanced scorecard approach places a heavy emphasis on continually updating strategy and measures to accurately reflect the changing operating environment.

Several government agencies, including the U.S. Customs Service, National Oceanic and Atmospheric Administration, Veterans Benefits Administration in the U.S. Department of Veterans Affairs, and the Department of Transportation have recognized the benefits of the balanced scorecard framework in their efforts to comply with the Government Performance and Results Act (GPRA), which requires federal agencies to submit five-year strategic plans as well as annual performance plans alongside their budget requests to Congress. By helping agencies link their strategic planning with performance measurement objectives, the balanced scorecard organizes efforts across business lines so that processes and goals are aligned with the overall departmental strategy as required by GPRA.

The administration offices of higher education institutions are also recognizing the value of the balanced scorecard, which serves the dual purpose of assessing for improvement and accountability. Offices in both the University of Southern California (USC) and the University of California at San Diego (UCSD) have incorporated the balanced scorecard approach as part of their larger efforts to improve the efficiency and effectiveness of their operations. Among other things, the balanced scorecard offers a way to streamline and prioritize activities as well as measure performance. Interestingly, the two schools are focusing on different aspects of their operations in their use of the scorecard; USC's Rossier School of Education is using the scorecard to measure academic quality, while UCSD's Business Affairs Office is focusing on measuring the productivity of its business operations.

Phase One

The balanced scorecard is a technique used by providers for self-assessment. Phase One may be conducted by a provider, but not using this technique. Thus, Phase One does not apply.

Phase Two

The balanced scorecard is an example of an approach used in Model 3 for provider-based self-assessment. The scorecard's emphasis on goal alignment, performance measurement, continuous improvement, and flexibility makes it an attractive option for self-assessment in organizations, particularly in contexts where involvement of multiple stakeholder is needed.

The balanced scorecard offers four perspectives from which to view organization effectiveness:

- financial
- internal business
- innovation and learning
- customer.

For each of these four perspectives, the organization must first identify goals then determine the measures and benchmarks that will capture the outcome of these goals.

Identify Goals for Education and Training

For each of the four perspectives that orient the focus of the scorecard assessment, goals and corresponding measures must be determined. The scope and number of goals can change as the operating environment of the institution changes.

The Veterans Benefits Administration has used the scorecard approach to align its five diverse lines of business and found that three main factors were important in its successful implementation: consensus on the effort, a flexible structure, and effective communication.

The balanced scorecard allows the provider to include as many stakeholders as necessary in the goal determination process. For instance, the School of Education at USC developed its goals with a small committee consisting of two faculty administrators. The committee relied on the balanced scorecard approach as a way to focus on the department's goals for the next five years. Modifying the approach somewhat to fit the context of an academic institution, the committee developed an "academic scorecard" that includes no more than five goals for each scorecard perspective. Its goal selection process was based on current priorities of both the university and the department. The committee adopted many department-specific goals mainly because in some instances university and department priorities did not match.[1]

---

[1]Efforts to improve accountability and effectiveness stemmed from the Provost's commitment to require "metrics of excellence" from all academic departments. Initially, the Graduate School of Education complied with this data-gathering effort, but did not commit itself seriously, mainly because none of the indicators correlated strongly with the department's decisions on resources and program development. In addition, the university followed an annual budget cycle and required each department to submit an academic plan in the fall and an academic budget in the spring. In theory, both the plan and the budget should complement one another, but they did not. Realizing that the Provost's request was not a passing fad, however, the department decided to develop meaningful measures internally that reflected its lines of business.

According to USC officials, the process of limiting the number of goals in each area imposed discipline upon the committee and forced the members to think about the priorities of the organization. Not everything is equally important, and there is a tendency for people to associate importance with anything that is measured. Also, in a complex organization such as a university, different levels of bureaucracy often require different scorecards. For instance, campus security is an important goal for a university but not for a department.

Some of the goals developed by the School of Education at USC are listed in Table K.3.1, by perspective.

Table K.3.1

USC School of Education Goals, by Perspective

Perspective	Goal
Academic management	Improve budget performance Improve school operations Improve management/leadership
Stakeholder	Quality of academic programs Student-centeredness Quality of faculty Value of money Alumni/employer satisfaction
Internal business	Improve faculty productivity Improve staff productivity Improve recruitment advisement Maintain responsibility to community
Innovation and learning	Improve quality of degree programs Increase student learning Improve quality of students Attract/keep talented faculty/staff Increase education innovation Faculty/staff development

SOURCE: O'Neil et al. (1999, p. 35).

Develop Measures of Quality and Productivity

The balanced scorecard framework encourages institutions to identify a limited number of metrics that relate to the goals they have established. The Veterans Benefits Administration settled on speed, accuracy, cost, customer satisfaction, and employee development as the right performance measures for all the lines of business, although the measures are weighted differently for each area. The process of introducing the balanced scorecard and developing measures and performance goals was intended to be flexible and iterative, allowing "refinement in the measures and the organization to become familiar with the scorecard" (Williams and Wall, 1999, p. 1).

Selection of measures is not fixed, so different institutions can adopt different strategies. What affects selection are the requirements most important to the institution. In selecting measures, USC's School of Education has incorporated the use of benchmarks based on comparisons to other university graduate programs. It has also relied heavily on the *U.S. News and World Report* academic program rankings and set goals for improvement to match those institutions that are currently ranked in the top ten of schools of education. USC's School of Education believes that the *U.S. News* rankings have a major influence on perception and "have become a de facto standard of excellence for prospective students and faculty" (O'Neil et al., 1999, p. 38). The measures have been based mainly on data already being collected on a regular basis.

Table K.3.2 is an example of the goals, measures, and benchmarks for one of the perspectives included in the USC School of Education academic scorecard.

The UCSD Business Affairs Office has taken a unique approach by combining the balanced scorecard with the National Association of Colleges and Universities Business Officers (NACUBO) benchmark program. NACUBO's benchmarking program was developed to

> provide college and university administrators and managers with performance measurement information . . . . [T]he program offers comparative operational performance data geared toward aiding administrators in sharing best practices and improving efficiency (Shepko and Douglas, 1998).

This component of UCSD's balanced scorecard approach enhances the usefulness of the balanced scorecard by not only informing the office of whether it is meeting its stated goals, but also how it measures against comparable institutions.

The Business Affairs Office at UCSD implemented the scorecard in 1993 in response to fiscal problems and a changing business environment. As the office sought to introduce reengineered processes and operations in its lines of business, the balanced scorecard allowed it to focus efforts on where and when reengineering should be utilized. For each of the 30 core campus business functions, NACUBO benchmarks were selected to compare UCSD's performance in these areas with that of other research universities and participating University of California campuses (Relyea, 1998). Table K.3.3 shows examples of business operations measured by the balanced scorecard and compared against benchmarks.

Table K.3.2

Stakeholder Perspective: How Do Stakeholders See Us? (USC)

Goal	Measure	Benchmark
Quality of academic programs	Ranking in *U.S. News and World Report*	Ascend to the top ten schools of education
	Teaching effectiveness	Equal average of top five of USC schools
Student-centeredness	Quality of student services is measured by student satisfaction with advisement, career development, job placement, course offerings, financial aid, etc.	
	School climate for special-population students, e.g., international, minority, and women	
Quality of faculty	Publications	Exceed average of publications per USC tenure-track faculty member
	Research funding	Equal average of top 11–20 in *U.S. News and World Report*
Value for money	Retention	Equal average of top five of USC graduate programs
	Reduced time to degree	Reduce time by 20 percent
	Return on student investment	Break even
Alumni satisfaction	To be developed	
Employer satisfaction	Quality of elementary and secondary school teachers	

SOURCE: O'Neil et al. (1999), p. 37. Reprinted by permission.

Evaluate Quality and Productivity Using Measures

Evaluation relies on the comparison of performance with that of external peers (benchmarking). Indeed, the need to benchmark and the availability of such benchmarking information influences the choice of performance measures as described in the previous subsection.

The process is a continuous one with goals being added or deleted as the operating environment changes. Once the scorecard has been completed, the organization must identify ways to implement it. At UCSD, results from the scorecard are the focus of an annual management retreat where leaders discuss the performance of the business functions against the benchmark institutions, "identified as either positive, neutral or negative. Negative performance gaps are

Table K.3.3

Examples of Business Operations Scorecard (UCSD)

Business Function	Measure
Internal Process Perspective: Are We Productive and Effective?	
Administrative computing	Ratio of number of workstations to number of employees
	Ratio of technical employees in central organizations to number of technical employees
Benefits	Ratio of department cost to faculty staff head counter
	Ratio of faculty staff head counter to department FTE
Human resources	Ratio of HR cost to faculty staff head counter
	Ratio of faculty staff head counter to HR FTE
	Percentage of active career staff vested
	Percentage of career staff turnover
Housing	Ratio of number of bed spaces to department FTE
	Ratio of housing cost to bed space
Staff education and development	Ratio of course contract hours to staff FTE
	SE&D cost to staff FTE
Innovation and Learning: How Do Our Employees Feel?	
Administrative computing	Each business function rated on a 5-point scale on:
Admin. computing service	communication
Data center	compensation
Benefits	customer service
Human resources	decisionmaking
Housing	diversity
Staff education and development	leadership
	morale
	performance management
	teamwork
	training and development
	vision, values, mission
Customer Perspective: How Do Our Customers See Us?	
Administrative computing	5-point satisfaction scale; surveyed academic and administrative staff separately
Benefits	5-point satisfaction scale; surveyed academic and administrative staff separately
Human resources	None
Housing	5-point student satisfaction scores
Staff education and development	5-point satisfaction scale; surveyed academic and administrative staff separately
Financial Perspective: How Do We Look to Resource Providers?	
Administrative computing	None
Benefits	None
Human resources	None
Housing	Profitability and efficiency ratios
Staff education and development	None

NOTE: See www.vcba.ucsd.edu/performance.

addressed with an action plan" (Relyea, 1998). The business functions needing attention are then prioritized, an action plan is set, and goals are established for the following year. At USC, academic reviews are conducted every six years and the scorecard framework within the USC School of Education is designed currently to fit this cycle. Scorecard information is for internal use mainly; however "success stories" are sometimes published for the benefit of others.

The scorecard approach can be successful if it attempts to desegregate the different aspects of an organization. In contrast, USC has not been able to undertake a systemwide effort to develop some of these indicators. Instead, the Provost at USC is aggregating the lines of business by asking for "mindless" accountability through data inputs. Unfortunately, the university does not have a centralized office of research to move these efforts along.

The whole point of the balanced scorecard approach is for managers to select high-level indicators that can help them monitor progress toward key goals. Thus, the results of the balanced scorecard should be linked to the general management of the organization. Implications can be broad or narrow depending on how comprehensive the framework process has been.

K.4. The Urban Universities Portfolio Project: Assuring Quality for Multiple Publics

Overview

Stakeholders of higher education are increasingly demanding that universities offer more information about their practices: Legislators require information to justify funding levels for these institutions; potential students and their families require information about which schools offer the best education and best fit their needs; and accreditation agencies seek to better classify institutions according to services being offered.

Urban public universities are one among many types of higher education institutions. Catering to a large segment of college students, these universities are essential players in the higher education market. Current ranking methods used by popular media and other entities compare these urban public institutions to more traditional research universities. However, such comparisons often overlook several important differences. First, at urban public universities, nontraditional students[1] (including students with diverse ethnic backgrounds, age ranges, and working and living circumstances) account for most of the population pool. Often, the parents of these students did not attend college. As a result, most of the coursework offered must accommodate the lives of these student consumers. Consequently, nontraditional practices such as distance, evening, and weekend courses are offered to provide maximum access to students whose lives place competing demands on their time. Urban public universities also tend to place greater emphasis on professional programs. These programs are created and maintained based on the type of students enrolled. A final characteristic of urban public universities is the use of the community as a teaching and learning tool. These characteristics distinguish urban public universities from the traditional ones.

Because the urban public universities view themselves as different, and these differences are not recognized by existing assessment methods, funding was

[1]Traditional students are generally thought of as full-time students in the 18–23 age range. Basically, they are students who go to college (usually a residential college) right after high school and do not work full time while attending school.

obtained from The Pew Charitable Trusts to develop a new method for assessing the effectiveness and quality of urban public universities. Six urban public universities from across the country are participating in this initiative (The Urban Universities Portfolio Project (UUPP)): Indiana University–Purdue University Indianapolis, University of Illinois at Chicago, Portland State University, California State University at Sacramento, University of Massachusetts at Boston, and Georgia State University.

The end product of the three-year project, which started in 1998, will be a web page for the project in general and a web page containing a portfolio for each participating university. The institutional portfolios (currently under development) will serve as vehicles for capturing the distinctive characteristics, work, and accomplishments of urban public universities and informing the public about these urban schools, particularly on how they differ from more-traditional institutions of higher learning. This project has two main emphases: (1) enhance understanding, among both internal and external stakeholders (such as potential students, lawmakers, and accreditors), of the distinguishing features and missions of urban public comprehensive universities; and (2) enhance the capacity of these universities to communicate, through the institutional portfolio, their effectiveness in achieving their missions.

The purpose of UUPP is both accountability and improvement. While this project is a collaboration among the six urban universities, each university is a provider and seeks to inform its own stakeholders and improve its own internal operations and quality. The portfolios are tools for accountability in that they include the evaluation of measures that capture the universities' own goals and objectives. Urban universities, in general, seek to be measured on variables that coincide with their own objectives and goals. Hopefully, once these portfolios are completed, there will be universal standards for assessing urban universities. Therefore, legislators can provide funding based on appropriate information and interpretations; accrediting associations can better classify these schools by services rendered; and students and families can determine whether or not an urban school fits their needs.

These portfolios will also be used as a self-assessment and correction tool for improving educational practices. Participating universities have found that creating an institutional portfolio brings about substantial internal benefits. The complexity of the project demands broad campus involvement, creating an occasion for large segments of the university to think together about how particular practices, programs, and initiatives connect with one another and contribute to the overall institutional mission. This collaboration is helping to build institutional identity and community, developing and reinforcing shared visions and commitments that lead to meaningful institutional change and improvement. Already, several participating universities have launched significant improvement initiatives resulting directly from their portfolio work. In addition, once the portfolios are completed, the participating universities will be able to compare themselves to each other, adding a dimension on which to base improvement.

In creating the portfolios, institutions rely on self-generated data. Each university has a team that includes a project director and institutional research staff who coordinate gathering these data; the university's provost selects and is a member of this team. The project has established two groups of external constituents who are knowledgeable about higher education. The National Advisory Board (NAB) and the Institutional Review Board (IRB) include distinguished leaders from business, government, and education. The project team selects members for both boards and asks participating universities to review the list.

NAB's role is to advise the project about its aims, practices, and progress by reviewing the evolving set of core goals, indicators, and measures, and to keep current on issues facing the urban public schools. Members of the board have strong backgrounds in funding and public endorsement; they include directors of accrediting associations and of foundations, a chancellor, a commissioner on a state coordinating board, and a president of a company.

The IRB members work closely with the six urban universities advising on the construction of the portfolios. Each IRB member is assigned to and works with one of the participating institutions. Members include college deans, directors of accrediting associations, professors, and provosts.

Figure K.4.1 charts these relationships.

This portfolio process for assessment differs from current practices, such as program review and traditional accreditation. Program reviews are designed to measure value of a specific program while accreditation reviews measure compliance to minimum standards. Typically accreditation self-studies reveal very little about the quality and efficiency of a whole university. Both types of review occur once every few years and are conducted by professionals within the higher education community. By contrast, the portfolio approach will offer ongoing internal and external reviews where the external evaluation will serve to educate all stakeholders and promote university-wide changes rather than specific programmatic ones.

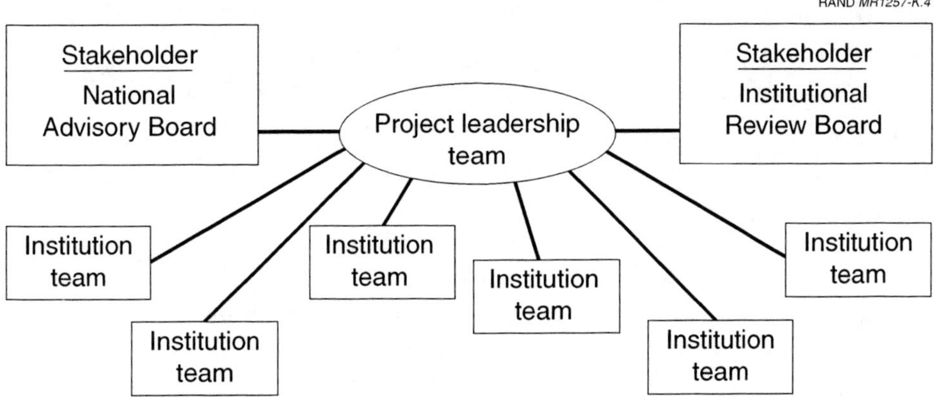

Figure K.4.1—UUPP Campus Team Structure

Implications of this assessment are widespread, provided that similar institutions adopt this approach. Such implications are the reasons that UUPP was conceptualized.

Phase One

Some examples of Phase One assessment are evident in this portfolio process of assessment. Part of this process focuses on determining common goals and measures of performance for an urban, public university through defining the specific mission elements and outcomes that uniquely characterize each of the institutions involved in the project. Although not all urban public universities are involved in this process at this point, the process itself is meant to be somewhat representative of this "system" of urban public universities.

Phase Two

This portfolio process for assessment is an example of Model 3. In this process, the providers are assessing themselves without use of an intermediary. However, providers do involve external stakeholders throughout the assessment process.

Identify Goals for Education and Training

As mentioned under "Phase One," the six institutions involved in UUPP have taken time to define the character of the public urban university. They have also spent time examining the goals for these universities and matching these goals to their characters and missions. In this process, they have involved external stakeholders through their National Advisory Board, part of whose role is to advise the project about its aims, practices, and progress by reviewing the evolving set of core goals. In addition to working on this task as a team, each university is developing goals at its own institutional level. The universities are at different stages in this process, but each has determined to link portfolio goals to strategic goals of its own university.

Most of the goals in UUPP have been focused on student learning outcomes. Project-wide efforts have been conducted to find common institution characteristics among the institutions involved and to determine common student learning goals. Several criteria for goal development were established: whether learning goals cut across programs and curricula, reflect external stakeholder concerns, contribute to common conversations about learning, and reflect what urban universities do differently. Examples of these goals for student learning outcomes include that students will have achieved appropriate skill levels in communication, critical thinking, and problem solving; and that students will have developed a sense of civic responsibility and an appreciation for pluralism and diversity.

Develop Measures of Quality and Productivity

Once goals have been established, the universities will focus on developing both project-wide and institution-specific evidence (i.e., measures) of the degree to which institutions have met their goals. These measures are the heart of the portfolio itself. External stakeholders, via the National Advisory Board, will review the measures as they evolve. Currently, models for documenting several fundamental learning outcomes are being developed. Any adopted measure must touch on the unique attributes of the urban public universities. Cooperation allows the six participating universities to learn from one another and to develop shared measures.

Evaluate Quality and Productivity Using Measures

Through this portfolio process of assessment, urban universities will be evaluated against their peers rather than against the entire university population of which some have a different agenda. If, eventually, all urban public universities adopt the portfolio approach, then relevant comparisons can be made among all appropriate peer institutions. Once the portfolios are completed, these six pioneering institutions will pilot an innovative type of institutional review based on the institutional portfolio and an on-site audit. This review process may eventually replace traditional accreditation processes.

Bibliography

Abernathy, D. J. (February 1999). Thinking outside the evaluation box. *Training & Development, 53*(2), 18–23.

Accrediting Commission of Career Schools and Colleges of Technology. www.accsct.org/standards/accred/accred_index.html.

ACT (1999). *Work Keys.* www.act.org/workkeys/index.html.

ACT (1997). *Work Keys: Targets for Instruction.* Iowa City, IA.

AETC Instruction 36-2201 (1998). *Training Evaluation.* Department of the Air Force.

AETC Instruction 36-2601 (1999). *Occupational Analysis Program.* Department of the Air Force.

Air Force Handbook 36-2235 (1993). *Information for Designers of Instructional Systems.* Department of the Air Force.

Air Force Policy Directive 36-22 (1993). *Military Training.* Department of the Air Force.

Albright, B. N. (Fall 1995). The accountability litmus test: Long-term performance improvement with contained costs. In G. H. Gaither (ed.) *New Directions for Higher Education: Assessing Performance in an Age of Accountability: Case Studies, Volume XXIII, Number 3.* San Francisco, CA: Jossey-Bass Publishers (Number 91, pp. 65–76).

American Psychological Association (1985). *Standards for Educational and Psychological Testing.* Washington, D.C.

American Society for Quality Control Standards Committee (1996). *Quality Assurance Standards—Guidelines for the Application of ANSI/ISO/ASQC Q9001 or Z9002 to Education and Training Institutions.*

Andersen, A. (2000). *U.S. DOT Training Program Review, Final Report.*

Anderson, R. E., & Meyerson, J. W. (eds.) (1992). *Productivity & Higher Education: Improving the Effectiveness of Faculty, Facilities, and Financial Resources.* Princeton, NJ: Peterson's Guides, Inc.

Aper, J. P., Cuver, S. M., & Hinkle, D. E. (1990). Coming to terms with the accountability versus improvement debate in assessment. *Higher Education, 20,* 471–483.

Aper, J. P., and Hinkle, D. E. (1991). State policies for assessing student outcomes: A case study with implications for state and institutional authorities. *Journal of Higher Education 62,* 539–555.

APQC Institute for Education Best Practices (1987). *Measuring Institutional Performance Outcomes*, final report. American Productivity and Quality Center.

Association of American Colleges Project on Redefining the Meaning and Purpose of Baccalaureate Degrees (1985). *Integrity in the College Curriculum: A Report to the Academic Community*. Washington, D.C.: Association of American Colleges.

Avery, Christopher, Resnick, Paul, & Zeckhauser, Richard (1999). The market for evaluations. *American Economic Review, 89*, 564–584.

Babbie, E. (1992). *The Practice of Social Research*. Belmont, CA: Wadsworth Publishing Company.

Banta, T. W. (1988). Assessment as an instrument of state funding policy. In T. W. Banta (ed.), *Implementing outcomes assessment: Promise and perils*. New Directions for Institutional Research, Vol. 59. San Francisco, CA: Jossey-Bass (pp. 81–94).

Banta, T. W., & Borden, V. M. H. (Summer 1994). Performance indicators for accountability and improvement. In V. M. H. Borden & T. W. Banta (eds.), *New Directions for Institutional Research: Using Performance Indicators to Guide Strategic Decision Making, Volume XVI, Number 2*. San Francisco, CA: Jossey-Bass Publishers (Number 82, pp. 95–106).

Banta, T. W. & Fisher, H. S. (1989). Tennessee's performance funding policy: L'Enfant terrible of assessment at age eight. In E. V. Johanningmeier (ed.), *Accountability and Assessment in Higher Education*. A Society of Professors of Education, John Dewey Society Publication.

Bassi, L. J. (May 2000). *Measuring ROI: The Business of Learning*. Proceedings from the Post-Conference Workshop of the Corporate Universities 2000: Benchmarks for a New Millennium, Las Vegas, NV.

Bassi, L. J., Scott, C., Lewis, Eleesha, Costa de Souza, Humberto Cesar, McDonald, Ian, Pickett, Les, & Elliott, Phillipa (November 1998). Trends in workplace learning: Supply and demand in interesting times. *Training & Development, 52*(11), 51–53.

Bassi, L. J., Scott, C., & McMurrer, Daniel (March 1998). A common standard for measuring training results. *Training & Development, 52*(3), 10–12.

Bassi, L. J., Scott, C., & Van Buren, Mark (November 1997). Training industry trends 1997. *Training & Development, 51*(11), 46–58.

Bassi, L. J., & Van Buren, Mark (January 1999a). The 1999 ASTD state of the industry report. *Training & Development, 53*(1), 1–27.

Bassi, L. J., & Van Buren, Mark (January 1999b). Sharpening the leading edge. *Training & Development, 53*(1) 23–28.

Benjamin, R., Carroll, S., Dewar, J., Lempert, R., Stockley, S., Hove, A., & Yoda, T. (2000). *Achieving the Texas Higher Education Vision*, Santa Monica, CA: RAND.

Bennett, W. J. (1984). *To Reclaim a Legacy: A Report on the Humanities in Higher Education.* Washington, D.C.: National Endowment for the Humanities.

Biglaiser, G. (1993). Middlemen as experts. *RAND Journal of Economics, 24,* 212–223.

Biglaiser, G., & Friedman, J. (1994). Middlemen as guarantors of quality. *International Journal of Industrial Organization, 12,* 509–531.

Birnbaum, R. (1992). The constraints on campus productivity. In R. E. Anderson & J. W. Meyerson (eds.), *Productivity and Higher Education: Improving the Effectiveness of Faculty, Facilities, and Financial Resources* (pp. 23–47). Princeton, NJ: Peterson's Guides, Inc.

Blair, Julie (2000). Study: College rankings affect aid packages. *Education Week.* www.edweek.org/ew/ewstory.cfm?slug=19rank.h19&keywords=College%20 Rankings.

Blankinship, D. A. E., & Denise, M. (Summer/Fall 1997). A general survey for obtaining participants' evaluations of professional development sessions. *SRA Journal, 29*(1,2), 17–24.

Boatright, K. J. (Fall 1995). University of Wisconsin's system accountability. In G. H. Gaither (ed.), *New Directions for Higher Education: Assessing Performance in an Age of Accountability: Case Studies, Volume XXIII, Number 3.* San Francisco, CA: Jossey-Bass Publishers (Number 91, pp. 51–64).

Borden, V. M. H., & Bottrill, K. V. (Summer 1994). Performance indicators: History, definitions, and methods. In V. M. H. Borden & T. W. Banta (eds.), *New Directions for Institutional Research: Using Performance Indicators to Guide Strategic Decision Making, Volume XVI, Number 2.* San Francisco, CA: Jossey-Bass Publishers (Number 82, pp. 5–21).

Borden, V. M. H., & Banta, T. W. (eds.) (1994). *New Directions for Institutional Research: Using Performance Indicators to Guide Strategic Decision Making, Volume XVI, Number 2.* San Francisco, CA: Jossey-Bass Publishers.

Bottrill, K. V., & Borden, V. M. H. (Summer 1994). Appendix: Examples from the literature. In V. M. H. Borden & T. W. Banta (eds.), *New Directions for Institutional Research: Using Performance Indicators to Guide Strategic Decision Making, Volume XVI, Number 2.* San Francisco, CA: Jossey-Bass Publishers (Number 82, pp. 107–119).

Boyer, C., Ewell, P., Finney, J., & Mingle, J. (1987). Assessment and outcomes measurement: A view from the states. *AAHE Bulletin, 39*(7), 8–12.

Brennan, R. (1996). Generalizability of performance assessments. In G. Phillips (ed.), *Technical Issues in Large-Scale Performance Assessment.* Washington, D.C.: U.S. Department of Education, Office of Educational Research and Improvement, NCES-802, pp. 19–58.

California State University (1997). *The Cornerstones Report V.*

California State University (1998). *Cornerstones Implementation Plan.*

Campbell, D. T., & Fiske, D. W. (1959). Convergent and discriminant validation by the multitrait-multimethod matrix. *Psychological Bulletin, 15*, 546–553.

Campbell, D. T., & Stanley, J. C. (1966). *Experimental and Quasi-Experimental Designs for Research.* Chicago, IL: Rand McNally.

Carnevale, D. (May 19, 2000). Two models for collaboration in distance learning. *The Chronicle of Higher Education.* chronicle.com.

Carnevale, A. P., Johnson, N. C., & Edwards, A. R. (April 10, 1998). Opinion: Performance-based appropriations: Fad or wave of the future? *The Chronicle of Higher Education.* chronicle.com.

Cavalluzzo, Linda C., & Cymrot, Donald J. (1998), *A Bottom-Up Assessment of Navy Flagship Schools (CRM 97-24).* Alexandria, VA: Center for Naval Analyses.

Chickering, Zelda, & Gamson, F. (eds.) (1991). *Applying the Seven Principles for Good Practice in Undergraduate Education.* San Francisco: Jossey-Bass, Inc.

Cohen, W. S. (1997). *Defense Reform Initiative Report.* Washington, D.C.: U.S. Department of Defense. www.defenselink.mil/pubs/dodreform.

Cole, H. P., Moss, J., Gohs, F. X., Lacefield, W. E., Barfield, B. J., & Blyethe, D. K. (1984). *Measuring Learning in Continuing Education for Engineers and Scientists.* Phoenix, AZ: Oryx Press.

Cole, J. J. K., Nettles, M. T., & Sharp, S. (1997). *Assessment of Teaching and Learning for Improvement and Accountability: State Governing, Coordinating Board and Regional Accreditation Association Policies and Practices.* Ann Arbor: University of Michigan, National Center for Postsecondary Improvement.

Cook, T. D. & Campbell, D. T. (1979). *Quasi–experimentation: Design and Analysis Issues for Field Settings.* Chicago, IL: Rand McNally.

Cornwell, T. (1997). Rising Phoenix ruffles feathers. *The Times Higher Education Supplement, 1306*, 8.

Cornwell, T. (1998). Phoenix takes a nosedive. *The Times Higher Education Supplement, 1352*, 14.

Council for Higher Education Accreditation (CHEA) (January 24–26, 2000). *2000 Annual Conference—Quality Assurance: Distance Learning and International Perspectives and Needs*, Washington, D.C.

Cousins, J. B. M., & Colla, J. (August 1998). Conceptualizing the successful product development project as a basis for evaluating management training in technology-based companies: A participatory concept mapping application. *Evaluation & Program Planning, 21*(3), 333–344.

Cronbach, L. J. (1971). Test validation. In R. L. Thorndike (ed.), *Educational Measurement.* Washington, D.C.: American Council on Education (2nd edition, pp. 443–507).

Cronbach, L. J. & Gleser, G. C. (1965). *Psychological Tests and Personnel Decisions* (2nd edition). Urbana, IL: University of Illinois Press.

Davis, J. R. D., & Adelaide, B. (May 1999). The test of training. *Security Management, 43*(5), 33–35.

Defense Reform Initiative Directive 41 Study (1998). *Blueprint for the Chancellor for Education and Professional Development.* Washington, D.C.: U.S. Department of Defense.

DeHayes, D. W., & Lovorinic, J. G. (Summer 1994). Activity-based costing model for assessing economic performance. In V. M. H. Borden & T. W. Banta (eds.), *New Directions for Institutional Research: Using Performance Indicators to Guide Strategic Decision Making, Volume XVI, Number 2.* San Francisco, CA: Jossey-Bass Publishers (Number 82, pp. 81–93).

Dickinson, T. L. (1986). *Performance Ratings: Designs for Evaluating Their Validity and Accuracy.* Interim Technical Paper for Period May–September 1983. Manpower and Personnel Division, Brooks Air Force Base, TX, AFHRL-TP-86-15.

Dickinson, T. L. & Hedge, J. W. (1989). *WCRK Performance Ratings: Measurement Test Bed for Validity and Accuracy Research.* Interim Technical Paper for Period June 1985–September 1987. Training Systems Division, Brooks Air Force Base, TX, AFHRL-TP-88-36.

Dill, D. (1999). *Implementing Academic Audits: Lessons Learned in Europe and Asia. Draft.* Chapel Hill: University of North Carolina.

Dill, David (2000a). Designing academic audit: Lessons learned in Europe and Asia. *Quality in Higher Education, 6* (3), 187–207.

Dill, David (2000b). www.unc.edu/courses/acaudit/whatisacademicaudit.html.

Dionne, P. (Fall 1996). The evaluation of training activities: A complex issue involving different stakes. *Human Resource Development Quarterly, 7*(3), 279–286.

Dolence, M. G., & Norris, D. M. (Summer 1994). Using key performance indicators to drive strategic decision making. In V. M. H. Borden & T. W. Banta (eds.), *New Directions for Institutional Research: Using Performance Indicators to Guide Strategic Decision Making, Volume XVI, Number 2.* San Francisco, CA: Jossey-Bass Publishers (Number 82, pp. 63–80).

Dooris, M. J., & Teeter, D. J. (Summer 1994). Total quality management perspective on assessing institutional performance. In V. M. H. Borden & T. W. Banta (eds.), *New Directions for Institutional Research: Using Performance Indicators to Guide Strategic Decision Making, Volume XVI, Number 2.* San Francisco, CA: Jossey-Bass Publishers (Number 82, pp. 51–62).

Dunn, N. J., & Wilson, L. S. (1994). New college leaders: Strategic shortcuts for short-term success. In J. W. Meyerson & W. F. Massy (eds.), *Measuring*

Institutional Performance in Higher Education. Princeton, NJ: Peterson's Guides, Inc. (pp. 99–129).

Ebenkamp, B. (February 8, 1999). Budget boost backs Eastpak upgrade. *Brandweek, 40*(6), 52.

Education Commission of the States (1997). *1997 State Postsecondary Education Structures Sourcebook: State Coordinating and Governing Boards.* Denver, CO: Education Commission of the States.

El-Khawas, E. (1995). *Campus Trends 1995.* Higher Education Panel Report No. 85. Washington, D.C.: America Council on Education.

Epstein, P. (1992). Measuring the performance of public services. In M. Holzer (ed.), *Public Productivity Handbook.* New York: Marcel Dekker, Inc.

Ewell, P. T. (1984). *The Self-Regarding Institution: Information for Excellence.* Boulder, CO: National Center for Higher Education Management Systems.

Ewell, P. T. (1985). *Levers for Change: The Role of State Government in Improving Quality of Postsecondary Education*. Paper presented at the Annual AAHE Assessment Forum.

Ewell, P. T. (1987a). *Assessment, Accountability, and Improvement: Managing the Contradiction*. Boulder, CO: National Center for Higher Education Management Systems.

Ewell, P. T. (1987b). Assessment: Where are we? The implications of new state mandates. *Change 19*(1), 23–28.

Ewell, P. T. (1990). *State Policy on Assessment: The Linkage to Learning*. Denver, CO: Education Commission of the States.

Ewell, P. T. (1991). Assessment and public accountability: Back to the future. *Change 23*(6), 12–17.

Ewell, P. T. (1993). The role of states and accreditors in shaping assessment practice. In T. W. Banta (ed.), *Making a Difference: Outcomes of a Decade of Assessment in Higher Education.* San Francisco, CA: Jossey-Bass Publishers (pp. 339–356).

Ewell, P. T. (1996). The current pattern of state-level assessment: Results of a national inventory. *Assessment Update, 8*(3), 1–15.

Ewell, P. T. (1997a). Identifying indicators of curricular quality. In G. Gaff & J. Ratcliff (eds.), *Handbook of the Undergraduate Curriculum.* San Francisco, CA: Jossey-Bass, Inc.

Ewell, P. T. (1997b). Accountability and assessment in a second decade: New looks or same old story? In *Assessing Impact: Evidence and Action—Presentations from the 1997 American Association for Higher Education Conference on Assessment and Quality.* Washington, D.C.: American Association for Higher Education.

Ewell, P. T. (1999a). Assessment of higher education and quality: Promise and politics. In Samuel J. Messick (ed.), *Assessment in Higher Education: Issues of Access, Quality, Student Development, and Public Policy*. Mahwah, NJ: Lawrence Erlbaum Associates.

Ewell, P. T. (1999b). *A Delicate Balance: The Role of Evaluation in Management.* Boulder, CO: National Center for Higher Education Management Systems (NCHEMS).

Ewell, P. T. (1999c). *Examining a Brave New World: New Accreditation Might be Different*. Washington, D.C.: Council on Higher Education Accreditation.

Ewell, P. T., & Jones, D. P. (Summer 1994). Data indicators, and the national center for higher education management systems. In V. M. H. Borden & T. W. Banta (eds.), *New Directions for Institutional Research: Using Performance Indicators to Guide Strategic Decision Making, Volume XVI, Number 2.* San Francisco, CA: Jossey-Bass Publishers (Number 82, pp. 23–35).

Ewell, P. T. & Wellman, J. (1997). *Refashioning Accountability: Toward a "Coordinated" System of Quality Assurance for Higher Education.* Policy Papers on Higher Education, ED 410 812. Denver, CO: Education Commission of the States.

Flynn, G. (November 1998). The nuts & bolts of valuing training. *Workforce, 77*(11), 80–82+.

Frederiksen, N., Jensen, O., & Beaton, A. E. (1972). *Prediction of Organizational Behavior*. New York: Pergamon Press.

Freeman, T. M. (Fall 1995). Performance indicators and assessment in the state University of New York system. In G. H. Gaither (ed.), *New Directions for Higher Education: Assessing Performance in an Age of Accountability: Case Studies, Volume XXIII, Number 3.* San Francisco, CA: Jossey-Bass Publishers (Number 91, pp. 25–49).

Gaither, G. H. (Fall 1995a). Some observations while looking ahead. In G. H. Gaither (ed.), *New Directions for Higher Education: Assessing Performance in an Age of Accountability, Volume XXIII, Number 3.* San Francisco, CA: Jossey-Bass Publishers (Number 91, pp. 97–101).

Gaither, G. H. (Fall 1995b). Suggestions for further reading. In G. H. Gaither (ed.), *New Directions for Higher Education: Assessing Performance in an Age of Accountability, Volume XXIII, Number 3.* San Francisco, CA: Jossey-Bass Publishers (Number 91, pp. 103–104).

Gaither, G. H. (ed.) (1995c). *New Directions for Higher Education, Volume XXIII, Number 3.* San Francisco, CA: Jossey-Bass Publishers.

Gilmore, J. L., & To, D. (1992). Evaluating academic productivity and quality. In C. S. Hollins (ed.), *Containing Costs and Improving Productivity in Higher Education.* San Francisco, CA: Jossey-Bass, Inc.

Glidden, R. (1998). *The Contemporary Context of Accreditation: Challenges in a Changing Environment.* Keynote address for 2nd CHEA "Usefulness"

Conference. Council for Higher Education Accreditation. www.chea.org/Events/Usefulness/98May/98_05Glidden.html.

Gonczi, A. (1994). Competency-based assessment in the professions in Australia. *Assessment in Education, 1*(1), 27–44.

Gordon, E. E., Ronald, R., & Ponticell, Judith A. (September 1995). The individualized training alternative. *Training & Development, 49*(9), 52–61.

Gouillart, F. J. (1994). The self-transformation of corporations: A lesson from industry? In J. W. Meyerson & W. F. Massy (eds.), *Measuring Institutional Performance in Higher Education.* Princeton, NJ: Peterson's Guides, Inc. (pp. 55–70).

Gray, G. R. H., McKenzie, E., Miller, M., & Shasky, C. (Summer 1997). Training practices in state government agencies. *Public Personnel Management, 26*(2), 187–202.

Greening, D.W., & Gray, B. (1994). Testing a model of organizational response to social and political issues. *Academy of Management Journal*, 467–498.

Gubernick, L. (1997). For-profit U. *Forbes Magazine, V*(159), 92.

Hackett, J. T. (1992). Productivity through privatization. In R. E. Anderson & J. W. Meyerson (eds.), *Productivity and Higher Education: Improving the Effectiveness of Faculty, Facilities, and Financial Resources.* Princeton, NJ: Peterson's Guides, Inc. (pp. 103–108).

Haine, S. F. (1999). Measuring the mission: Using a scorecard approach in not-for-profit organizations. *Journal of Strategic Performance Measurement, 3*(2), 13–19.

Hambleton, R. K., & Novick, M. R. (1973). Toward an integration of theory and method for criterion-referenced tests. *Journal of Educational Measurement, 10*(3), 159–170.

Hayes, C. R. (Fall 1995). Development of evaluation indicators: Three universities of the Texas A&M system. In G. H. Gaither (ed.), *New Directions for Higher Education: Assessing Performance in an Age of Accountability: Case Studies, Volume XXIII, Number 3.* San Francisco, CA: Jossey-Bass Publishers (Number 91, pp. 91–96).

Hebel, S. (May 28, 1999). Government & politics: Virginia board wants to link state aid for colleges to their performance in key areas. *The Chronicle of Higher Education.* chronicle.com.

Hedley, T. P. (March 1998). Measuring public sector effectiveness using private sector methods. *Public Productivity & Management Review, 21*(3), 251–258.

Heimovics, R. D., Herman, R. D., & Jurkiewicz Coughlin, C. L. (1993). Executive leadership and resource dependence in nonprofit organizations: A frame analysis. *Public Administration Review, 53*, 419–427.

Holton, E. F. I. (Fall 1996). New employee development: A review and reconceptualization. *Human Resource Development Quarterly, 7*(3), 233–252.

Houston, G. R. J. (1992). Achieving productivity gains in financial management. In R. E. Anderson & J. W. Meyerson (eds.), *Productivity and Higher Education: Improving the Effectiveness of Faculty, Facilities, and Financial Resources.* Princeton, NJ: Peterson's Guides, Inc.

Hutchins, G. (1993). *ISO 9000: A Comprehensive Guide to Registration, Audit Guidelines, and Successful Certification.* Bases Junction, VT: Oliver Wright.

Inter-Agency Advisory Group of Federal Personnel Directors and the Chief Financial Officers Council. *Using the Balanced Scorecard to Improve Performance.* www.financenet.gov/fed/cfo/gpra/cfocover/b8balanc.htm.

Izadi, Mahyar, Ali, Kashef E., & Stadt, Ronald W. (1996). Quality in higher education: Lessons learned from the Baldrige Award, Deming Prize, and ISO 9000 registration. *Journal of Industrial Teacher Education, 33*(2), 60–76.

Jacobi, M., Astin, A., & Ayala, F. (1987). *College Student Outcomes Assessment: A Talent Development Perspective.* ASHE-ERIC Higher Education Report No. 7. Washington, D.C.: Association for the Study of Higher Education.

Jaeger, R. M. (1989). Certification of student competence. In R. L. Linn (ed.), *Educational Measurement* (3rd edition). New York: American Council on Education/Macmillan, pp. 485–514.

Jaeger, R. M., Mullis, I. V. S., Bourque, M. L., & Shakrani, S. (1996). Setting performance standards for performance assessments: Some fundamental issues, current practice, and technical dilemmas. In G. Phillips (ed.), *Technical Issues in Large-Scale Performance Assessment*. Washington, D.C.: U.S. Department of Education, Office of Educational Research and Improvement, NCES-802, pp. 79–116.

Joint Staff for the Committee (1957). *A Study of the Need for Additional Centers of Public Higher Education in California.* California: California State Department of Education.

Jones, D. P., & Ewell, P. (1993). *The Effect of State Policy on Undergraduate Education: State Policy and College Learning*. Boulder, CO: Education Commission of the States.

Jongbloed, B. W. A., & Westerheijden, D. F. (Summer 1994). Performance indicators and quality assessment in European higher education. In V. M. H. Borden & T. W. Banta (eds.), *New Directions for Institutional Research: Using Performance Indicators to Guide Strategic Decision Making, Volume XVI, Number 2.* San Francisco, CA: Jossey-Bass Publishers (Number 82, pp. 37–50).

Kaiser, H. H. (1992). Increasing productivity in facilities management. In R. E. Anderson & J. W. Meyerson (eds.), *Productivity and Higher Education: Improving the Effectiveness of Faculty, Facilities, and Financial Resources.* Princeton, NJ: Peterson's Guides, Inc. (pp. 95–108).

Kaplan, R. S., & Norton, D. (1996). Using the balanced scorecard as a strategic management system. *Harvard Business Review, 74*(1), 75–85.

Kidder, P. J. R., & Janice, Z. (Spring 1997). Evaluating the success of a large-scale training effort. *National Productivity Review, 16*(2), 79–89.

Kirkpatrick, D. L. (1998). *Evaluating Training Programs: The Four Levels*. San Francisco, CA: Barrett-Koehler Publishers.

Koretz, D., Stecher, B., Klein, S., McCaffrey, D., & Deibert, E. (1994). *Can Portfolios Assess Student Performance and Influence Instruction? The 1991–92 Vermont Experience*. RP-259, Santa Monica, CA: RAND. (Originally published in Los Angeles, CA: National Center for Research on Evaluation, Standards, and Student Testing, UCLA, CSE Technical Report 371.)

Landgon, D. (February, 1999). Objectives? Get over them. *Training & Development, 53*(2), 54–58.

Lawler, E. E., III (1967). The multi-trait multi-rater approach to measuring managerial job performance. *Journal of Applied Psychology, 51*, 369–381.

Leatherman, C. (1998). University of Phoenix faculty members insist they offer high-quality education. *The Chronicle of Higher Education, 45*(8), A14–A16.

Lee, C. (September 1998). Certified to train. *Training, 35*(9), 32–40.

Leebern, D. (1997). *Board of Regents University System of Georgia Comprehensive Plan*. Georgia: Board of Regents University System of Georgia.

Leland, H. (1979). Quacks, lemons, and licensing: A theory of minimum quality standards. *Journal of Political Economy, 87*, 1328–1346.

Lenth, C. S. (1996). What political leaders expect from postsecondary assessment. In National Center for Higher Education Management Systems, *The National Assessment of College Student Learning: An Inventory of State-Level Assessment Activities*. Boulder, CO: NCHEMS (pp. 157–164).

Levine, S. (May 26, 1997). Desktop degrees: University of Phoenix takes education on-line. *Telephony, V*(232), 50.

Levy, Dina, et al. (forthcoming). *Strategic and Performance Planning for the Office of the Chancellor for Education and Professional Development*. Santa Monica, CA: RAND.

Light, R. J., Singer, J. D., & Willett, J. B. (1990). *By Design: Planning Research on Higher Education*. Cambridge, MA: Harvard University Press.

Lively, K. (February 26, 1999). Money & management: U. of Florida's "Bank" rewards colleges that meet key goals. *The Chronicle of Higher Education*. chronicle.com.

Lizzeri, Allesandro (1999). Information revelation and certification intermediaries. *RAND Journal of Economics, 30*, 214–231.

Loan-Clarke, J. (December 1997). The implications for organizations of in-house management qualifications: A case study. *Management Learning, 28*(4), 439–454.

London, M. S., & James, W. (Spring 1999). Empowered self-development and continuous learning. *Human Resource Management, 38*(1), 3.

Lupton, R. A. W., John, E., & Peterson, Robin T. (January 1999). Sales training evaluation model (STEM): A conceptual framework. *Industrial Marketing Management, 28*(1), 73–86.

MacCordy, E. L. (1992). Managing technology transfer. In R. E. Anderson & J. W. Meyerson (eds.), *Productivity and Higher Education: Improving the Effectiveness of Faculty, Facilities, and Financial Resources.* Princeton, NJ: Peterson's Guides, Inc. (pp. 109–120).

Mager, R. F. (1997). *Preparing Instructional Objectives.* Atlanta, GA: Center for Effective Performance.

Mann, R. B. (Winter 1996–1997). Seven questions to ask before investing in a training program. *Small Business Forum, 14*(3), 50–60.

Maratuza, V. R. (1977). *Applying Norm-Referenced and Criterion-Referenced Measurement in Education.* Boston: Allyn and Bacon.

Marcus, J. (1999). Rise of the fast food learning model. *The Times Higher Education Supplement, 1400*, 11.

Massy, W. F. (1992). Improvement strategies for administration and support services. In R. E. Anderson & J. W. Meyerson (eds.), *Productivity and Higher Education: Improving the Effectiveness of Faculty, Facilities, and Financial Resources.* Princeton, NJ: Peterson's Guides, Inc. (pp. 49–83).

Massy, W. (1994a). *Resource Allocation in Higher Education.* Ann Arbor: University of Michigan Press.

Massy, W. F. (1994b). Measuring performance: How colleges and universities can set meaningful goals and be accountable. In J. W. Meyerson & W. F. Massy (eds.), *Measuring Institutional Performance in Higher Education.* Princeton, NJ: Peterson's Guides, Inc. (pp. 29–54).

Massy, W. F. (1999). *Energizing Quality Work: Higher Education Quality Evaluation in Sweden and Denmark.* Stanford, CA: National Center for Postsecondary Improvement, Stanford University.

Massy, W. F., & French, N. (May 1997). *Teaching and Learning Quality Process Review: A Review of the Hong Kong Program.* Paper presented at the International Network for Quality Assurance Agencies in Higher Education.

Massy, W. F., & French, N. (May 1999). *Teaching and Learning Quality Process Review: What Has the Programme Achieved in Hong Kong?* Paper presented at the International Network for Quality Assurance Agencies in Higher Education.

Massy, W. F., & Meyerson, J. W. (1994). *Measuring Institutional Performance in Higher Education.* Princeton, NJ: Peterson's Guides, Inc.

Master Plan Survey Team (1960). *A Master Plan for Higher Education in California, 1960–1975.* California: California State Department of Education.

McGuinness, A. C., Jr. (1997). Essay: *The Functions and Evaluations of State Coordination and Governance in Postsecondary Education.* Denver, CO: National Center for Postsecondary Management Systems.

Meister, J. C. (1998). *Corporate Universities: Lessons in Building a World Class Work Force.* New York: McGraw-Hill, Inc.

Mendel, P. (2000). *Global Models of Organization: International Management Standards, Reforms, and Movements.* Unpublished dissertation proposal, Stanford University.

Messick, S. (1975). The standard problem: Meaning and values in measurement and evaluation. *American Psychologist, 30,* 955–966.

Messick, S. (1989). Validity. In R. L. Linn (ed.), *Educational Measurement* (3rd edition). New York: Macmillan Press (pp. 13–103).

Messick, S. (1996). Validity of performance assessments. In G. Phillips (ed.), *Technical Issues in Large-Scale Performance Assessment.* Washington, D.C.: U.S. Department of Education, Office of Educational Research and Improvement, NCES-802, pp. 1–18.

Meyer, J. W., & Rowan, B. (1991). Institutionalized organizations: formal structure as myth and ceremony. In W. W. Powell and P. J. DiMaggio (eds.), *The New Institutionalism in Organizational Analysis.* Chicago, IL: The University of Chicago Press (pp. 41–62).

Meyerson, J. W., & Johnson, S. L. (1994). Introduction: Change in higher education: Its effect on institutional performance. In J. W. Meyerson & W. F. Massy (eds.), *Measuring Institutional Performance in Higher Education.* Princeton, NJ: Peterson's Guides, Inc. (pp. 1–13).

Miller, M. (May 1999). Evaluate training on these four levels. *Credit Union Magazine, 65*(5), 25–26.

Murray, B. R., Gary C. (Fall 1997). Single-site, results-level evaluation of quality awareness training. *Human Resource Development Quarterly, 8*(3), 229–245.

National Center for Higher Education Management Systems (NCHEMS). (1996). *The National Assessment of College Student Learning: An Inventory of State-Level Assessment Activities.* Boulder, CO: NCHEMS.

National Institute for Standards and Technology (NIST), Baldrige National Quality Program (1995). *Malcolm Baldrige National Quality Award 1995 Criteria.* Gaithersburg, MD.

National Institute for Standards and Technology (NIST), Baldrige National Quality Program (1999). *Education Criteria for Performance Excellence.* Gaithersburg, MD. www.quality.nist.gov.

National Institute of Education (1984). *Involvement in Learning: Realizing the Potential of American Higher Education.* Washington, D.C.: National Institute of Education.

Neal, J. E. (Fall 1995). Overview of policy and practice: Differences and similarities in developing higher education accountability. In G. H. Gaither (ed.), *Assessing Performance in an Age of Accountability: Case Studies, Volume XXIII, Number 3.* San Francisco, CA: Jossey-Bass Publishers (Number 91, pp. 5–10).

The Need for Public Communication and Evidence Annual Report (1998–1999). Project home page www.imir.iupui.edu/portfolio/.

New Jersey Commission on Higher Education (1996). *NJ's Renewable Resource: A Systemwide Accountability Report.* New Jersey: New Jersey Commission on Higher Education.

Nunnally, J. C. (1970). *Introduction to Psychological Measurement.* New York: McGraw-Hill.

Office of Management and Budget (OMB) (1998). *Preparation and Submission of Strategic Plans and Annual Performance Plans,* Circular No. A-11, Part 2. Washington D.C.

Oliver, C. (1991). Strategic responses to institutional processes. *Academy of Management Review, 16,* 145–179.

O'Neil, H., Bensimon, E., Diamond, M., & Moore, M. (1999). Designing and implementing an academic scorecard. *Change Magazine, Nov/Dec* 34–40.

Ory, J. C. (1991). Suggestions for deciding between commercially available and locally developed assessment instruments. *North Central Association Quarterly 66*(2), 451–457.

Palomba, Catherine A., & Banta, Trudy W. (1999). *Assessment Essentials: Planning, Implementing, and Improving Assessment in Higher Education.* San Francisco, CA: Jossey-Bass Publishers.

Paulson, K., & Ewell, P. (1999). *21st Century Skills for Community College Education: The Critical Role of Competencies.* National Center for Higher Education Management Systems (NCHEMS).

Pencavel, J. H. (1992). Higher education and efficient resource allocation. In R. E. A. Anderson & J. W. Meyerson (eds.), *Productivity and Higher Education: Improving the Effectiveness of Faculty, Facilities, and Financial Resources.* Princeton, NJ: Peterson's Guides, Inc. (pp. 121–134).

Pfeffer, J. & Salancik, G. (1978). *The External Control of Organizations: A Resource Dependence Perspective.* New York: Harper and Row.

Phillips, G. (1996). Foreword. In G. Phillips (ed.), *Technical Issues in Large-Scale Performance Assessment*. Washington, D.C.: U.S. Department of Education, Office of Educational Research and Improvement, NCES-802, pp. iii–vi.

Phillips, J. J. (July 1997). A rational approach to evaluating training programs . . . including calculating ROI. *Journal of Lending & Credit Risk Management, 79*(11), 43–50.

Phillips, J. J. P., & Patti, F. (December 1997). The seven key challenges facing training and development. *Journal of Lending & Credit Risk Management, 80*(4), 25–30.

Pottinger, P. S., & Goldsmith, J. (eds.) (1979). *Defining and Measuring Competence.* San Francisco, CA: Jossey-Bass, Inc.

Prewitt, P. L. (September 1997). Army job standard v. training standard. *Training & Development, 51*(9), 52–53.

Reisberg, L. (August 28, 2000). Assailed substance of "U.S. News" college rankings. *The Chronicle of Higher Education.* chronicle.com.

Relyea, S. W. (1998). From gutter balls to strikes. *NACUBO Business Officer.* Washington, D.C.: National Association of College and University Business Officers. www.nacubo.org/website/members/bomag/9806/scorecard.html.

Resnick, L. (April 1990). *Psychometricians' Beliefs About Learning: Discussion.* Presented at the annual meeting of the American Educational Research Association, Boston.

Richardson, Richard (1994). Illinois. In S. Ruppert (ed.), *Charting Higher Education Accountability: A Sourcebook on State-Level Performance Indicators.* Denver: Education Commission for the States.

Rossett, A. (August 1998). No cheers for corporate U. *Training, 35*(8), 96–98.

Rowden, R. W. (Summer 1998). A practical guide to assessing the value of training in your company. *Employment Relations Today, 25*(2), 65–74.

Ruppert, S. S. (ed.) (1994). *Charting Higher Education Accountability: A Sourcebook on State-Level Performance Indicators*. Denver: Education Commission for the States.

Ruppert, S. S. (Fall 1995). Roots and realities of state-level performance indicator systems. In G. H. Gaither (ed.), *New Directions for Higher Education: Assessing Performance in an Age of Accountability: Case Studies, Volume XXIII, Number 3.* San Francisco, CA: Jossey-Bass Publishers (Number 91, pp. 11–23).

Rush, S. (1992). Productivity and higher education: Improving the effectiveness of faculty, facilities, and financial resources. In R. E. Anderson & J. W. Meyerson (eds.), *Productivity & Higher Education: Improving the Effectiveness of Faculty, Facilities, and Financial Resources.* Princeton, NJ: Peterson's Guides, Inc. (pp. 1–13).

Rush, S. C. (1994). Benchmarking—How good is good? In J. W. Meyerson & W. F. Massy (eds.), *Measuring Institutional Performance in Higher Education.* Princeton, NJ: Peterson's Guides, Inc. (pp. 83–97).

Schank, R. C. (December 1998). Basic training. *Chief Executive* (140), 54–57.

Schapiro, M. O. (1993). The concept of productivity as applied to U.S. higher education. In M. S. McPherson, M. O. Schapiro, & G. C. Winston (eds.), *Paying the Piper: Productivity, Incentives, and Financing in U.S. Higher Education.* Ann Arbor: University of Michigan Press.

Schmidt, P. (July 2, 1999). Government & politics: A state transforms colleges with "performance funding." *The Chronicle of Higher Education.* chronicle.com.

Schulz, W. G. (August 26, 1996). Alliance of industry, academia, labor leads skill standards movement. *Chemical & Engineering News, 74*(35), 39–41.

Scott, R. H. (1994). Measuring performance in higher education. In J. W. Myerson & S. L. Johnson (eds.), *Measuring Institutional Performance in Higher Education.* Princeton, NJ: Peterson's Guides, Inc. (pp. 15–27).

Scott, W. R., & Meyer, J. W. (1991). The organization of societal sectors: Propositions and early evidence. In W. W. Powell and P. J. DiMaggio (eds.), *The New Institutionalism in Organizational Analysis.* Chicago, IL: The University of Chicago Press (pp. 108–140).

Shepard, L. A. (1990). *Psychometricians' Beliefs About Learning.* Presented at the annual meeting of the American Educational Research Association, Boston.

Shepko, R., & Douglas, B. (December 1998). Reframing for crisis. *NACUBO Business Officer.* Washington, D.C.: National Association of Colleges and Universities Business Officers. www.nacubo.org/website/members/bomag/9812/benchmarking.html.

Singleton, R. A., Jr., Straits, B. C., & Miller Straits, M. (1993). *Approaches to Social Research,* (2nd edition). New York, NY: Oxford University Press.

Smith, M. L. (1989). *The Role of External Testing in Elementary Schools.* Los Angeles: Center for Research on Evaluation, Standards, and Student Testing, UCLA.

Snow, R. E. (1974). Representative and quasi-representative designs for research on teaching. *Review of Educational Research, 44,* 265–291.

Snow, R. E. (1993). Construct validity and constructed response tests. In R. E. Bennett & W. C. Ward, Jr. (eds.), *Construction Versus Choice in Cognitive Measurement: Issues in Constructed Response, Performance Testing, and Portfolio Assessment.* Hillsdale, NJ: Erlbaum (pp. 45–60).

Spanbauer, S. J. (1992). *A Quality System for Education.* Milwaukee, WI: American Society for Quality Control Standards.

Steele, J. M., & Lutz, D. A. (1995). *Report of ACT's Research on Postsecondary Assessment Needs.* Iowa City, IA: American College Testing.

Stein, R. B., & Fajen, A. L. (Fall 1995). Missouri's funding for results initiative. In G. H. Gaither (ed.), *New Directions for Higher Education: Assessing Performance in an Age of Accountability: Case Studies, Volume XXIII, Number 3.* San Francisco, CA: Jossey-Bass Publishers (Number 91, pp. 77–90).

Stevens, J., & Hamlett, B. D. (1983). State concerns for learning: Quality and state policy. In J. R. Warren (ed.), *Meeting the New Demands for Standards.* San Francisco, CA: Jossey-Bass Publishers (pp. 29–38).

Strosnider, K. (June 6, 1997). For-profit university challenges traditional colleges. *The Chronicle of Higher Education.* chronicle.com.

Tannenbaum, S. I., & Yukl, G. (1992). Training and Development in Work Organizations. *Annual Review of Psychology, 43,* 399–441.

Taylor, P. J. L., Aaron, Vincent, & O'Driscoll, Michael P. (October 1998). The validity of immediate and delayed self-reports in training evaluation: An exploratory field study. *Applied Psychology: An International Review, 47*(4), 459–479.

Terenzini, P. T. (1989). Assessment with open eyes: Pitfalls in studying student outcomes. *Journal of Higher Education 60,* 644–664.

Testa, A. M. (November 1999). Design and Delivery of Distance Delivered Competency Based Degree Programs. *Proceedings from the 1999 Assessment Institute.* Indianapolis, IN: Western Governors University, The 1999 Assessment Institute.

Thorndike, R. L. (ed.) (1971). *Educational Measurement* (2nd edition). Washington, D.C.: American Council on Education.

Trachtenberg, S. J. (1992). Productivity and the academic "business." In R. E. Anderson & J. W. Meyerson (eds.), *Productivity and Higher Education: Improving the Effectiveness of Faculty, Facilities, and Financial Resources.* Princeton, NJ: Peterson's Guides, Inc. (pp. 15–21).

University of California at San Diego (nd). *Business Affairs Performance Measurements.* www.vcba.ucsd.edu/performance.

The Urban Universities Portfolio Project (1998). *Final Proposal.* www.imir.iupui.edu/portfolio.

The Urban Universities Portfolio Project (1999). *Annual Report (1998–1999).* www.imir.iupui.edu/portfolio.

U.S. Air Force Academy (April 1997a). *U.S. Air Force Academy Educational Outcomes Assessment Working Group, Phase 2, Final Report.* Colorado Springs, CO.

U.S. Air Force Academy, Department of Management (July 1997b). *Accreditation Plan.* Colorado Springs, CO.

U.S. Air Force Academy, Department of Management (August 1999a). *Candidacy School Profile Sheet, American Assembly of Collegiate Schools of Business Annual Report.* Colorado Springs, CO.

U.S. Air Force Academy, Department of Management (October 1999b). *Assessment Program.* Colorado Springs, CO.

U.S. Department of Labor, Secretary's Commission on Achieving Necessary Skills (SCANS) (1991). *What Work Requires of Schools: A SCANS Report for America 2000.* Washington, D.C.

U.S. Department of Labor, Secretary's Commission on Achieving Necessary Skills (SCANS) (1992a). *What Work Requires of Schools: A SCANS Report for America 2000.* Washington, D.C.

U.S. Department of Labor, Secretary's Commission on Achieving Necessary Skills (SCANS) (1992b). *A Blueprint for High Performance: A SCANS Report for America 2000.* Washington, D.C.

U.S. Department of Transportation (DOT) (1997a). *Learning and Development Framework.* dothr.dot.gov/L&D_Framework/toc1.html, and dothr.ost.dot.gov/L&D_Framework/evaltoc.htm.

U.S. Department of Transportation (1997b). *United States Department of Transportation Strategic Plan for Fiscal Years 1997–2002.* Washington, D.C. www.dot.gov/hot/dotplan.html.

U.S. Department of Transportation (1999). *Procurement Balanced Scorecard.* Washington, D.C. www.dot.gov/ost/m60/scorecard/ppmsrev.htm.

U.S. General Accounting Office (GAO) (1996). *Executive Guide: Effectively Implementing the Government Performance and Results Act,* (GAO/GGD-96-118). Washington, D.C.

U.S. News and World Report (August 30, 1999). America's best colleges. *U.S. News and World Report, 127*(8), 84–105.

Vandenberge, D. G. (1995). An undergraduate quality management and control class for engineers. *ASEE Annual Conference Proceedings, 1,* 1229–1233.

Western Association of Schools and Colleges (1998). *An Invitation to Dialogue.* Alameda, CA. www.wascweb.org/senior/invite/dialogue.htm.

Western Association of Schools and Colleges (1999a). *Invitation to Dialogue II: Proposed Framework for a New Model of Accreditation.* Alameda, CA.

Western Association of Schools and Colleges (April 12–13, 1999b). *Summary of Small Group Sessions and Feedback from the Accreditation Liaison Officer's (ALO) Meeting,* Alameda, CA, April 12–13, 1999. www.wascweb.org/senior/alomtg.html.

Western Association of Schools and Colleges (2000a). *Proposed WASC Capacity Standards: Part One of the Revision of the Handbook of Accreditation.* Alameda, CA. www.wascweb.org/senior/capacitystandards/capacity.html.

Western Association of Schools and Colleges (2000b). *The Senior College Commission Addressing the Core Commitments to Institutional Capacity and Educational Effectiveness*. Alameda, CA. www.wascweb.org/senior.

Western Association of Schools and Colleges (2001). *Handbook of Accreditation*. Alameda, CA.

Williams, C., & Wall A. (Fall 1999). Balanced Scorecards at the Veterans Benefits Administration, *The Business of Government*, Arlington, VA: The PricewaterhouseCoopers Endowment for the Business of Government, 2-5.

Winer, B. J. (1971). *Statistical Principles in Experimental Design*. New York: McGraw-Hill.

Winston, G. C. (1994). New dangers in old traditions: The reporting of economic performance in colleges and universities. In J. W. Meyerson & W. F. Massy (eds.), *Measuring Institutional Performance in Higher Education*. Princeton, NJ: Peterson's Guides, Inc. (pp. 71–81).

Wirth, I. A., & Scott, J. (1996). Distance learning for project management. *Transactions of AACE International*, PM11–PM15.

Wolfe, A. (December 4, 1998). How a for-profit university can be invaluable to the traditional liberal arts. *The Chronicle of Higher Education*. chronicle.com.

Wolff, Ralph, (January 2000). *Re-Visioning WASC Accreditation*, one-page handout from Council for Higher Accreditation Conference, Washington, D.C.

Wright, B. (1997). Evaluating learning in individual courses. In J. G. Gaff, J. L. Ratcliff, and Associates, *Handbook of the Undergraduate Curriculum: A Comprehensive Guide to Purposes, Structures, Practices, and Change*. The Association of American Colleges and Universities. San Francisco, CA: Jossey-Bass Publishers.

Yang, H. S., Paul, R., & Arvey, Richard D. (Fall 1996). Statistical power and cost in training evaluation: Some new considerations. *Personnel Psychology, 49*(3), 651–668.

Online Bibliography

Accreditation Board of Engineering and Technology	www.abet.org
Accreditation Council for Graduate Medical Education	www.abet.org
Accreditation Council on Continuing Medical Education	www.accme.org
ACT	www.act.org/workkeys/index.html
American Bar Association	www.abanet.org
American Dental Association	www.ada.org
American Medical Accreditation Program	www.ama-assn.org/med-sci/amapsite/index.htm
American Medical Association	www.ama-assn.org
American Psychological Association	www.apa.org
Annual Data Profile for Public Community and Technical Colleges of Texas	www.thecb.state.tx.us/divisions/ctc
Association of Universities in the Netherlands (VSNU)	www.vsnu.nl
Berkeley Extension	www.unex.berkeley.edu
College Profiles for Public Community and Technical Colleges of Texas	www.thecb.state.tx.us/divisions/ctc/ie/ctcprof/ctcprof.htm
CUNY Queens College	www.qc.edu
Department of Agriculture	www.usda.gov
Department of Education	www.ed.gov
Department of Transportation	www.dot.gov
The European Commission on Education, Training and Youth	europa.eu.int/comm/dgs/education_culture/index_en.htm
Forest Service	www.fs.fed.us
H-530.947 AMA Structure, Governance and Operations	www.ama-assn.org
Harvard Extension	extension.dce.harvard.edu
Health and Human Services	www.hhs.gov
Institutional Effectiveness Measures and Standards: On-Site Review for Texas Community and Technical Colleges	www.thecb.state.tx.us/divisions/ctc/ie/ctciems/Measures.pdf
Liaison Committee on Medical Education	www.lcme.org
Michigan State University	www.msue.msu.edu
New England Association of Schools and Colleges, Inc., Standards for Accreditation	www.neasc.org/cihe/stancihe.htm
North Central Association of Colleges and Schools Commission on Institutions of Higher Education	www.ncacihe.org/mission/index.html
Proxion Research Group Limited	www.connect.ab.ca/~praxiom/intro.htm

The Quality Assurance Agency for Higher Education	www.qaa.ac.uk
Social Security Administration	www.ssa.gov
Stanford Extension	continuingstudies.stanford.edu
Texas Higher Education Institutional Effectiveness	www.thecb.state.tx.us/divisions/ctc/ie
UCLA Extension	www.unex.ucla.edu
United States House of Representatives Majority Leader	freedom.house.gov
United States Postal Service	www.usps.gov
University of Massachusetts at Amherst	www.umass.edu
University of Phoenix	www.phoenix.edu
University of Texas at Austin	www.utexas.edu/cee
The Urban Universities Portfolio Project	www.imir.iupui.edu/portfolio
Western Governors University	www.wgu.edu